DATE DUE

THE QUALITY OF
CONSUMER INSTALMENT CREDIT

NATIONAL BUREAU OF ECONOMIC RESEARCH

Studies in Consumer Instalment Financing

1. *Personal Finance Companies and Their Credit Practices*
   Ralph A. Young and associates
2. *Sales Finance Companies and Their Credit Practices*
   Wilbur C. Plummer and Ralph A. Young
3. *Commercial Banks and Consumer Instalment Credit*
   John M. Chapman and associates
4. *Industrial Banking Companies and Their Credit Practices*
   Raymond J. Saulnier
5. *Government Agencies of Consumer Instalment Credit*
   Joseph D. Coppock
6. *The Pattern of Consumer Debt, 1935–36: A Statistical Analysis*
   Blanche Bernstein
7. *The Volume of Consumer Instalment Credit, 1929–1938*
   Duncan McC. Holthausen in collaboration with Malcolm L. Merriam and
   Rolf Nugent
8. *Risk Elements in Consumer Instalment Financing*
   David Durand
9. *Consumer Instalment Credit and Economic Fluctuations*
   Gottfried Haberler
10. *Comparative Operating Experience of Consumer Instalment Financing Agencies
    and Commercial Banks, 1929–41*
    Ernst A. Dauer
11. *Consumer Credit Costs, 1949–59*
    Paul F. Smith
12. *Consumer Credit Finance Charges: Rate Information and Quotation*
    Wallace P. Mors
13. *The Quality of Consumer Instalment Credit*
    Geoffrey H. Moore and Philip A. Klein

THE QUALITY OF CONSUMER INSTALMENT CREDIT

GEOFFREY H. MOORE
NATIONAL BUREAU OF ECONOMIC RESEARCH

AND

PHILIP A. KLEIN
THE PENNSYLVANIA STATE UNIVERSITY AND
NATIONAL BUREAU OF ECONOMIC RESEARCH

NATIONAL BUREAU OF ECONOMIC RESEARCH
NEW YORK, 1967
Distributed by COLUMBIA UNIVERSITY PRESS
NEW YORK AND LONDON

RELATION OF THE DIRECTORS TO THE WORK AND PUBLICATIONS OF THE NATIONAL BUREAU OF ECONOMIC RESEARCH

1. The object of the National Bureau of Economic Research is to ascertain and to present to the public important economic facts and their interpretation in a scientific and impartial manner. The Board of Directors is charged with the responsibility of ensuring that the work of the National Bureau is carried on in strict conformity with this object.
2. To this end the Board of Directors shall appoint one or more Directors of Research.
3. The Director or Directors of Research shall submit to the members of the Board, or to its Executive Committee, for their formal adoption, all specific proposals concerning researches to be instituted.
4. No report shall be published until the Director or Directors of Research shall have submitted to the Board a summary drawing attention to the character of the data and their utilization in the report, the nature and treatment of the problems involved, the main conclusions, and such other information as in their opinion would serve to determine the suitability of the report for publication in accordance with the principles of the National Bureau.
5. A copy of any manuscript proposed for publication shall also be submitted to each member of the Board. For each manuscript to be so submitted a special committee shall be appointed by the President, or at his designation by the Executive Director, consisting of three Directors selected as nearly as may be one from each general division of the Board. The names of the special manuscript committee shall be stated to each Director when the summary and report described in paragraph (4) are sent to him. It shall be the duty of each member of the committee to read the manuscript. If each member of the special committee signifies his approval within thirty days, the manuscript may be published. If each member of the special committee has not signified his approval within thirty days of the transmittal of the report and manuscript, the Director of Research shall then notify each member of the Board, requesting approval or disapproval of publication, and thirty additional days shall be granted for this purpose. The manuscript shall then not be published unless at least a majority of the entire Board and a two-thirds majority of those members of the Board who shall have voted on the proposal within the time fixed for the receipt of votes on the publication proposed shall have approved.
6. No manuscript may be published, though approved by each member of the special committee, until forty-five days have elapsed from the transmittal of the summary and report. The interval is allowed for the receipt of any memorandum of dissent or reservation, together with a brief statement of his reasons, that any member may wish to express; and such memorandum of dissent or reservation shall be published with the manuscript if he so desires. Publication does not, however, imply that each member of the Board has read the manuscript, or that either members of the Board in general, or of the special committee, have passed upon its validity in every detail.
7. A copy of this resolution shall, unless otherwise determined by the Board, be printed in each copy of every National Bureau book.

(Resolution adopted October 25, 1926,
as revised February 6, 1933, and February 24, 1941)

Contents

Tables

Tables

Charts

Acknowledgments

The genesis of this study was a paper written during 1956 for the Conference on Regulation, which the National Bureau of Economic Research organized as a part of the Federal Reserve Board's study, *Consumer Instalment Credit* (Washington, 1957). In the intervening years that original paper has been enlarged and revised a number of times as data became available from new sources and made possible a fuller examination of instalment credit quality.

Authors of empirical studies are perpetually dissatisfied with the state of the data on which they must base their findings. Always they long for material with which to test new relationships of possible importance, in the hope of being able to produce a definitive solution to whatever problem they are examining. It was this hope which persuaded us to wait until now to present our findings, though we realize that there are still important gaps in our knowledge, the filling in of which must await data not now available.

We have incurred obligations of many kinds and to many persons and institutions in the process of obtaining and analyzing the data for this study. We are indebted, first of all, to those who assisted in the preparation of the 1956 paper, and to whom we there expressed our thanks. We are especially indebted to our coauthor in that initial endeavor, Thomas R. Atkinson. Not only are many of his original insights still to be found in the pages which follow but also he was kind enough to read an early version of the present manuscript and to make many helpful suggestions.

We would be remiss were we not to thank once more the American Bankers Association, the Association of Reserve City Bankers, the American Finance Conference, and the Research Staff of the Board of Governors of the Federal Reserve System for their patience and cooperation in enabling us to obtain the basic data utilized here. It is impossible to name all the individuals in these organizations, as well as in the many sales finance companies and banks we have been able to include in our sample, who have our gratitude. Three who were especially helpful, however, were Arthur L. Broida of the Research Staff of the Federal Reserve Board, Madeline McWhinney of the Research Department of the New York Federal Reserve Bank, and Seymour Marshak of National Analysts, Incorporated.

A special word of appreciation must go to James S. Earley, director of the National Bureau's general study of the quality of credit, of which this study of instalment credit is a part. Earley read our draft manuscript with great care and perceptiveness, and is responsible for many improvements in the presentation of our material. We should also like to thank Wallace J. Campbell, Melvin G. de Chazeau, Edgar R. Fiedler, Jack M. Guttentag, Harold G. Halcrow, and Paul F. Smith for their critical review of the manuscript and their helpful comments.

At the National Bureau we are indebted to many other individuals. Jacob Mincer gave valuable advice on the most useful mode of presenting some of the data. James F. McRee, Jr., edited the manuscript. Martha Jones and Dora Thompson were in charge of the IBM computations carried out at the Bureau. Maude Pech, Elizabeth Jenks, and Georgette Welscher were our chief research assistants and carried out much of the work of computation and data checking. Muriel De Mar was the patient and perennially cooperative secretary, and typed many of the chapters in more versions than any of us care to remember. The charts are the work of H. I. Forman, who performed with his customary skill and efficiency.

The National Bureau's study of the quality of credit has been supported by a grant from the Merrill Foundation for Advancement of Financial Knowledge, Inc., and it is a pleasure to acknowledge its indispensable assistance.

G. H. M.
P. A. K.

Foreword

I feel unduly honored to be asked to provide a brief foreword to this volume, placing it in its context within the National Bureau's quality of credit program as a whole. Its authors, and especially Geoffrey Moore, have had much more to do with the design of that program than I, and their study of consumer instalment credit was well under way before I became director of the program. I played a very small role in the design and execution of this study.

Nevertheless, it has special importance, and I should like to stress its contributions. The credit quality program has had several objectives. It sought first of all to effect improvements in the data relating to credit quality, which earlier National Bureau studies had shown were seriously inadequate. Second, it sought to devise methods by which "quality" could be quantified, so that "credit quality" could be measured statistically. Third, it sought to analyze the relationships between changing credit quality and business cycles, and to assess the significance of the changes that have occurred since World War II.

The several studies that have constituted the credit quality program— three have been issued and a half-dozen are under way—should be seen as building blocks designed in combination to work toward these objectives.[1] But the present volume deserves special mention for its contributions to the data and to methods of analyzing them, as well as because of the importance of the credit sector that it investigates.

The months and indeed years of work the authors devoted to collecting the statistics set forth in their study have in fact resulted in

---

[1] The published reports are by Albert M. Wojnilower, *The Quality of Bank Loans: A Study of Bank Examination Records*, 1962, Martin H. Seiden, *The Quality of Trade Credit*, 1964, and Thomas R. Atkinson, *Trends in Corporate Bond Quality*, 1967. In preparation are reports on corporate direct placements, municipal bonds, agricultural credit, residential mortgage credit, a statistical compendium on credit quality, and a summary volume.

substantial improvements in instalment credit quality data, both private and governmental. In their final chapter, the authors urge a program of still further improvement in the statistics of instalment credit, to whose potential value their work attests.

This volume develops the concepts of *ex ante* and *ex post* credit quality, first set forth in a pioneering article by Moore in 1956.[2] These concepts provide much of the methodological framework of the other credit quality studies. In addition, throughout the volume there are methodological innovations designed to measure and test changing credit quality on both a "cross-sectional" and a time-series basis.

Finally, there is the growing importance of instalment credit in the contemporary American scene. Instalment debt, like household debt in general, has expanded more rapidly than other major types of debt over the postwar years. In addition, the ratios between aggregate consumer instalment debt and debt service, on the one hand, and aggregate consumer income, on the other, have so risen in the postwar years as to cause some concern. This concern takes one or both of two forms. One is lest the household sector become overburdened by indebtedness, with a consequent weakening of credit performance. A different, but no less serious, concern is lest the relatively high plateau that has been reached in recent years in the ratio of consumer debt service to personal income may mean that the buoyancy contributed to the economy by the steady rise in instalment credit in the postwar years can no longer be anticipated.

Moore and Klein draw no definite conclusions regarding these latter matters. But their work will be of interest to those who wish to form judgments regarding them.

[2] "The Quality of Credit in Booms and Depressions," *Journal of Finance*, May 1956.

JAMES S. EARLEY
Director, Quality of
Credit Program

1. Instalment Credit in Perspective

Instalment credit for use in purchasing consumer durable goods, and more recently services as well, is firmly established in the American economy. From time to time, however, concern has been voiced about the possible overextension of consumer credit and its consequences. This concern arises not solely because variations in the volume of consumer credit are now a highly potent factor in the economy but also because deterioration in its quality might have widespread, untimely repercussions. This book attempts to measure and to analyze the variations that have occurred in consumer credit quality.

The effect of changes in the volume of credit on economic growth, stability, and prices has already received much attention. It is the problem that Rolf Nugent and Gottfried Haberler dealt with in their pioneering works, and it was examined again in the 1957 Federal Reserve study.[1] On the other hand, the impact of cyclically and secularly changing credit quality on economic stability, growth, and the level of prices has been relatively neglected. An initial exploration of this question was undertaken in a paper prepared for the Federal Reserve study just cited.[2] This book updates and expands that study through further analysis of additional data.

We begin with a consideration of some of the broad changes in the quantity and quality of consumer instalment credit. But first, what is meant by credit quality? Since the next chapter will consider this matter in some detail, here we merely note that quality concerns itself

[1] Rolf Nugent, *Consumer Credit and Economic Stability*, New York, Russell Sage Foundation, 1939; Gottfried Haberler, *Consumer Instalment Credit and Economic Fluctuations*, New York, National Bureau of Economic Research, 1942; Board of Governors of the Federal Reserve System, *Consumer Instalment Credit*, Washington, 1957.

[2] Geoffrey H. Moore, Thomas R. Atkinson, and Philip A. Klein, "Changes in the Quality of Consumer Instalment Credit," in *Consumer Instalment Credit*, Part II, Volume 1, pp. 70–157.

ultimately with the degree of risk that attaches to credit transactions. Such risk may be viewed prospectively at the time the credit is extended, or retrospectively in terms of collection experience. Viewed prospectively, credit quality can be measured by credit terms (down payment or loan-to-value ratios, or maturities) and by borrower characteristics such as income or occupation—in short, by such aspects of the credit transaction as are known to be associated with risk. Viewed retrospectively, credit quality can be measured by delinquency, repossession, and loss experience. Hence an examination of credit quality must deal with the conditions that determine risk. We need to consider the changing volume of instalment credit, on what terms credit has been extended and how they have changed, what kind of people use consumer credit and how the borrowing population has changed, and how collection experience on instalment loans has varied over the years.

Historically, instalment credit has been most closely associated with the purchase of consumer durables, especially automobiles, although in recent years it has spread to various consumer services, such as travel and education. Both total consumer credit and its chief component, instalment credit, have grown in three waves—in the late 1920's, the 1930's, and most rapidly in the decade following the Second World War. This pattern of growth in outstanding debt is shown in Chart 1, which shows as well the growth of the economy as measured by total personal income and consumer expenditures.[3]

The growth of the 1920's was reversed by the Great Depression, at which time the decline in personal income was accompanied by even larger declines in expenditures on consumer durables as well as in instalment debt. Economic recovery, reversed briefly but sharply during the 1937–38 recession, produced new highs in personal income, durable goods expenditures, consumer debt, and instalment debt by the beginning of the Second World War. The imposition of Regulation W (see note 6), governing the use of instalment credit, together with

[3] There are many excellent discussions of the growth in instalment credit. Among the classics in the field are E. R. A. Seligman, *The Economics of Instalment Selling* (1927), and the volumes cited in note 1. More recently the growth of consumer instalment credit has been traced in Volume 1, Parts I and II, of the Federal Reserve study, *Consumer Instalment Credit*. See also the report by F. Thomas Juster, *Household Capital Formation and Financing, 1897–1962*, NBER, New York, 1966.

CHART 1

Personal Income, Consumer Expenditures, and Consumer Debt
Outstanding, 1920–65

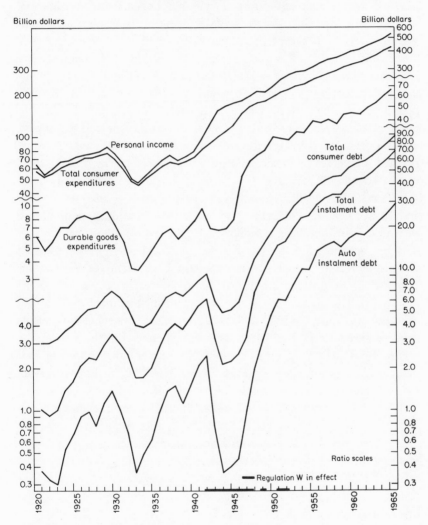

SOURCE: Table 1 and its sources.

reductions in the availability of new automobiles and other consumer durables, caused a drop in the use of credit during 1942–45. Since 1945, consumer credit has expanded spectacularly. Total consumer debt, instalment debt, and its largest component, automobile paper, have all grown at a faster rate than either personal income or total sales of durables. By the end of 1965, total consumer debt outstanding was 16 per cent of annual personal income, whereas it was 7 per cent in 1948 and 8 per cent in 1929 (Table 1). Instalment debt was 13 per cent of income in 1965, 4 per cent in 1948 and in 1929.

It is illuminating to consider not only the growth in the accumulated debt but also the rate at which it is extended and repaid. The extensions, of course, constitute a supplement to income and the repayments a drain upon it.[4] Instalment credit extensions, as Table 1 shows, reached a level 14 per cent as large as total personal income in 1965, compared with 7 per cent thirty-four years before. The repayments were somewhat smaller in each year: 6 per cent of income in 1929 and 13 per cent in 1965. The net increase in instalment debt during each year was, therefore, a rather small fraction of income: about half of 1 per cent in 1929, 1.5 per cent in 1965.[5] These figures show that the primary function of consumer credit is to facilitate transactions rather than to provide additional funds—in recent years, for every hundred dollars of income the net increment in instalment debt during the year was only about a dollar. Nevertheless, these net increments have persisted year after year, and this accounts for the rise in the accumulated debt relative to income. Moreover, it is probable that many purchases made with the use of credit might not be made at all in the absence of available credit.

In part, the growth of consumer credit has merely facilitated transactions at higher prices. But Table 1 shows that the price rise by no means accounts for the increase. Prices of consumer goods and services in 1965 were nearly twice their 1929 level, but instalment credit extensions were thirteen times their 1929 level. Neither total expenditures nor those on durable goods alone have risen as fast as the rate of credit extension.

[4] The estimates of repayments in Table 1 include not only periodic and final repayments but also repayments of obligations that are immediately refinanced. These refinancings are, of course, also included in the extensions.

[5] Extensions, repayments, and net change are larger fractions of *borrowers'* income, of course, than of total income. Repayments apparently have not risen relative to borrowers' income. See Table 9.

TABLE 1

Consumer Credit, Consumer Expenditures, and Personal Income, Selected Dates, 1920–65

(dollars in billions)

| | Consumer Debt Outstanding, End of Year | | | Consumer Instalment Credit | | | Consumer Expenditures | | Personal Income | Price Index for Consumer Expenditures (1958:100) | |
| | Total Debt | Instalment Debt | | Exten-sions | Repay-ments | Net Change | Total | Durable Goods | | Total | Durable Goods |
		Total	Auto								
1920	3.0	1.0	0.4	--	--	+0.2	58.7	6.1	65.4	66	70
1929	7.1	3.5	1.4	5.8	5.4	+0.4	77.2	9.2	85.9	55	56
1937	6.9	4.1	1.5	6.3	5.9	+0.4	66.5	6.9	74.1	46	46
1941	9.2	6.1	2.5	9.4	8.9	+0.6	80.6	9.6	96.0	49	50
1948	14.4	9.0	3.0	15.6	13.3	+2.3	173.6	22.7	210.2	82	86
1953	31.4	23.0	9.8	31.6	28.0	+3.6	230.0	33.2	288.2	92	94
1957	45.0	33.9	15.3	42.0	39.9	+2.1	281.4	40.8	351.1	98	98
1960	56.0	42.8	17.7	49.6	46.0	+3.6	325.2	45.3	401.0	103	101
1963	70.5	54.2	22.4	61.3	55.2	+6.1	375.0	53.9	465.5	106	100
1964	78.4	60.5	25.2	67.5	61.1	+6.4	401.4	59.4	496.0	107	100
1965	87.9	68.6	28.8	75.5	67.5	+8.0	431.5	66.1	535.1	109	100
Ratio, 1965 to 1929	12.4	19.6	20.6	13.0	12.5	20.0	5.6	7.2	6.2	1.9	1.8

(continued)

TABLE 1 (concluded)

Percentage Ratios

	Total Debt to Income	Instalment Debt to Income Total	Instalment Debt to Income Auto	Instalment Credit Extensions to Income	Instalment Credit Repayments to Income	Net Change in Instalment Debt to Income	Durable Goods Expenditures to Total Expenditures	Instalment Credit Extensions to Total Expenditures	Net Change in Instalment Debt to Total Expenditures
1920	5	2	1	--	--	+0.3	10	--	+0.3
1929	8	4	2	7	6	+0.5	12	8	+0.5
1937	9	6	2	9	8	+0.5	10	9	+0.6
1941	10	6	3	10	9	+0.6	12	12	+0.7
1948	7	4	1	7	6	+1.1	13	9	+1.3
1953	11	8	3	11	10	+1.2	14	14	+1.6
1957	13	10	4	12	11	+0.6	14	14	+0.7
1960	14	11	4	12	11	+0.9	15	15	+1.1
1963	15	12	5	13	12	+1.3	14	16	+1.6
1964	16	12	5	14	12	+1.3	15	17	+1.6
1965	16	13	5	14	13	+1.5	15	17	+1.9

Notes to Table 1

Source: Consumer credit: 1920–62, "Section 16 (new) Consumer Credit Statistics," p. 33, prepared by Board of Governors of the Federal Reserve System from *Supplement to Banking and Monetary Statistics;* 1963–65, *Federal Reserve Bulletin,* June 1966, pp. 874, 876.

Consumer expenditures, total: 1920–28, estimated as the same percentage of personal income as shown by the ratio of consumers' outlay to aggregate payments to individuals including entrepreneurial savings, Kuznets, *National Income and Its Composition, 1919–1938,* p. 137; 1929–61, *Survey of Current Business,* August 1965; p. 24, 30, 52; 1962–65, *Survey,* July 1966, pp. 11, 13, 38.

Consumer expenditures, durable goods: 1920–28, estimated as the same percentage of consumer expenditures as shown by the ratio of consumer expenditures on durable goods to total flow of goods to consumers, Variant III, Kuznets, *Capital in the American Economy: Its Formation and Financing,* pp. 486, 502; 1929–65, from the sources indicated for consumer expenditures.

Personal income: 1920, extrapolated from 1921 by aggregate payments to individuals including entrepreneurial savings, Kuznets, *National Income and Its Composition,* p. 137; 1921–28, Barger, unpublished worksheets; 1929–65, from the sources indicates for consumer expenditures.

Price indexes: 1920–28, extrapolated from 1929 by the series implicit in Kuznets series for Variant III, *Capital,* pp. 486, 487, 502, 504; 1929–65, from the sources indicated for consumer expenditures.

TRENDS IN CREDIT TERMS

In the 1920's instalment credit was associated primarily with the purchase of such consumer durables as pianos, sewing machines, and automobiles, and the chief source of credit then was the sales finance company. In recent years commercial banks have become prominent in this field, providing a large volume of personal instalment loans, automobile loans, and other types of instalment credit. At the end of 1965, total instalment credit stood at $68.6 billion, of which commercial banks held $29.2, sales finance companies $16.1, credit unions $7.5, consumer finance companies $5.6, department stores $4.5, and other institutions $5.6 billion. Automobile paper amounted to $28.8 billion, other consumer goods paper $17.7, personal loans $18.4, and home repair and modernization loans $3.7 billion.

A survey of the changes in instalment credit terms should, therefore, encompass the several types of financial institutions that provide such credit and the wide variety of types of credit extended. In view of the limitations of available data, however, we shall concentrate upon the trend in terms on automobile paper as reported by banks and sales finance companies. Although even these data are not fully comparable, they do provide a conspectus of the changing character of credit terms in a major sector of the market.

As Table 2 indicates, there has been a marked trend, at least since the twenties, toward a lengthening of contract maturities on automobile paper. In 1929, for example, the group of sales finance companies included in the sample reported that 85 per cent of their automobile paper (by dollar volume for both new and used cars) had a maturity of twelve months or less. Very little went beyond eighteen months. Maturities changed relatively little during the Great Depression. By 1937, however, when the volume of credit had more than regained the 1929 level, only 32 per cent had a maturity as short as twelve months. Considering new-car contracts alone, 22 per cent were for twelve months or less and 35 per cent were for more than eighteen months. If the war and the Regulation W periods are omitted, by 1953, with new-car volume reaching new highs, the volume of contracts being written for over eighteen months had jumped to 83 per cent. By 1957, 80 per cent of new-automobile contracts were for over twenty-four months, and 44 per cent had maturities in excess of thirty months. By 1965, 86 per cent were in this category. The trend toward longer contracts has applied to both new and used cars, but used-car contracts have remained substantially shorter in maturity than new-car contracts.

Chart 2 shows in somewhat greater detail that the long-run trend toward lengthening terms has continued in recent years, though at a moderate pace since 1959. This trend was broken sharply only when Regulation W was reimposed in 1950–51 during the Korean War.[6]

Table 3 and Chart 3 reveal that much the same trend toward easier terms is evidenced by down payment percentages. A lower down payment relative to the retail price of the car is, of course, indicative of a more liberal advance of credit. Substantial shifts toward smaller down payment ratios occurred between 1934 and 1937 and between 1953 and 1955. Since 1957, however, there has been little further easing,

[6] This Federal Reserve regulation was in effect during the following periods: September 1, 1941, to November 1, 1947; September 20, 1948, to June 30, 1949; and September 18, 1950, to May 7, 1952. It imposed maximum maturities and minimum down payments for instalment credit.

TABLE 2

Percentage Distribution of Dollar Volume of Automobile Contracts by Length of Contract, Sales Finance Companies, Selected Years, 1925–65

Length of Contract	Statement Date, End of Year									
	1925	1929	1934	1937	1953	1955	1957	1960	1963	1965
New and Used Cars										
1. 12 mos. or less	81[a]	85[a]	70[a]	32[a]	--	--	--	--	--	--
2. 13 mos. and over	19	15	30	68	--	--	--	--	--	--
New Cars										
3. 12 mos. or less	--	--	62[a]	22[a]	--	--	--	--	--	--
4. 13 mos. and over	--	--	38	78	--	--	--	--	--	--
5. 18 mos. or less	--	--	--	65[b]	17[b]	9[b]	6[b]	--	--	--
6. 19 mos. and over	--	--	--	35	83	91	94	--	--	--
7. 24 mos. or less	--	--	--	95[a]	81[c]	32[b]	20[b]	--	--	--
8. 25 mos. and over	--	--	--	5	19	68	80	--	--	--
9. 30 mos. or less	--	--	--	--	--	--	56[b]	19[b]	15[b]	14[b]
10. 31 mos. and over	--	--	--	--	--	--	44	81	85	86
Used Cars										
11. 12 mos. or less	--	--	85[a]	51[b]	14[b]	17[b]	11[b]	--	--	--
12. 13 mos. and over	--	--	15	49	86	83	89	--	--	--
13. 24 mos. or less	--	--	--	99[a]	99[c]	95[c]	65[b]	33[b]	21[b]	21[b]
14. 25 mos. and over	--	--	--	1	1	5	35	67	79	79

(continued)

Notes to Table 2

[a]National Association of Sales Finance Companies, "Composite Experience of Sales Finance Companies and Automobile Dealers, 1939."

[b]First National Bank of Chicago, "Ratios of the Instalment Sales Finance and Small Loan Companies," and Supplements. Percentages shown are simple averages of the percentages reported by each company. Used-car figures from 1957 include only models up to two years old.

[c]*Consumer Instalment Credit*, Part II, Vol. 1, pp. 123—124. New-car figures are based on percentage distribution of number of contracts for five companies, which in 1955 had 57.1 per cent of the automobile paper extensions by all sales finance companies. Used-car figures are for four companies, which in 1955 had 55.8 per cent of the automobile paper. Percentage distribution by dollar volume not available.

Note: For additional detail see Appendix Tables A-1 — A-3.

judging from the percentage of sales finance contracts in which the amount of credit advanced exceeded the cost of the automobile to the dealer (or, in the case of used cars, its wholesale value). This ratio, termed the "dealer cost ratio," is an improvement upon the down payment percentage in that it avoids the inflation inherent in the latter when trade-in allowances (included in the down payment) are raised relative to the actual cash value of the trade-in. It is similar to the loan-to-value ratio used in mortgage credit analysis.[7]

Statistics on trends in the characteristics of automobile credit extended by commercial banks are assembled in Tables 4, 5, and 6. Table 4 indicates that since 1956 there has been a steady lengthening in maturities on both new- and used-car contracts and on contracts which the banks issue themselves as well as those purchased from dealers and other lenders. However, for direct loans the proportion with long maturities is much lower, a point worth bearing in mind because we shall find a corresponding difference in collection experience. Note also that the maturities are shorter for used-car than for new-car loans, just as in the sales finance company figures. Data for the same period but covering a different sample of commercial banks yield similar results (see Table A-4).

---

[7] For further discussion and comparison of the down payment percentage and dealer cost ratio, see Chapters 2, 7, and Appendix H.

CHART 2

Percentage of New-Car Sales Contracts in Excess of 18, 24, and 30 Months'
Maturity, Sales Finance Companies, 1935–65

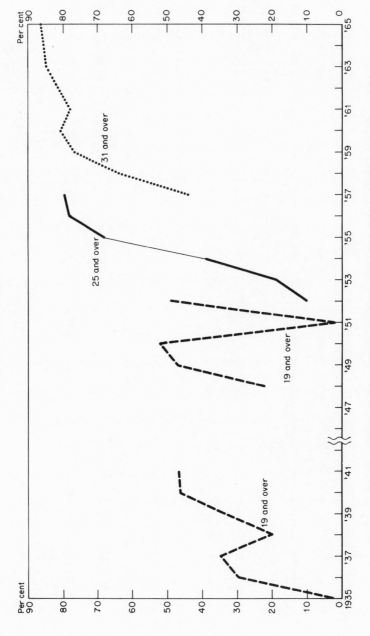

SOURCE: 1935–41, 1955–65, Table A-2 (percentages based on dollar volumes); 1948–54, Table
A-3 (percentages based on number of contracts).
NOTE: The figures for 1951 are significantly affected by Regulation W. Cf. note 6.

TABLE 3

Percentage Distribution of Dollar Volume of Automobile Contracts by Down Payment Percentage and by Dealer Cost Ratio, Sales Finance Companies, Selected Years, 1925–65

	Statement Date, End of Year									
	1925	1929	1934	1937	1953	1955	1957	1960	1963	1965
New and Used Cars										
1. Down Payment under 33-1/3%	19[a]	8[a]	18[a]	23[a]	--	--	--	--	--	--
2. Down Payment 33-1/3% and over	81	92	82	77	--	--	--	--	--	--
New Cars										
3. Down Payment under 33-1/3%	--	--	17[a]	22[b]	30[b]	52[b]	60[b]	--	--	--
4. Down Payment 33-1/3% and over	--	--	83	78	70	48	40	--	--	--
5. Dealer cost ratio 1.01 and over	--	--	--	--	--	--	32[b]	32[b]	38[b]	40[b]
6. Dealer cost ratio 1.00 or less	--	--	--	--	--	--	68	68	62	60
Used Cars										
7. Down Payment under 40%	--	--	21[a]	--	--	--	--	--	--	--
8. Down Payment 40% and over	--	--	79	--	--	--	--	--	--	--
9. Down Payment under 33-1/3%	--	--	--	28[b]	31[b]	38[b]	54[b]	--	--	--
10. Down Payment 33-1/3% and over	--	--	--	72	69	62	46	--	--	--
11. Dealer-cost ratio 1.01 and over	--	--	--	--	--	--	59[c]	39[b]	53[b]	52[b]
12. Dealer-cost ratio 1.00 or less	--	--	--	--	--	--	41	61	47	48

Notes to Table 3

[a]National Association of Sales Finance Companies, "Composite Experience of Sales Finance Companies and Automobile Dealers, 1939."

[b]First National Bank of Chicago, "Ratios of the Instalment Sales Finance and Small Loan Companies," and Supplements, Percentages shown are simple averages of the percentages reported by each company. The dealer-cost ratio is the ratio of the amount of credit advanced to the cost of the car to the dealer (for new cars) or to its wholesale value (for used cars). Hence an increase in the percentage of contracts with dealer-cost ratios in excess of 1.00 indicates an easing of credit similar to that implied by an increase in contracts with down payments less than 33 per cent of the retail price of the car.

[c]Related to low book value. (The First National Bank of Chicago, "Supplementary Ratios," June 1960 release.)

Table 4 suggests that the trend toward more liberal maturities which sales finance company data have revealed since the 1920's has also characterized commercial bank loans in the recent past. The only bank data available for a longer period are the estimated average loan durations shown in Table 5. While the method of estimation introduces certain biases, they are not so serious as to cast doubt upon the broad trends. It is clear that the average maturity on automobile contracts from all sources lengthened over time both in the prewar era and again in the years since 1946. Banks, however, have adhered to somewhat more conservative terms, especially on their direct loans, than sales finance companies. In 1965, for example, banks reported 80 per cent of their purchased paper and 64 per cent of their direct loans had maturities of more than thirty months, whereas the corresponding figure for sales finance companies was 86 per cent (see Chart 4).

The limited information available on down payment percentages or dealer cost ratios suggests that banks also have participated in the trend toward more liberal credit advances. Table 6 shows that since 1957 the proportion of bank loans on which the contract balance exceeded dealer cost or wholesale value has increased quite steadily, for purchased and direct loans on new cars as well as on used cars. Comparison of the dealer cost ratios for banks with those for sales finance companies (Table 3)—a hazardous comparison because the sources and method of averaging are different—suggests that bank terms have eased

CHART 3

Percentage of New-Car Sales Contracts (Dollar Volume) with Down Payment Less Than 33 Per Cent or Balance in Excess of Dealer Cost, Sales Finance Companies, 1935–65

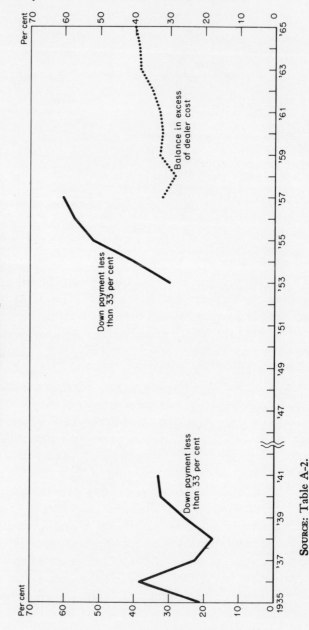

SOURCE: Table A-2.

TABLE 4

Percentage of Automobile Loans With Long Maturities,
Commercial Banks, 1956–65

	New Cars (per cent with maturities 31 months and over)			Used Cars (per cent with maturities over 25 months)		
	All Loans	Purchased Paper	Direct Loans	All Loans	Purchased Paper	Direct Loans
1956	38.4	45.2	18.2	13.2	17.0	5.2
1957	40.7	50.5	19.9	14.2	17.6	5.2
1958	49.7	59.6	29.1	17.7	23.1	7.4
1959	58.6	67.7	38.1	24.8	30.9	10.2
1960	62.6	71.2	43.9	25.8	31.0	12.8
1961	63.4	71.9	44.7	24.8	30.4	13.1
1962	67.9	75.4	52.1	28.9	35.4	15.6
1963	70.9	77.4	56.8	33.9	40.4	21.3
1964	73.8	79.6	60.8	38.1	44.4	25.0
1965	75.2	80.2	63.9	43.1	49.6	29.7

Source: NBER estimates based on unpublished data for a sample of commercial banks from the Board of Governors of the Federal Reserve System. All percentages are averages of twelve monthly figures.

more widely and steadily since 1957, but still remain more conservative, on the whole, than the terms on sales finance company credit. In any case, it seems clear that the long-run trend toward more liberal credit terms has been a general one.

The trend toward longer maturities and larger relative credit advances in the prewar period and the similar shift in the postwar period has been such that average monthly instalment payments on automobile contracts remained relatively constant in each period, though they shifted to a higher absolute level postwar than had been customary before the war. That is to say, repayment periods have increased roughly in proportion to the larger debt obligations, leaving payments per month about the same. Typical monthly payments on new cars in the postwar period have been $70–$80, and on used cars

TABLE 5

Average Duration Of Loan, Automobile Paper (New And Used Cars),
1928–65
(months)

	Average Term on Contracts Written, Automobile Dealers (1)	Computed Average Duration of Loan[a]					
		All Holders (2)	Auto Dealers[b] (3)	Commercial Banks			Sales Finance Companies (7)
				Direct (4)	Pur- chased (5)	Total (6)	
1928	12.4	--	--	--	--	--	--
1929	12.5	12.2	--	--	--	--	--
1930	12.6	11.5	--	--	--	--	--
1931	13.0	11.7	--	--	--	--	--
1932	13.1	11.9	--	--	--	--	--
1933	13.3	14.0	--	--	--	--	--
1934	13.8	13.5	--	--	--	--	--
1935	14.3	14.4	--	--	--	--	--
1936	16.2	14.4	--	--	--	--	--
1937	17.4	14.1	--	--	--	--	--
1938	16.8	14.6	--	--	--	--	--
1939	--	15.1	--	--	--	--	--
1940	--	16.2	--	--	--	--	--
1941	--	16.4	--	--	--	--	--
1942	--	12.3	--	12.5	13.1	12.8	--
1943	--	6.6	--	9.1	8.9	9.0	--
1944	--	9.2	--	9.6	10.1	9.8	--
1945	--	9.2	--	10.5	9.8	10.2	--
1946	--	10.2	11.0	11.3	10.3	10.9	9.4
1947	--	11.8	12.4	12.4	11.1	11.8	11.9
1948	--	13.8	14.0	14.0	13.7	13.9	13.8
1949	--	15.4	15.0	14.8	15.4	15.1	15.9
1950	--	17.6	16.8	17.0	18.3	17.6	18.0
1951	--	15.1	15.0	14.9	15.5	15.2	15.0
1952	--	14.8	14.5	14.2	15.2	14.7	15.1
1953	--	18.9	17.6	17.5	19.6	18.6	19.7
1954	--	18.6	17.1	17.2	18.7	18.0	19.5
1955	--	20.5	18.4	18.6	19.8	19.2	22.0
1956	--	22.2	20.0	20.0	22.1	21.3	23.6
1957	--	22.1	20.0	20.0	22.4	21.5	23.1
1958	--	21.7	20.1	20.1	22.2	21.4	22.5
1959	--	22.6	20.7	20.9	22.7	22.1	23.9
1960	--	24.4	21.8	22.4	24.6	23.8	25.6
1961	--	24.2	22.5	22.4	24.4	23.7	25.2
1962	--	24.1	19.3	22.8	24.8	24.0	25.1
1963	--	25.0	14.6	24.2	26.1	25.4	26.4
1964	--	25.5	n.a.	24.2	26.2	25.4	27.3
1965	--	25.8	n.a.	24.8	26.7	26.0	27.8

Notes to Table 5

Source: Column 1 —— Duncan McC. Holthausen, *The Volume of Consumer Instalment Credit, 1929–38*, NBER, 1940, p. 46; Columns 2–7 —— Federal Reserve *Supplement to Banking and Monetary Statistics*, "Section 16 (new), Consumer Credit"; *Federal Reserve Bulletin*, May 1966; Federal Reserve Releases G.18 and G.20; computed as follows:

$$1929{-}39: \frac{\text{Average outstandings at end of preceding and current year} \times 2}{\text{Repayments during year} \div 12} - 1.$$

$$1940{-}65: \text{Four-quarter average of } \frac{\text{Average outstandings at end of preceding and current quarter} \times 2}{\text{Repayments during quarter} \div 3} - 1.$$

[a]These estimates are subject to a downward bias when new loan extensions decline sharply, reducing outstandings relative to repayments, and to an upward bias when extensions rise sharply. Also, since the repayment figures include refinancing, the calculated durations are necessarily shorter than the average maturities of the original obligations. The figures for certain years in the period 1946–52 are importantly affected by Regulation W. Cf. note 6.

[b]Information on repayments of auto loans held by dealers is not published separately. The Federal Reserve estimate is based on the assumption that the monthly collection ratio is the same as that for direct auto loans held by commercial banks. While this assumption was valid several years ago there is no recent information on this point; hence the computed durations for the most recent period are of uncertain validity and are necessarily nearly identical with those for direct bank loans.

n.a. = not available.

$45–$50. In the prewar period the amounts were roughly half these levels.

Finally, it is important to bear in mind that the trend toward easier terms since the 1920's which has just been outlined does not necessarily mean that credit quality has declined proportionately. Other factors that affect credit quality or risk must be taken into consideration. The higher level and greater stability of incomes, the broader distribution of liquid assets, the longer life of the average car, the greater necessity of owning an automobile for transportation to work in our expanding suburban areas, and many other factors need to be considered before one reaches broad conclusions based on the simple association of loan

CHART 4

Terms on New-Car Contracts: Sales Finance Companies and Commercial Banks, 1956–65

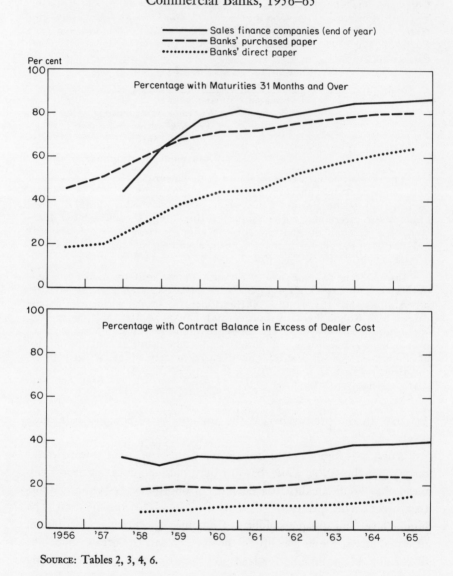

—————— Sales finance companies (end of year)
——————— Banks' purchased paper
••••••••••• Banks' direct paper

Per cent

Percentage with Maturities 31 Months and Over

Percentage with Contract Balance in Excess of Dealer Cost

Source: Tables 2, 3, 4, 6.

TABLE 6

Percentage of Automobile Loans With Contract Balance in Excess of
Dealer Cost, Commercial Banks, 1956–65

	New Cars			Used Cars[a]		
	All Loans	Purchased Paper	Direct Loans	All Loans	Purchased Paper	Direct Loans
1956	12.9	––	––	24.1	––	––
1957	12.4	––	––	24.0	––	––
1958	14.5	17.5	7.1	26.4	33.5	12.7
1959	16.2	19.2	8.0	30.0	36.9	14.2
1960	16.3	18.6	9.9	32.4	38.0	19.0
1961	16.8	18.7	10.9	35.9	40.0	26.0
1962	17.7	20.3	10.5	37.9	45.9	20.2
1963	19.9	22.6	11.0	40.3	47.3	23.5
1964	12.2	23.8	12.2	39.5	45.2	24.9
1965	21.6	23.6	14.5	38.3	43.6	24.2

Source: NBER estimates based on unpublished data for a sample of commercial banks from the Board of Governors of the Federal Reserve System. Percentages are averages of twelve monthly figures (except 1956, which is an average of the last 3 months of the year).

[a]Percentage with contract balance in excess of wholesale value.

terms with credit quality. Among these factors, consideration of borrower characteristics, to which attention is directed in the next section, is of critical importance.

BORROWER CHARACTERISTICS

As just noted, loan quality viewed prospectively at the time loans are made requires consideration not alone of the terms on which loans are extended but also of those characteristics of the borrowers which pertain to their ability and willingness to repay. The degree of risk which attaches to loans with identical down payment and maturity requirements can, of course, vary radically depending on the borrowers to whom the loans are extended. Improvements in the level and stability of borrowers' incomes, for example, can lead to better collection experience. Such changes in the characteristics of borrowers may occur because of shifts in the willingness of lenders to grant credit to different segments of the population, because of changes in the desire of different groups to borrow, and, lastly, because of changes that occur in the characteristics of the population itself.

It is much more difficult to summarize changes in borrower characteristics than in loan terms. First, the relevant characteristics are by no means as clearly defined or as commonly agreed upon as are loan terms. In the second place, few financial institutions keep systematic statistical records even of the more obvious characteristics of their borrowers, such as income and occupational status, despite the value such records would have not only in analyzing risk but also in defining the market. It is, furthermore, difficult to trace changes in borrower characteristics over a long period of time, because most of the available information is to be found in the Survey of Consumer Finances, which began in the postwar period. Moreover, the questions asked by the survey have varied somewhat from year to year, the method of presenting the results has also varied, and the definition of indebtedness, crucial for our purposes, has varied considerably as well. Nonetheless, it is possible through the survey data, and with a few other sources of information, to arrive at certain broad conclusions concerning changes in borrower characteristics.

In her study of the pattern of consumer debt for 1935–36, Blanche Bernstein found that 26 per cent of the families with instalment debt had incomes under $1,000 a year. Forty-eight per cent of the instalment debt holders had incomes between $1,000 and $2,000, and only 27 per cent had incomes over $2,000. Table 7 compares Bernstein's results with the distribution of instalment debt holders by income in 1941, 1956, and 1962. A rough adjustment for the change in the cost of living has been incorporated by making use of the fact that prices paid by consumers rose only moderately between 1935–36 and 1941 but approximately doubled by 1956 and 1962. Thus Table 7 suggests that, even bearing in mind the great changes in price levels since the mid-1930's, the distribution of debt has shifted to a marked degree toward higher real-income groups, largely in accordance with the rising real incomes of the entire population. The use of instalment debt has increased sharply in all income groups since the mid-thirties, but more so in the middle and upper income range than in the lower groups. In all

TABLE 7

Instalment Debt Holders by Income Group,
1935–36, 1941, 1956, and 1962

Income in 1935–36 or 1941 Dollars	Income in 1956 or 1962 Dollars	1935–36	1941	1956	1962	Change 1935–36 to 1956	Change 1956 to 1962
				All Households,			
				Percentage Distribution			
Under 1,000	Under 2,000	35	23	21	15	-14	-6
1,000-1,999	2,000-3,999	40	31	24	21	-16	-3
2,000-4,999	4,000-9,999	21	41	47	49	+26	+2
5,000 and over	10,000 and over	3	5	8	15	+5	+7
Total		100	100	100	100		
				All Households,			
				Percentage with Instalment Debt			
Under 1,000	Under 2,000	17	15	24	22	+7	-2
1,000-1,999	2,000-3,999	28	32	45 } 56		+17 }	+1
2,000-4,999	4,000-9,999	28	37	60 }		+32 }	
5,000 and over	10,000 and over	15	24	35	46	+20	+11
Average		24	30	47	50	+23	+3
				Instalment Debt Holders,			
				Percentage Distribution			
Under 1,000	Under 2,000	26	12	11	7	-15	-4
1,000-1,999	2,000-3,999	48	34	23 } 80		-25 }	-3
2,000-4,999	4,000-9,999	25	51	60 }		+35 }	
5,000 and over	10,000 and over	2	4	6	14	+4	+8
Total		100	100	100	100		

Notes to Table 7

Source: 1935–36, Blanche Bernstein, *The Pattern of Consumer Debt, 1935–36: A Statistical Analysis,* NBER, 1940, Table A-1, p. 124. Data refer to families having a net change in instalment debt during the year.

1941, Reavis Cox, "Instalment Buying by City Consumers in 1941," BLS *Bulletin 773,* p. 3. Data refer to consumer units having a net increase in their outstanding instalment-purchase obligations during the year.

1956, "Survey of Consumer Finances," *Federal Reserve Bulletin,* August 1957, pp. 892, 896, 900. Data refer to spending units; income data pertain to 1956, instalment indebtedness to date of interview, early 1957.

1962, *1963 Survey of Consumer Finances,* Monograph No. 34, Survey Research Center, Institute for Social Research, The University of Michigan, pp. 20, 65, and 66. Data refer to spending units; income data pertain to 1962, instalment indebtedness to date of interview, early 1963.

Since the consumer price index was 48 in 1935–36, 51 in 1941, and 95 in 1956 and 105 in 1962 (1957–59:100), doubling the 1935–36 and the 1941 incomes makes them roughly comparable in real terms with 1956 and 1962.

Note: Detail may not add to total because of rounding.

years, however, the majority of instalment debt holders have been in the middle income groups.

One can, of course, ignore the position of borrowers at either end of the income scale and consider the median incomes of spending units with debt and without it. Such figures for a number of years are shown in Table 8. It is seen that in every year surveyed the median income of debtors has been higher than the median income of the total spending population, and instalment debt holders have higher median incomes than all personal debt holders. Instalment debt is not typically associated with very low income. Moreover, movements in median incomes for debtors and nondebtors have not been sharply divergent. Between 1948 and 1963 median incomes of spending units with instalment debt and of all spending units both more than doubled.

We are interested in changes in income primarily because they are relevant to consideration of the burden that instalment debt represents for the borrower and his ability to repay it. According to Table 1, the ratio of instalment loan repayments to total personal income has risen sharply since the end of the Second World War. However, it is the

TABLE 8

Median Incomes: Spending Units with Debt and All Spending Units, 1935–36, 1941, and 1948–63

	Spending Units			Ratio	
	With Personal Debt[a] (1)	With Instalment Debt (2)	All (3)	Col. 1 to Col. 3 (4)	Col. 2 to Col. 3 (5)
1935–36	— —	$1,461	$1,286	— —	1.14
1941	— —	2,126	1,863	— —	1.13
1948	$3,305	3,216	2,840	1.16	1.13
1949	3,155	— —	2,700	1.17	— —
1950	3,402	— —	3,000	1.13	— —
1951	3,547	— —	3,200	1.11	— —
1952	3,666	— —	3,420	1.07	— —
1953	4,152	4,310	3,780	1.10	1.14
1954	4,059	4,125	3,700	1.10	1.11
1955	4,257	4,442	3,960	1.08	1.12
1956	4,712	4,936	4,250	1.11	1.16
1957	4,868	n.a.	4,350	1.12	n.a.
1958	4,891	5,082	4,400	1.11	1.16
1959	— —	5,498	4,860	— —	1.13
1960	— —	6,008	5,170	— —	1.16
1961	— —	5,790	5,000	— —	1.16
1962	— —	5,996	5,300	— —	1.13
1963	— —	6,640[b]	5,900[b]	— —	1.13

Source: Computed from data from Bernstein, *Pattern of Consumer Debt,* for 1935–36; Cox, "Instalment Buying," for 1941; "Survey of Consumer Finances," *Federal Reserve Bulletins* for 1948–58; and Monographs 24, 32, 34, 39 of *Survey of Consumer Finances,* Survey Research Center, University of Michigan, for 1959–63.

[a]Personal debt excludes mortgage debt in all years except 1948 and 1949; in 1950, figure may include some cases with only business debt or with only charge accounts. In other years those with business debt or charge accounts only are excluded. In 1951, all owners of unincorporated businesses and farm operators are excluded from calculations whether or not they had consumer debt; in later years they are included.

[b]In 1963 the Survey was conducted on a family-unit basis.

TABLE 9

Two Estimates of the Ratio of Instalment Debt Repayments to Income of Instalment Debtors, 1935–63

	Total Personal Income (bil. $) (1)	Per Cent of Spending Units with Instalment Debt (2)	Ratio of Median Incomes, Instalment Debtors to All Spending Units (3)	Estimated Personal Income of Instalment Debtors (bil. $) (4)	Repayments on Instalment Debt (bil. $) (5)	Repayments as Percentage of Personal Income of Instalment Debtors (6)	Median Percentage, Repayments to Preceding Year's Disposable Income of Debtors (7)
1935–36	64.5	24	1.14	17.6	4.0	23	n.a.
1941	96.0	30	1.13	32.6	8.9	27	n.a.
1952	272.5	38	1.14e	118.0	25.4	22	n.a.
1953	288.2	40e	1.14	131.4	28.0	21	n.a.
1954	290.1	43	1.11	138.5	30.5	22	14
1955	310.9	44	1.12	153.2	33.6	22	14
1956	333.0	45	1.16	173.8	37.1	21	14
1957	351.1	47	1.16e	191.4	39.9	21	15
1958	361.2	48	1.16	201.1	40.3	20	13
1959	383.5	48	1.13	208.0	42.6	20	14
1960	401.0	48	1.16	223.3	46.0	21	13
1961	416.8	47	1.16	227.2	47.7	21	12
1962	442.6	46	1.13	230.1	50.2	22	13
1963	465.5	50	1.13	263.0	55.2	21	13

Notes to Table 9

e   = estimated by interpolation or extrapolation.
n.a. = not available.
Source: Columns 1 and 5 — Table 1, above.
Columns 2 and 7 — *1963 Survey of Consumer Finances,* pp. 65 and
68; and earlier Surveys. Figures in Column 7 for 1954, 1956, 1957,
and 1959 computed by NBER from frequency distributions published
in earlier surveys.
Column 3 — Table 8, above.
Column 4 — Column 1 x Column 2 x Column 3 ÷ 100.
Column 6 — Column 5 ÷ Column 1 x 100.

ratio of repayments to borrowers' income rather than to all income
that is relevant for consideration of the ability of borrowers to repay
their loans. In view of the facts demonstrated in Tables 7 and 8 that
the average income of borrowers has increased at least as much as the
average income of the whole population, and that the number of borrowers has increased relative to the population, it seems likely that the
aggregate income of borrowers has risen faster than total personal
income. Hence the ratio of debt repayments to *borrowers'* income,
while much higher than the ratio to total income, has not risen as fast
as that ratio has. Indeed, some rough calculations, together with direct
survey evidence, suggest that the average ratio of instalment debt repayments to borrowers' income may not have risen at all (Table 9
and Chart 5). The calculations suggest that instalment debt repayments have absorbed about 21 per cent of the aggregate income of
borrowers each year since 1952. Estimates for 1935–36 and 1941 are
somewhat higher. The median ratio of instalment debt repayments to
disposable income of borrowers as reported by the Survey of Consumer Finances is a much lower figure, around 13 per cent, but it too
has remained roughly constant over the years for which it has been
reported (since 1955).[8] One of the factors that has prevented an increase in the repayment-income ratio is, of course, the extension of

[8] One of the principal reasons for the higher level of our calculated ratio compared with the median ratio reported by the survey is that our figures on repayments include repayment of debt that is refinanced, whereas the survey ratios
do not include such "repayments." Other factors seem to work in the opposite
direction. Since the calculated ratio is, in effect, an average of repayment to
income ratios weighted by income, and since repayment ratios are probably higher
in the heavily populated low income groups, one might expect the median
ratio to be higher than the weighted average. Furthermore, our calculation uses,

CHART 5

Ratios of Consumer Instalment Credit to Income, 1920–65

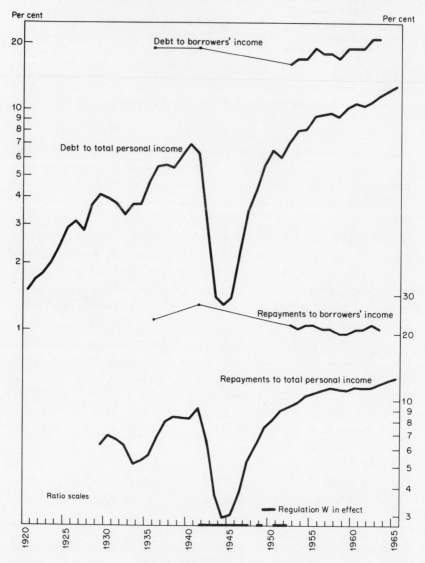

SOURCE: Worksheets for Tables 1 and 9.

maturities. The ratio of instalment debt to borrowers' income has undoubtedly increased, though only moderately. Between 1953 and 1963, the ratio of instalment debt at the end of the year to instalment debtors' income as estimated in Table 9 rose from 17.5 per cent to 20.6 per cent. In short, the obligation assumed by borrowers has increased relative to their income, although the immediate burden of that obligation has not.

Data on the occupational characteristics of the borrowing population are available for even fewer years than are the income characteristics. Comparisons reflecting changes over a fairly long period are possible only by utilizing the Bernstein data for the mid-1930's and the Survey of Consumer Finances data for the 1950's. Bernstein classified nonfarm occupations into two groups, wage-earning and other. The latter includes not only the professional and managerial groups but also clerical and sales—occupations now usually included with wage earners. In Table 10 the distribution of instalment debt borrowers in the farm and two nonfarm classes is shown for 1935–36 and for 1956, together with more detail for 1956 alone.

The incidence of debt holding has increased substantially in all occupational groups during this twenty-year period, though relatively more for wage earners and least for farmers (cols. 3 and 4). This shift, plus the dramatic reduction in farm households (cols. 1 and 2), has meant that borrowers in the wage-earner group have increased relative to those in other occupations, while farm borrowers have decreased.[9] Since wage earners have generally had a poorer than average record in repaying consumer debt, and the farm group better than average (see Chapter 4), this shift in itself would contribute to a deterioration in credit quality. However, an offsetting factor, no doubt, has been the substantial relative increase in wage-earner income during this period.

not the ratio of mean incomes of debtors to those of the whole population, but the ratio of their median incomes. One might expect the ratio of mean incomes to be lower than the ratio of medians, but this would reduce the estimate of borrowers' income and hence raise the calculated ratio of repayments to borrowers' income. Finally, our calculated ratio is to total personal income, whereas the survey ratio is to disposable income; correction for this difference would make the discrepancy still larger. Estimates of the median ratio for borrowers on new-auto contracts, of 17 per cent for 1953 and 19 per cent for 1957, are given in Table 35, below.

[9] For some evidence that this trend has continued since 1956, cf. Table A-5.

TABLE 10

Instalment Debt Holders by Occupation Group, 1935–36 and 1956

Occupation Of Family Head	All Households				Instalment Debt Holders, Percentage Distribution	
	Percentage Distribution		Percentage with Instal-ment Debt			
	1935-36 (1)	1956 (2)	1935-36 (3)	1956 (4)	1935-36 (5)	1956 (6)
Wage earners	40	46	30	60	49	57
Skilled and semiskilled	--	34	--	62	--	43
Unskilled and service	--	13[a]	--	56[a]	--	14[a]
Other nonfarm occupations	35	47	26	42	39	40
Professional and semiprofessional	--	13	--	47	--	13
Managerial	--	8	--	47	--	7
Clerical and sales	--	15	--	44	--	14
Self-employed	--	11	--	30	--	7
Farmers						
Operators and laborers	25	--	12	--	12	--
Operators	--	6	--	18	--	2
Total employed	100	100	24	49	100	100

Source: Bernstein, *Pattern of Consumer Dept.*, pp. 28, 31, 130, 146, 147; "Survey of Consumer Finances," *Federal Reserve Bulletin*, July 1956, p. 705. The latter source also covers instalment debt holders among those not employed, with the following results (1956):

	All Households		Instalment debt holders, percentage distribution
	Percentage distribution	Percentage with instal-ment debt	
Employed	80	49	88
Retired	9	13	3
Unemployed, students, housewives, and protective service workers	11	40	10
Total	100	45	100

[a]Includes farm laborers.
Note: Detail may not add to total because of rounding.

One borrower characteristic which is of considerable importance in connection with ability to repay debt is the holding of liquid assets. There are good reasons to suppose, and some empirical evidence as well (presented in Chapter 4), that the existence of liquid assets reduces the degree of risk attached to consumer credit. Although we have not been able to put together a usable series showing changes in the debt-to-liquid-asset ratio among borrowers, it is possible to examine the change in liquid-asset holdings for the whole population, and to compare it with the change either in total consumer credit or in instalment credit outstanding (Table 11). It appears that, despite the great increase in liquid assets held by nonfarm households generally, their debt has risen faster still. The ratio of debt to assets in 1963 was higher than in any year on record, and was almost as high in 1964. However, since 1957, the increase in the ratio has been relatively small. It is, of course, necessary to bear in mind that the liquid assets shown in the table include all liquid assets held, not simply those held by the users of consumer credit.

A recent picture of borrowers' holdings of liquid assets in relation to their debt is provided by Table 12. For borrowers in the lower income groups, personal debt is typically greater than liquid assets. The percentage of borrowers with debt in excess of their liquid assets declines quite steadily as one moves up the income scale (cols. 7 and 10). The fact that debt is usually at a more conservative level in relation to liquid assets in the case of higher income groups may help to explain why credit experience is generally better in high than in low income groups.

Finally, one might inquire how indebtedness has spread among age groups, since the borrower's age has some bearing on his financial responsibility and economic prospects. Table 13 indicates that the holding of debt within all age groups became more common between 1951 and 1959, but that the frequency of indebtedness increased most in the younger groups. This doubtless reflects the recent trend toward marriage at younger ages and the consequent necessity for establishing households. An offsetting factor has been the shift in the age distribution of the population toward the older, with the net effect that the distribution of debt holders by age was substantially the same in 1959 as in 1951. Recently published data for 1962 show that the frequency of debt holding has remained high at the younger ages. In

TABLE 11

Consumer Credit and Liquid-Asset Holdings by Nonfarm Households, Selected Years, 1929–64

End of Year	Liquid Assets Held by (billion dollars)		Consumer Credit Outstanding		Debt to Asset Ratios (per cent)			
					Nonfarm Households		Consumer and Nonprofit Organizations	
	Nonfarm Households	Consumer and Nonprofit Organizations	Total	Instalment Credit	Total ÷(1)	Instalment Debt (4)÷(1)	Total (3)÷(2)	Instalment Debt (4)÷(2)
	(1)	(2)	(3)	(4)	(5)	(6)	(7)	(8)
1929	44.2	--	7.3	3.5	16.5	7.9	--	--
1933	43.9	--	3.9	1.7	8.9	3.9	--	--
1939	53.8	--	7.2	4.5	13.4	8.4	--	--
1945[a]	170.8	--	5.7	2.5	3.3	1.5	--	--
1945[b]	162.4	--			3.5	1.5	--	--
1949	178.6	--	17.4	11.6	9.7	6.5	--	--
1953	206.5	--	31.4	23.0	15.2	11.1	--	--
1955	225.4	--	38.8	28.9	17.2	12.8	--	--
1957	245.9	--	45.0	33.9	18.3	13.8	--	--
1958	260.5	272.1	45.1	33.6	17.3	12.9	16.6	12.3
1959	--	293.0	51.5	39.2	--	--	17.6	13.4
1960	--	302.0	56.0	42.8	--	--	18.5	14.2
1961	--	320.5	57.7	43.5	--	--	18.0	13.6
1962	--	351.0	63.2	48.0	--	--	18.0	13.7
1963	--	369.1	70.5	54.2	--	--	19.1	14.7
1964	--	412.5	78.4	60.5	--	--	19.0	14.7

(continued)

Notes to Table 11

Source: Column 1 —— *Studies in the National Balance Sheet of the United States,* Volume II, Raymond W. Goldsmith, Robert E. Lipsey, and Morris Mendelson, Princeton Press for NBER, 1963, Table Ia, pp. 78–85 and Table III-1, pp. 118–119. Liquid assets include currency and demand deposits, other bank deposits and shares, and U.S. government securities.

Column 2 —— *Flow of Funds Accounts, 1945–62, 1963 Supplement,* Board of Governors of the Federal Reserve System, Table 8, p. 4, and *Federal Reserve Bulletin,* November 1965, p. 1622.   Liquid assets include demand deposits and currency, savings accounts, and U.S. government securities. The differences between column (1) and column (2) represent principally bank deposits and shares and savings bonds held by farm households and revisions in the Federal Reserve data.

Columns 3 and 4 —— Table 1.

^aComparable with preceding years.

^bComparable with following years.

that year 80 per cent in the group under 35 and 20 per cent in the group 65 and over had personal debt.[10]

Data on other borrower characteristics are too fragmentary, or too remotely related to credit quality, to justify detailed consideration. What evidence there is concerning these characteristics, as well as more detailed materials on the characteristics presently considered, are presented in Table A-5.

It is apparent from this brief review of the admittedly scanty evidence on the changing characteristics of borrowers that there has been a substantial increase in recent decades in the incidence of both instalment and noninstalment debt among all income, occupation, and age groups. The over-all increase is indeed more striking than the redistribution among income, age, or occupation groups. Whether the incidence has shifted in such a way as to reduce repayment difficulties substantially is difficult to say. As between the prewar period and the late 1950's, the shift toward higher income groups, the continued increase in the use of credit in the better paid and more stable occupations, and the greater stability in aggregate income and employment have no doubt tended to reduce risk, thereby compensating at least in part for the easing of terms. During the postwar period alone, how-

[10] Dorothy S. Projector and Gertrude S. Weiss, *Survey of Financial Characteristics of Consumers,* Board of Governors of the Federal Reserve System, August 1966, p. 126.

TABLE 12

Distribution of Spending Units by Income And by Relation of Personal Debt to Liquid-Asset Holdings, 1959 and 1962

Income Before Taxes[a] (dollars)	1959, All Spending Units: Percentage with				1959, Spending Units with Debt: Percentage with			1962, Consumer Units with Debt: Percentage with		
	No Personal Debt (1)	Personal Debt Less than Liquid Assets (2)	Personal Debt Equal to or Greater than Liquid Assets (3)	Total (4)	Personal Debt Less than Liquid Assets (5)	Personal Debt Equal to or Greater than Liquid Assets (6)	Total (7)	Personal Debt Less than Liquid Assets (8)	Personal Debt Equal to or Greater than Liquid Assets (9)	Total (10)
Under 1,000	58	5	37	100	12	88	100			
1,000–1,999	57	5	38	100	12	88	100	9	91	100
2,000–2,999	44	15	41	100	27	73	100			
3,000–3,999	36	17	47	100	27	73	100	21	79	100
4,000–4,999	32	21	47	100	31	69	100			
5,000–5,999	30	25	45	100	36	64	100	24	76	100
6,000–7,499	29	27	44	100	38	62	100			
7,500–9,999	31	31	38	100	45	55	100	29	71	100
10,000 and over	49	26	25	100	51	49	100	40	60	100
All	40	20	40	100	33	67	100	24	76	100

Source: "Survey of Consumer Finances," *Federal Reserve Bulletin*, July 1959, p. 721, Supplementary Table 19; *Survey of Financial Characteristics of Consumers* by Dorothy S. Projector and Gertrude S. Weiss, Board of Governors of the Federal Reserve System, August 1966, p. 17.

[a] 1958 income, for distribution by debt–liquid assets in early 1959; 1962 income, for distribution by debt–liquid assets on December 31, 1962.

TABLE 13

Consumer Indebtedness by Age of Borrower, 1951 and 1959

	All Households						Personal Debt Holders, Percentage Distribution		
Age of Head of Spending Unit (years)	Percentage Distribution			Percentage with Personal Debt					
	1951	1959	Change, 1951–59	1951	1959	Change, 1951–59	1951	1959	Change, 1951–59
18–24	8	8	0	46	70	+24	8	10	+2
25–34	21	20	–1	62	80	+18	27	26	–1
35–44	23	23	0	62	71	+9	30	27	–3
45–54	19	18	–1	47	64	+17	19	20	+1
55–64	16	16	0	36	41	+5	12	11	–1
65 and over	13	15	+2	19	26	+7	5	7	+2
Total or average	100	100		48	60	+12	100	100	

Source: "Survey of Consumer Finances," *Federal Reserve Bulletin*, December 1951, p. 1522; July 1959, pp. 712, 721. In 1951 personal debt includes charge accounts, instalment debt, and all other debt not secured by real estate. In 1959 it includes all short- and intermediate-term consumer debt other than charge accounts and excludes mortgage and business debt.

Note: Detail may not add to total because of rounding.

ever, the appreciable rise in the debt-to-income and debt-to-liquid-asset ratios suggests that the net effect of the changes in borrower characteristics has been to heighten rather than to lessen the risk attendant upon easier loan terms.

COLLECTION EXPERIENCE

It is clear that there has been considerable easing of loan terms during the past thirty years, especially on automobile credit. It is also clear that there has been a great increase in the use of instalment credit by all classes of consumers, though whether this use has been concentrated among particular groups of borrowers in such a way as to increase lending risks is less easy to say. This matter will require further consideration of the relation among loan terms, borrower characteristics, and prospective risk. To begin with, however, some direct evidence on lending risks may be obtained by examining briefly the level and trend in collection experience on instalment loans.

The major indicators of collection experience are delinquency rates, repossession rates, and loss rates.[11] The initial indication of collection difficulties is shown by the delinquency rate. The American Bankers Association has collected such information on automobile loans monthly since the 1940's and bimonthly since 1964; annual averages of these rates both for direct bank loans and for loans which banks acquire from automobile dealers are shown in Table 14. The trend of these rates has been downward since 1947, though the decline seems to have halted in 1957 or 1959. Indirect bank loans throughout show poorer delinquency experience than direct loans. In each business recession, i.e., in 1949, 1954, 1958, and 1961, delinquencies have risen, then declined when prosperity returned. During the period as a whole, there has been no dramatic rise in delinquency rates comparable with the easing in loan terms.

The ultimate measure of collection experience is the loss rate. The available information here pertains to sales finance companies, and it extends considerably farther back than the bank delinquency data (Table 15). The data from the study by Winchester summarized in the first column suggest a long-run diminution in loss rates for the period

---

[11] For further discussion of these and other measures of collection difficulty, cf. Chapter 3 and Appendix C. Data on repossession rates covering a long period are not available; some figures for 1948–56 are given in Table 47, below.

TABLE 14

Delinquency Experience on Automobile Loans,
Commercial Banks, 1948–65

	Loans Delinquent 30 Days and Over as Percentage of Loans Outstanding at End of Month (Annual Average)	
	Direct	Indirect
1948	1.64	2.05
1949	1.75	2.24
1950	1.42	1.96
1951	1.23	1.73
1952	.93	1.47
1953	.98	1.65
1954	1.05	1.71
1955	.82	1.41
1956	.76	1.36
1957	.75	1.35
1958	.84	1.53
1959	.78	1.31
1960	.94	1.46
1961	1.05	1.49
1962	.95	1.33
1963	.94	1.42
1964	.94	1.50
1965	1.14	1.57

Source: "Delinquency Rates on Bank Instalment Loans," bi-monthly reports compiled by Instalment Credit Committee, American Bankers Association.

Data represent unweighted averages of delinquency rates reported separately in nine regions from 1948-54, and in ten regions from 1955-64. 1965 is extrapolated from 1964-65 change in weighted average (the present form of the published data).

TABLE 15

Net Losses on Retail Paper, Sales Finance Companies, 1929–65

Year	Outstanding Automobile Paper (5 companies) (1)	All Retail Paper Liquidated (19 companies) (2)
	Ratio of Net Loss to	
1929	1.15	––
1930	2.08	––
1931	1.69	––
1932	1.63	––
1933	.60	––
1934	.68	––
1935	.57	.75
1936	.44	.92
1937	.60	.89
1938	.97	1.70
1939	.48	.82
1940	.50	.92
1941	.50	.68
1942	1.07	––
1943	(1.51)[a]	––
1944	(.07)[a]	––
1945	.33	––
1946	.20	––
1947	.28	.48
1948	.30	.66
1949	.50	1.57
1950	.21	.58
1951	.31	.44
1952	––	.76
1953	––	1.40
1954	––	1.18
1955	––	.64
1956	––	.72
1957	––	.74
1958	––	1.35
1959	––	1.07
1960	––	1.71
1961	––	1.73
1962	––	1.28
1963	––	1.08
1964	––	1.21
1965	––	1.22

Notes to Table 15

Source:　Column 1 – James P. Winchester, *Consumer Installment Loan Losses and Valuation Reserves* (Bankers Publishing Company, Cambridge, Mass., 1955), Table 10, p. 33.

Column 2 – First National Bank of Chicago, *Ratios of the Instalment Sales Finance and Consumer Finance Companies,* February 1961, pp. 20–25, and current releases.

[a]Recoveries from loans previously charged off exceeded the gross write-offs.

1929–50, although the rates for 1930–32 were obviously raised during the Great Depression. The estimates compiled by the First National Bank of Chicago, which begin somewhat later and continue to the present, rise in each business recession since 1938. Unlike the bank delinquency rates, the sales finance company loss rates do not show a downward trend. Indeed, loss rates have risen somewhat during the postwar period.

Thus it emerges that a revolution in the terms on which instalment credit is extended and in the type of borrower to whom it is extended, as well as a vast increase in the sheer volume of lending, have occurred without any striking increase in delinquency or loss rates. Of course, some dangers may lie ahead, either on a national scale or in particular areas or markets. For this reason, an examination of the relationship between evidence of potential risk and actual experience, and how it is affected by economic conditions generally, is warranted.

2. The Concept of Credit Quality

In most discussions of consumer "credit quality," first consideration is given to the terms on which credit is granted. In 1955 Allan Sproul, then president of the New York Federal Reserve Bank, directed attention to the problem in this way: "I am disturbed not by the total amount of consumer credit, but by the fact or the indication that successive relaxation of terms has been largely responsible for keeping the ball in the air. This is a process which cannot go on indefinitely." [1]

There is a strong suggestion here that quantitative changes were being brought about by changes in quality,[2] and that the process might have undesirable consequences. Analysis of this process will be aided by defining and measuring credit quality as precisely as possible, so that the effect of changes in it can be identified.

The consumer credit industry has long recognized the need for maintaining "sound terms," but there has never been any agreement within the industry on how to define these terms. Some early attempts were made to use specific characteristics of the loan contract for this purpose, but these broke down because the guidelines were never very clear. Again, there have been efforts within the industry to define credit terms as sound if the loan was granted on a collateralized basis. The collateralized definition suggests that terms may safely be liberalized as long as the value of the note outstanding will at no time during the life of the contract exceed the market value of the commodity covered by the loan.[3] Others emphasize the character and capacity of

[1] Allan Sproul, "Reflections of a Central Banker," *Journal of Finance*, March 1956, p. 11.

[2] For some evidence on this point, see Appendix G.

[3] For a brief statement of this position, see Thomas W. Rogers, *Easy Credit Can be Tough*, American Finance Conference, December 1955.

the borrower, rather than the terms on which he borrows, as the essential ingredient of loan quality.[4]

Loan terms and borrower characteristics, however, constitute only one aspect of the concept of credit quality, albeit an important one. To quote an earlier paper, "Deterioration of credit quality can . . . mean at least four different things: (1) a decline in actual quality, as indicated by loss rates, foreclosure rates, default or delinquency rates determined after the event . . . (2) a decline in estimated quality as indicated by loss reserves, interest differentials, examiners' appraisals, and the like; (3) a shift toward types of loan contracts or types of borrowers that may be expected to involve higher delinquency or loss rates; or (4) a change for the worse in the economic prospects of debtors." [5]

It is important to note that deterioration in credit quality is not necessarily synonymous with a reduction of standards on the part of lenders. Such a reduction may be the cause of the deterioration described in the first definition cited, and it is suggested by the third definition (although the shift mentioned may take place not because lenders relax their standards but because the relative volume of credit handled by lenders with lower standards increases). The other two definitions of quality deterioration do not necessarily imply a lowering of standards on the part of lenders, although the second definition does imply a shift in the way lenders appraise their standards.

This distinction between credit standards and credit quality is important because some deterioration in quality may well be viewed as a necessary accompaniment to any expansion in credit. The major policy implications have to do with the question of how far the credit deterioration can safely go. This in turn can be answered only if we know how far it has in fact gone and what the consequences may be.

The distinction between credit standards and credit quality can perhaps be clarified by the distinction between *ex ante* and *ex post* quality, a distinction utilized extensively in the analysis below. By *ex ante* quality is meant the *prospective* risk attached to a given volume of credit. A decline in *ex ante* quality, therefore, means an increase in

---

[4] Otto C. Lorenz, in *The American Banker*, April 25, 1957, stated: "Successful consumer credit operators will tell you, quite simply, that loan quality is the customer's character, ability, and willingness to pay. That's basic."

[5] Geoffrey H. Moore, "The Quality of Credit in Booms and Depressions," *Journal of Finance*, May 1956, p. 293.

loans which possess characteristics of one sort or another which may be *expected on the basis of past experience at the time the loans are made* to result in increased delinquency, repossession, or loss rates. The bases upon which these expectations are formulated are indicated in the third definition cited above, and the credit market's actual evaluation of them is described by the measures in the second definition.

Ex ante quality may be said to deteriorate when there is deterioration in the conditions of lending that pertain to risk. These conditions in turn consist of the terms on which credit is extended and the characteristics of the borrowers who obtain it. Credit terms, as used in this study, include primarily the percentage which the down payment constitutes of the amount paid for the product, the number of months for which the credit contract is drawn, and related variables such as the cash selling price of the car or the trade-in allowance (which is sometimes taken into consideration by expressing the down payment as a ratio to the "real" car price rather than to the contract price, which may include an inflated trade-in allowance). The borrower characteristics relevant to *ex ante* quality are those that pertain to or reflect willingness and ability to repay debt. In the following pages much attention will be directed to the question of whether greater risk is attached to borrowers possessing such characteristics as youth, low income, or unstable employment than to other borrowers not possessing these characteristics. The hallmark of *ex ante* quality deterioration, therefore, is a change in loan terms or borrower characteristics such that, other things remaining the same, worsened collection experience may be expected to result.

Ex post quality, on the other hand, refers to actual collection experience on a given volume of loans and is measured by such factors as delinquency rates, repossession rates, and loss rates (cf. the first definition above). Though it may be a major determinant, *ex ante* quality is not the sole determinant of *ex post* quality. The latter is determined partly by changes in economic conditions or collection policy *subsequent* to the granting of the loans whose quality is under consideration (as the fourth definition implies). Hence it is possible that a deterioration in *ex ante* quality, brought about, say, by a change in credit standards, may not be followed by a decline in *ex post* quality if economic conditions improve sufficiently to offset the change.

In short, to analyze prospective risk and actual collection experience on a given volume of loans, one must study lending terms and borrower characteristics at the time the loans were made as well as subsequent changes in economic conditions and collection policy. It is to the isolation, analysis, and evaluation of these strategic variables that the present study is devoted. We shall not, incidentally, concern ourselves with a related question—namely, to what extent lenders attempt to offset the greater risk of easier credit standards by charging higher rates. The National Bureau's study of consumer finance rates, under the direction of Robert P. Shay, is concerned, in part, with this problem. Shay's tentative results do not suggest that there is any close adjustment of rates to prospective risk as indicated by credit terms or borrower characteristics.[6]

Before turning in Chapter 3 to a consideration of the relations between credit conditions and collection experience, it is appropriate to consider briefly the interrelations among the several aspects of credit conditions. These aspects—down payments, maturities, and various borrower characteristics—together make up what we have termed *ex ante* quality. Conceivably, easier terms may be associated with an improvement in the borrower's creditworthiness, so that these shifts in *ex ante* quality offset one another. Or longer maturities may go hand in hand with larger down payments, so that an easing in one direction is offset by tightening in another. But is this usually the case, or is the opposite association more typical? By first looking at the evidence on this point, we shall be in a better position to study the relation be-

[6] For example, in our analysis of the 1954–55 Federal Reserve survey of new-auto contracts (Table 36), we find that repossession and delinquency rates vary sharply with the size of down payment and the liquid assets held by the borrower. But the finance rates paid do not appear to vary systematically with either down payments or liquid asset holdings, or, indeed, with the corresponding repossession and delinquency rates. The average finance rates corresponding to the entries in Table 36 are:

Liquid Asset Holdings ($)	Effective Down Payment (%)		
	Under 30	30–39	40 and over
None	11.1	11.1	10.2
1–499	11.2	10.6	12.1
500–1,999	11.0	10.6	11.4
2,000 & over	10.7	11.2	10.5

tween credit conditions and collection experience, because much of the evidence on the latter takes into account only one kind of condition at a time.

MATURITIES AND DOWN PAYMENTS

Data provided by a large sales finance company for the United States as a whole and for separate regions make it possible to examine the interrelation between down payments and contract maturities.[7] Table 16 shows the median maturity for new-automobile credit contracts classified according to down payment percentage in July 1956. The results, both for the country as a whole and for the individual regions, suggest that (1) the contracts in the highest down payment group (50 per cent and over) have decidedly shorter maturities than those with smaller down payments; (2) maturities are progressively longer the smaller the down payment, up to a point; and (3) beyond that point (down payments about 25 per cent) maturities tend to be somewhat shorter. In general, low down payment contracts have longer maturities than high down payment contracts; that is, terms are eased in both directions at once. The relation noted has been tested by means of chi-square analysis and has been found to be statistically significant in each region.[8]

Table 17 shows the median down payment percentage for contracts classified by maturity. Again the conclusion which emerges is that the down payment percentages are typically larger when the maturities are shorter, and smaller when the maturities are longer. This relationship is evident to some extent for every region as well as for the United States as a whole. It is noteworthy, however, that the very longest maturity contracts often have somewhat higher down payment percentages than those of intermediate maturity, just as the very smallest down payment contracts had somewhat shorter maturities than those with down payments of intermediate proportions. This sug-

[7] The regional data utilized here and in subsequent sections are based on samples of actual contracts purchased through the branch offices of a large sales finance company, and consist of all contracts purchased during the first ten days of the month, collected periodically since 1953. We have examined three of these surveys, for June 1953, July 1956, and July 1957, but the present discussion is confined to the July 1956 survey. See Appendix B.

[8] For an explanation of the chi-square test, see Appendix B. The 5 per cent level of significance is used throughout this study.

TABLE 16

Median Maturity of New-Automobile Contracts Classified by Down Payment, United States Total and Nine Regions, A Large Sales Finance Company, July 1956

Median Maturity[a] (months)

Down Payment as a percentage of Cash Selling Price	Pacific	Mountain	West North Central	West South Central	East South Central	East North Central	South Atlantic	Middle Atlantic	New England	Total U.S.
Under 20	37.2*	29.1	38.0*	30.5	30.7	30.8	30.0	39.9*	39.2*	32.2
20–24	38.3*	31.0	38.0*	31.0	31.4	32.1	31.1	40.3*	40.0*	33.7
25–29	39.7*	31.1	38.0*	31.2	31.1	33.3	31.2	40.8*	40.3*	35.8
30–34	39.1*	32.2	37.8*	30.1	30.0	32.3	30.5	39.7*	39.0*	34.8
35–49	37.2*	31.1	29.3	27.8	26.5	28.8	24.6	38.2*	39.2*	30.5
50 and over	33.2	19.9	20.5	22.5	24.0	19.0	20.8	23.0	18.6	21.7
All contracts[b]	38.6*	30.4	37.4*	30.5	30.4	31.4	30.1	39.6*	38.9*	33.2
No. of contracts[b]	551	248	680	1,078	548	1,824	1,059	1,211	313	7,512

Source: Appendix Table B-2.

[a] Medians were calculated from the frequency distributions. Where the median value fell in the class 36 months and over (marked with an *) it was interpolated on the assumption that there were no loans with maturities more than 46 months. Other evidence for this period suggests this is a reasonable assumption..

[b] Excludes contracts for which either down payment or maturity was not stated.

Note: For states included in the various regions see Appendix Table B-1. Chi-square results significant for all regions and for total United States at the 5 per cent level (App. Table B-2).

TABLE 17

Median Down Payment Percentage, New Automobile Contracts Classified by Maturity, United States Total and Nine Regions, A Large Sales Finance Company, July 1956

Maturity (mos.)	Median Down Payment as Percentage of Cash Selling Price[a]									
	Pacific	Mountain	West North Central	West South Central	East South Central	East North Central	South Atlantic	Middle Atlantic	New England	Total U.S.
12 and under	28.8	52.3*	37.5	35.8	32.5	44.6	29.8	51.7*	53.4*	40.2
13–24	30.0	30.8	29.3	24.1	28.2	30.0	31.4	40.8	34.7	30.2
25–35	24.2	26.0	23.6	22.9	24.2	23.1	24.8	27.8	29.3	23.8
36 and over	26.1	31.1	23.9	23.8	25.3	26.0	26.3	27.5	27.6	26.2
All contracts[b]	25.7	28.1	24.4	23.5	25.4	24.7	26.1	28.6	28.9	25.7
No. of contracts[b]	551	248	680	1,078	548	1,824	1,059	1,211	313	7,512

Source: Appendix Table B-2.

[a]Medians were calculated from the frequency distributions. Where the median value fell in the open-end class (marked with an *) it was interpolated on the assumption that all contracts were accounted for by limiting the open-end class to 65 per cent of the cash selling price.

[b]Excludes contracts for which either down payment or maturity was not stated.

Note: For states included in the various regions see Appendix Table B-1. Chi-square results significant for all regions and for total United States at the 5 per cent level (App. Table B-2).

CHART 6

Change in Down Payments and Maturities on New-Automobile
Contracts, Twelve Metropolitan Areas, 1953–56

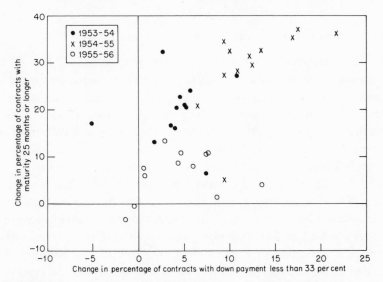

Source: Table G-1. Data from a large sales finance company; 1955–56 based on
January and April.

gests that lenders place some restriction on one dimension of the credit
contract when the other is being extended, presumably to limit the
risk.

The regional evidence that small down payments and long maturities
tend to occur together is supported by examination of local area data
on changes in these two aspects of credit quality. Chart 6, based on
data from another large sales finance company for twelve metropolitan
areas, illustrates the point well.[9] Whereas the regional evidence pertained to only one point in time, Chart 6 relates to changes over time.
Year-to-year changes in the percentage of contracts issued with maturities twenty-five months or longer are compared with corresponding changes in the proportion of contracts with down payments less
than 33 per cent. For all areas and for all three yearly changes a large
increase in long-maturity paper is generally associated with a large

[9] For a list of the areas and the basis for their selection, see Appendix F.

increase in low-down-payment paper, and vice versa. The positive association justifies the conclusion that these two factors, more often than not, move together so as to magnify rather than offset the qualitative implications of either one.

Do the borrowers who obtain credit contracts involving low down payments or long maturities differ in relevant characteristics from those who obtain credit on less easy terms? It is important to consider this question because it is a necessary step in determining whether any observed relation between credit terms and collection experience merely reflects an association between the terms and some more fundamental characteristic of the borrowers, or whether the terms themselves have an independent bearing on collection experience. There is another reason also. If it can be shown that those borrower characteristics that are associated with poor collection experience are often found in loans with terms that are also associated with poor collection experience, these two factors may reinforce one another in accounting for changes in *ex post* quality. If the reverse is true, they may offset one another. We wish, therefore, to know what types of borrowers obtain the "easiest" terms.

Our data enable us to consider five borrower characteristics and the down payment and maturity requirements associated with them. Tables 18 through 22, on which the discussion will be based, are derived from the tables in Appendix B which present the results of a chi-square analysis of the significance of the relations considered. The data pertain to contracts made in June 1953 and in July 1957. One of their most striking features, but one which we shall ignore for the moment, is the decrease in average down payment and the increase in average maturity between these two dates. This change, which pervades all types of borrower groups, is far wider than any variation we shall discover among the borrower groups at either date. Nevertheless, we shall for the present concentrate attention on the variations among borrowers.

Table 18 shows a fairly consistent tendency for borrowers in the lowest and in the highest income brackets to obtain shorter maturities, and the relation is statistically significant in both 1953 and 1957. As for down payments, there appears to be no statistically significant

TABLE 18

Median Maturity and Down Payment, New-Automobile Contracts
Classified by Income of Borrower, 1953 and 1957,
A Large Sales Finance Company

Monthly Income (dollars)	June 1953	July 1957	June 1953	July 1957
	Median Maturity (mos.)		*Number of Contracts*	
Under 250	20.1	37.0*	491	509
250–349	21.1	37.8*	1,245	1,609
350–499	21.2	37.5*	1,475	3,315
500–999	20.3	36.1*	983	2,489
1,000 and over	19.7	31.3*	125	281
All contracts	20.8	37.2*	4,319	8,203
Chi-square test	S	S		
	Median Down Payment (per cent)		*Number of Contracts*	
Under 250	38.3	33.1	489	510
250–349	38.1	32.0	1,244	1,612
350–499	37.8	31.9	1,482	3,311
500–499	38.4	32.1	988	2,484
1,000 and over	38.6	32.9	123	278
All contracts	38.1	32.1	4,326	8,195
Chi-square test	N	N		

Source: Appendix Tables B-3 and B-4.
Chi-square test (S = significant, N = not significant, at the .05 level) is based on data in the appendix tables.
*Median value falls in open-end class. Cf. note a, Table 16.

relationship to income, although in both years borrowers in the middle income brackets made slightly smaller down payments (as a percentage of purchase price) than the lower or higher income groups, on the average. Some further evidence on this point, pertaining to 1954–55 and utilized in another connection in Chapter 5, suggests that low in-

TABLE 19

Median Maturity and Down Payment, New-Automobile Contracts
Classified by Sex of Borrower, 1953 and 1957,
A Large Sales Finance Company

Sex	June 1953	July 1957	June 1953	July 1957
	Median Maturity (mos.)		*Number of Contracts*	
Male	20.7	37.1*	4,207	7,870
Female	20.4	37.0*	393	620
All contracts	20.7	37.1*	4,600	8,490
Chi-square test	N	N		
	Median Down Payment (per cent)		*Number of Contracts*	
Male	36.1	32.2	4,215	7,853
Female	36.0	32.0	391	623
All contracts	36.1	32.2	4,606	8,476
Chi-square test	N	N		

Source: Appendix Tables B-5 and B-6.
Chi-square test (S = significant, N = not significant, at the 0.5 level) is based on data in the appendix tables.
*Median value falls in open-end class. Cf. note a, Table 16.

come borrowers typically make smaller down payments than high income borrowers, but that the longest maturities go to borrowers in the middle income range.[10] It does not appear, therefore, that credit

[10] The proportions of new-auto contracts with low down payments and long maturities are as follows (Tables 36 and 37):

	Income of Borrower in Year of Purchase			
	Under $3,000	*$3,000– $4,999*	*$5,000– $7,499*	*$7,500 & over*
Percentage with:				
Down payment under 30 per cent	59	55	53	48
Maturity 30 months and over	49	53	48	37

TABLE 20

Median Maturity and Down Payment, New-Automobile Contracts
Classified by Marital Status of Borrower, 1953 and 1957,
A Large Sales Finance Company

Marital Status	June 1953	July 1957	June 1953	July 1957
	Median Maturity (mos.)		Number of Contracts	
Married	20.8	37.2*	3,779	7,215
Single	20.2	36.4*	790	1,244
Divorced-Widowed	28.1	a	15	a
All contracts	20.7	37.1*	4,584	8,459
Chi-square test	S	S		
	Median Down Payment (per cent)		Number of Contracts	
Married	38.3	32.2	3,783	7,205
Single	38.8	32.1	792	1,246
Divorced-Widowed	33.8	a	16	a
All contracts	38.3	32.2	4,591	8,451
Chi-square test	N	N		

Source: Appendix Tables B-7 and B-8. Chi-square (S = significant,
N = not significant, at the .05 level) is based on data in the appendix
tables.
aData not collected.
*Median value falls in open-end class. Cf. note a, Table 16.

agencies offset to any marked degree whatever greater risk is associated with low income borrowers by requiring higher down payments or shorter repayment periods, although there may be a modest
tendency of this sort, particularly with respect to maturities. As a rule,
the highest income groups make the largest down payments and the
shortest commitments.

Here, as in the case of other borrower characteristics, it is important to bear in mind that the contracts being analyzed reflect the

TABLE 21

Median Maturity and Down Payment, New-Automobile Contracts
Classified by Age of Borrower, 1953 and 1957,
A Large Sales Finance Company

Age (yrs.)	June 1953	July 1957	June 1953	July 1957
	Median Maturity (mos.)		*Number of Contracts*	
30 and under	20.7	37.4*	1,452	2,678
31–40	21.1	37.4*	1,446	2,774
41–50	20.4	36.6*	1,058	1,964
Over 50	20.1	36.0*	612	1,052
All contracts	20.7	37.1*	4,568	8,468
Chi-square test	S	S		
	Median Down Payment (per cent)		*Number of Contracts*	
30 and over	35.7	31.4	1,450	2,679
31–40	39.0	31.9	1,450	2,765
41–50	38.8	32.6	1,061	1,959
Over 50	41.7	34.1	615	1,053
All contracts	38.3	32.1	4,576	8,456
Chi-square test	S	S		

Source: Appendix Tables B-9 and B-10.

Chi-square test (S = significant, N = not significant, at the .05 level) is based on data in the appendix tables.

*Median value falls in open-end class. Cf. note a, Table 16.

terms agreed upon by borrower and lender. Borrowers' demands are tempered in the light of what terms are offered, and the offers are governed in part by what borrowers demand. That the result of this process can change dramatically is indicated by the marked shift between 1953 and 1957 in the terms accepted by both parties.

The terms of new-automobile contracts in our sample do not seem to differ significantly according to whether the borrowers were men

TABLE 22

Median Maturity and Down Payment, New-Automobile Contracts
Classified by Occupation of Borrower, 1953 and 1957,
A Large Sales Finance Company

Occupation	June 1953	July 1957	June 1953	July 1957
	Median Maturity (mos.)		*Number of Contracts*	
Farm				
Operators	14.5	28.3	150	205
Wage earners	18.0	32.8	49	86
Nonfarm				
Proprietors	19.5	33.7	493	632
Professional	20.2	35.3	269	462
Salaried	20.9	37.3*	1,544	2,809
Wage earners	21.4	37.5*	1,726	3,796
Miscellaneous	20.9	37.3*	346	492
All contracts	20.7	37.1*	4,577	8,482
Chi-square test	S	S		
	Median Down Payment (per cent)		*Number of Contracts*	
Farm				
Operators	42.1	38.0	148	213
Wage earners	41.0	35.0	48	88
Nonfarm				
Proprietors	39.4	33.6	495	630
Professional	39.1	32.9	270	461
Salaried	37.6	31.2	1,540	2,795
Wage earners	38.2	32.1	1,728	3,791
Miscellaneous	37.6	32.8	350	490
All contracts	38.3	32.2	4,579	8,468
Chi-square test	S	S		

Source: Appendix Tables B-11 and B-12.
Chi-square test (S = significant, N = not significant, at the .05 level) is based on data in the appendix tables.
*Median value falls in open-end class. Cf. note. a, Table 16.

or women, although the great majority of borrowers were men (Table 19). With regard to marital status, Table 20 suggests that while married borrowers tend to obtain loans with significantly longer maturities, the difference is not great. Moreover, marital status is not significantly associated with stringent or liberal down payment terms. On balance, the evidence does not suggest that one can attach great importance to the interrelation of loan terms with this borrower characteristic.

The classification of borrowers by age reveals consistent and significant associations with loan terms. Younger borrowers obtain more liberal terms, i.e., longer maturities as well as lower down payments. This result appears both in 1953 and in 1957 (Table 21).

We find occupation to be one of the borrower characteristics most consistently associated with loan terms. Table 22 indicates the median down payment and the median maturity associated with each occupational class in the two periods. The most striking finding is that not only are the maturities and down payments quite different for the various occupations, but the longer maturities and smaller down payments are concentrated in the same occupational classes in both 1953 and 1957.

The shortest maturities and largest down payments, i.e., the most conservative terms, are found in the farm operator group, with farm wage earners next. Somewhat longer maturities and smaller down payments characterize the nonfarm proprietor and professional groups. Salaried workers and nonfarm wage earners secure the easiest terms, the salaried group making smaller down payments than the wage earner group but receiving slightly shorter maturities, on the average. These findings pertain to samples considered on a national basis, without regard to the region where they originate. Analysis of separate samples for each region yields broadly similar conclusions (Table 23).

The over-all conclusion which emerges from this examination of the interrelationship of credit contract terms and borrower characteristics is that terms vary systematically with the age and occupation of the borrower, to a lesser extent with his income, and scarcely at all with the borrower's sex or marital status. These results obtained both before the extensive liberalization of lending terms that occurred in 1954–55 as well as after. It is unfortunate that data are not available to test the relations of loan terms to the liquid asset holdings, net worth, and life cycle status of the borrowers, because there is evidence that these borrower characteristics, as well as those we have just considered, are significantly related to collection experience (cf. Chapter 4). Moreover, it would be useful to study the impact on credit quality of social and economic instability, as indicated by such factors as the borrowers' length of residence, marital stability (divorce rate), whether they live in their own or a rented home, and the average number of times the borrowers have changed employment in the recent past. There is reason to think these factors might affect credit quality, but we have not been able to examine the possible relationships.

To return to the question asked at the beginning of this section: Is consumer credit extended in such a way that liberality in one dimension is accompanied by liberality in another, or is it generally true that an easing in one direction is offset by tightening in another? We can offer only a partial answer at this point. Although we have observed some offsetting tendencies, for the most part easier down payments and longer maturities go together. The relation of these factors, separately and together, to credit risk will be examined in Chapter 3. We have found also that easier terms are significantly associated with certain borrower characteristics. Whether this association offsets or reinforces prospective lender risk must await the analysis of Chapter 4, which examines the relation between borrower characteristics and collection experience.

TABLE 23

Summary of Regional Evidence on the Association Between Credit Terms and Borrower Characteristics, New-Automobile Contracts, 1953 And 1957, A Large Sales Finance Company

June 1953 Sample

	Pacific	Mountain	West North Central	West South Central	East South Central	East North Central	South Atlantic	Middle Atlantic	New England	Total U.S.[a]
Maturity as compared with										
Income per month	N	S	N	S*	N	S	N	N*	N	S
Sex	N	N	N	N	N	N	N	N	N	N
Marital status	N	N	N	S	N*	N*	N	N*	N	S
Age	N	N*	N	S*	N	S*	N*	N	N	S
Occupation	N	S	S*	S	N	S	S*	N	N	S
Down Payment as percentage of cash selling price as compared with										
Income per month	N	N	N	N	S	N	N	N	N	N
Sex	N	S	N	N	N	N	S	N	S	N
Marital status	N	N	N	S	N*	S	N	N*	N	N
Age	N	N	N	N	N	S*	N	N*	N	S
Occupation	N	N	N*	N	N	N	N	N	N	S

(continued)

TABLE 23 (concluded)

July 1957 Sample

	Pacific	Mountain	West North Central	West South Central	East South Central	East North Central	South Atlantic	Middle Atlantic	New England	Total U.S.[a]
Maturity as compared with										
Income per month	S*	N	S*	S*	N	S*	S*	S*	S	S
Sex	N	N	N	N	N	N	N	N	N	N
Marital status	N*	N*	N*	N	N*	S	N*	N*	N	S
Age	N*	S	N*	S*	N	S*	S*	S*	S*	S
Occupation	S	S*	S*	S	S*	S	S*	S	S	S
Down Payment as percentage of cash selling price as compared with										
Income per month	S	N	S	N	N	N	N	N	N	N
Sex	N	N	N	N	N	N	N	N	N	N
Marital status	N	N	S*	N*	N	N	N	S*	N	N
Age	N	N	S*	S	S*	S*	S	N	N	S
Occupation	S	N	S*	S	N	S	N	S	S	S

[a]For states included in each region, see Appendix Table B-1.

S = Chi-square values are significant at the .05 level.

N = Chi-square values are not significant at the .05 level.

* = Regional pattern is similar to the U.S. pattern (where it was significant). The measure of similarity is the percentage of like signs in the regional and U.S. patterns. Where this percentage is 75 or more, an asterisk is shown.

3. Credit Terms and Subsequent Collection Experience

The question treated in this and the next chapter is whether the ultimate collection experience with a particular group of instalment credit contracts (though not the ultimate experience on any single contract) can be approximately determined at the time the credit is advanced. If a favorable answer can be given, it should be possible to establish whether, for many lenders or for the country as a whole, loan quality is deteriorating or improving to a significant extent at any given time. It should also be possible to establish whether loan quality is related to changes in loan volume, as well as to other objective factors in the consumer credit situation.

The existence and significance of such relationships, of course, remain to be established. At this point we wish merely to inquire whether the lender is able to predict to some degree the ultimate experience with a group of loans meeting certain standards with respect to loan terms or borrower characteristics.

We must state at once, however, that an affirmative answer to this question does not necessarily imply that the actual experience with a given group of loans is closely predictable. This actual experience may depend importantly on the character of the business situation that develops while the loans are outstanding, as well as on other developments affecting the borrowers' ability to repay. What we are seeking to answer is whether, *given* the character of the future situation, the experience with one group of loans is likely to be better than with another and by how much. If the future situation is prosperous, experience may be favorable with all groups, though relatively less with some than others; if a depression comes along, experience may be unfavorable with all groups, but again relatively less so with some than others. Can this *relative* experience be determined approximately in advance?

It is not intended here to discuss at length the process whereby credit standards are determined by individual lenders and loans are actually made. Nevertheless, it is important to touch upon the thinking involved in lending and fixing loan standards in order to explain the empirical evidence that follows. To begin with, it is self-evident that loans are screened in some fashion to assure the lender that the loan is being sought in good faith with every intention of repayment. Thus, a substantial proportion of every credit investigation is devoted to verifying the honesty of would-be borrowers with respect to their business dealings. Beyond these minimum requirements for the prevention of fraud, however, lenders must satisfy themselves as to the present and future ability of the borrower to repay the loan, the likelihood that the borrower will remain willing to repay, and the adequacy of collateral or legal remedies in the event that the borrower does not repay. Lenders have for years summarized this by saying that lending standards are based upon the "character, capacity, and collateral" of the borrower. The borrower's income, his previous commitments, the stability of his occupation, and whether he is at a station in life in which the desire and social pressure to repay the debt are paramount—all these factors may be considered. Often, however, judgments must be based on rather sketchy evidence and analysis.

The fixing of credit standards rests in part on certain general lines of reasoning. Obviously the risk of default is greater the smaller the borrower's equity and the longer the time for repayment, since a longer period may encompass more drastic changes in ability to repay. Obviously, persons in occupations with regular and predictable income tend to be better risks than those in occupations with variable and unpredictable incomes. Less obvious but still amenable to logical analysis is the tendency for the lender's risk on a loan for a durable good to increase as maturities are lengthened and down payments reduced, because the market value of a consumer durable depreciates more rapidly in the earlier than in the later part of its life. Out of such considerations are forged the credit standards of individual lenders, modified, of course, by competitive pressures, by actual loss and recovery experience, by changing evaluations of risk, and by changing opportunities to recoup losses from finance charges or to shift risks to others.

In considering the evidence on loan experience, it is again necessary to take into consideration the fact that the statistical record is based on loans that have already been subjected to lender selection. All the loans making up the experience have already been screened for moral risk, terms have normally been adjusted to make repayment possible within the scope of the purchaser's budget, and unusual risks in one direction may have been balanced by more strict loan or collateral conditions in another direction. Preselection of loans and tailoring to counterbalance unusual risks with stricter conditions accordingly are reflected in the experience statistics.

It is important to note also that only rarely is the avoidance of loan losses and collection difficulties the prime determinant of lending standards. While each lender differs somewhat in what he regards as his policy, those who try to maximize their net revenue generally will lend to a given class of borrowers if the anticipated return at least covers the additional expense of the loan including collection difficulties and the additional expected losses to be incurred by accepting poorer quality loans. In some circumstances individual lenders will accept poorer quality credit risks at a higher schedule of finance charges. For example, most lenders accept loans secured by used cars at higher interest rates than on loans on new cars. Moreover, for the economy as a whole, an informal structure of lending institutions exists, with some firms taking mostly prime quality consumer paper, others taking less attractive loans at higher rates, and still others lending to extremely poor risks at high and sometimes illegal rates of interest. Accordingly, quality changes may take place not only through shifts in the individual lender's loan standards but also through shifts in the volume of business done by financing institutions with differing standards.

There is a great deal of scattered (and frequently unsatisfactory or unreliable) material which purports to relate collection difficulty or loss to the terms of the loan, the characteristics of the borrower, and even the type and condition of the collateral. While its examination here is neither complete nor definitive, we attempt to view these relations in more consistent fashion than has heretofore been possible.

We have chosen to use two convenient methods of quantifying loan experience as a measure of loan quality. The first method, that of calculating delinquency, repossession, or loss rates, involves computing for each category of loan—say those on which the down payment was less than one-third—the percentage that loans with collection difficulty or loss constituted of total outstandings or volume per period in that same category. The second method, that of computing "bad loan relatives," requires that the percentage a particular category of loans makes up of total bad loans (loans on which collection difficulty or loss is sustained) be divided by the percentage that this same category makes up of total good loans. If, for example, 40 per cent of the bad loans were in the group on which a down payment of less than one-third had been obtained, whereas among the good loans only 20 per cent were in this low down payment category, the bad-loan relative would be $40/20 = 2.0$. It would indicate that the actual bad-loan rate (derived by the first method) on low-down-payment loans would be about twice as high as the average rate on all loans.[1] Occasionally, we shall use the percentage distribution of all loans, instead of good loans, for the denominator of the bad-loan relative. This makes the bad-loan relative a precise index of the actual bad-loan rate when the samples of good and bad loans are in proper proportions, but in practice the two variants of bad-loan relatives yield similar results. The relation between the first measure and the two variants of the second is shown by the following hypothetical example:

	Down Payment Percentage		
Item	Under 33 per cent	33 per cent and over	Total or Average
Number of loans:			
1. Repossessed	1,000	1,500	2,500
2. Not repossessed	9,000	38,500	47,500
3. Total	10,000	40,000	50,000
Percentage distribution of loans:			
4. Repossessed	40	60	100
5. Not repossessed	19	81	100
6. Total	20	80	100
Repossession rate (method 1):			
7. Line 1 ÷ line 3	10.00	3.75	5.00
Bad-loan relatives (method 2):			
8. Line 4 ÷ line 5	2.11	0.74	1.00
9. Line 4 ÷ line 6 (or line 7 ÷ col. 3)	2.00	0.75	1.00

[1] The second method does not require information on the actual proportion of bad loans, and provides only an index of the way this proportion varies among categories. The advantage of this method for studies of loan experience

If we are to utilize the several available samples, we cannot adopt a uniform definition of a bad loan or unfavorable collection experience. Several sources provide repossession rates, one covers repossession as well as other forms of delinquency, others give actual loss rates or loans charged off, and one allows the lender to define unfavorable collection experience.[2] It is conceivable, accordingly, that inconsistent results will appear if loans of a given class result in a great deal of delinquency but little dollar loss because of the ultimate collection of most of the funds in question. For the purpose of extending the available data, some experience on unsecured loans has been included even though these types of loans are ordinarily not used for the purchase of durable goods, the type of transaction upon which this report is focused.

A final shortcoming of most of the available data must be mentioned. With rare exceptions the loan experience samples are classified by only one criterion at a time. That is, they show the experience on loans with less than one-third down payment, or on loans with a term of more than thirty months, but not on loans with less than one-third down *and* a term of more than thirty months. The evidence discussed in Chapter 2 showed, however, that the several characteristics by which loans are classified are associated with one another—e.g., long maturities and low down payments often go together. As a result, it is difficult to determine to what extent differences in loan experience are associated with the particular characteristic being observed rather than with some other one that is tied to it. In some cases the influence of the other factor or factors may completely obscure that of the characteristic underlying the given distribution. We shall illustrate some important instances of this sort below, but the possibility of effects of this sort should be kept in mind throughout.

In reviewing the evidence on the relation between the terms on which loans are made (primarily the size of the down payment and the length of time the loan contract has to run) and the subsequent

is that it permits oversampling of bad loans, which ordinarily occur infrequently, thereby reducing sampling variability and increasing the firmness of conclusions concerning the characteristics differentiating good and bad loans.

[2] The analytical advantages and disadvantages of four major measures of collection difficulty are discussed in Appendix C. One of these, renegotiations of loans with an extension of the repayment period, has not been included in our bad-loan category because such extensions are ambiguous—they can reflect credit difficulty or simply the desire to free funds for further purchases. Moreover, few data are available on loan extensions.

collection experience, we shall first deal briefly with the various analyses of this material that have appeared since the 1920's. Next we shall
consider new data that have been developed from the Federal Reserve
Survey of New Car Purchases in 1954–55. Finally, we shall analyze
certain new data on loan terms and collection experience in different
sections of the country.

CONSPECTUS OF EVIDENCE
FROM THE 1920's TO THE 1950's

The several analyses of the relations between loan terms and subsequent collection experience developed by previous investigators enable us to consider separately the relation of down payments and of
maturities to collection experience for a number of periods scattered
over a thirty-year span.

Table 24 presents the earliest data we have found bearing on the
relation of down payment percentages and collection experience. It
shows clearly that in the earlier history of automobile instalment credit,
repossession rates were consistently higher for loans with a small down
payment than for those with a substantial down payment in terms of
percentage of purchase price.

This relation has not changed markedly from the 1920's to recent
years. All the evidence in Chart 7 and Table 25, as well as in Table 28
in the next section, shows that repossession and loss rates are higher,
on the average, when the down payment is small than when it is large.
This is true of used cars as well as new cars, although collection experience with a given down payment percentage is materially worse
for used than for new cars. Since the data are so varied and the
samples so limited, it is not possible to make precise comparisons. For
example, the practice of "writing up" both the trade-in and the purchase price of the new car and thereby raising the down payment
percentage, a practice that probably became more prevalent in the
1950's than formerly, makes doubtful the precise comparability of the
figures, both within a given sample and from year to year.[3]

---

[3] To avoid some of these problems the Federal Reserve Board in 1956 began
collecting data on contract balance as a percentage of dealer cost, a type of
loan-to-value ratio, thereby avoiding the problem of defining the "true down
payment" altogether. Although this "dealer cost ratio" is analytically more precise, its introduction has had the unfortunate effect of making comparisons with
earlier data on down payment percentage virtually impossible.

TABLE 24

*The Relation of Down Payment Percentage to Repossession Rate,
New and Used Automobiles, 1925–30*

Down Payment Percentage	1925	1926	1927	1928	1929	1930	Average, 1925–30
			Repossession Rate (per cent)				
New cars:							
Under 25 per cent	11.0	11.5	n.a.	n.a.	n.a.	n.a.	12.0[a]
25 per cent	3.8	4.0	5.9	4.1	5.1	4.6	4.6
33 1/3 per cent	1.7	2.1	2.7	2.8	2.8	3.6	2.6
Used cars:							
35 per cent or less	6.2	8.6	6.9	10.9	9.0	9.8	8.6
40 per cent	3.0	4.3	5.2	5.3	5.3	6.5	4.9

Source: "Composite Experience of Finance Companies and Automobile Dealers," a mimeograph statement of the National Association of Finance Companies, April 13, 1931.

[a] Estimated by raising the 1925–26 average by 0.7 percentage points, which is the excess of the 1925–30 average over the 1925–26 average for the other two down-payment classes.

n.a. = not available.

Evidence from one large sales finance company that repossession rates are lower the lower the dealer cost ratio on new cars and the lower the percentage of wholesale value financed on used cars is given for 1958 and 1959 in Paul W. McCracken, James C. T. Mao, and Cedric V. Fricke, *Consumer Instalment Credit and Public Policy*, Ann Arbor, Mich., 1966, p. 138. For more comprehensive but indirect evidence, see our analysis of the dealer cost ratio in Chapter 7 and Appendix H. As noted below, even though the down payment percentage is an imperfect measure of borrowers' equity, every study of it has shown it to be closely associated with loan experience.

The relation between loan experience and the length of time given for repayment seems to be more complicated. The earliest evidence bearing on this, pertaining as before to 1925–30, suggests that the

CHART 7

The Relation of Down Payment Percentage to Subsequent Repossession and Loss Experience

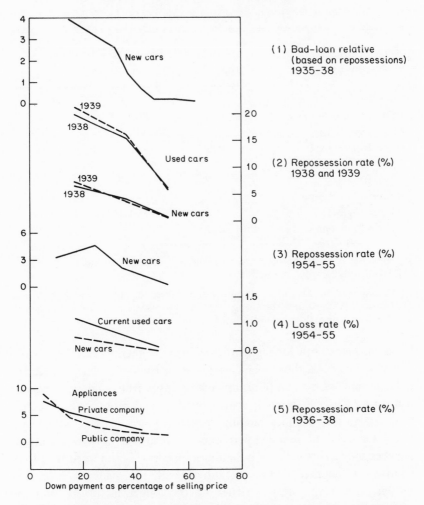

SOURCE: (1) David Durand, *Risk Elements in Consumer Instalment Financing*, New York, NBER, 1941, Table 9, p. 61. (2) G. A. Ames, "Our Responsibility to Consumer Credit," talk given at the National Instalment Credit Conference, sponsored by the American Bankers Association, Chicago, March 25, 1953. (3) See Table D-1. Unpublished lender report data from National Analysts Survey of New Car Purchases for Federal Reserve Board, 1954–55. (4) E. F. Wonderlic, "Control of Losses in Instalment Credit," *Time Sales Financing*, February 1956. (5) Wilbur C. Plummer and Ralph A. Young, *Sales Finance Companies and Their Credit Practices*, New York, NBER, 1940, Table 46, p. 184.

TABLE 25

Bad-Loan Relatives by Down Payment Percentage, Based on Repossessions, Automobile Contracts, 1954–56

Down Payment Percentage	Bad-Loan Relative[a]		
	Jan. 1954	Jan. 1955	Jan. 1956
New cars:			
Under 33 per cent	3.3	2.5	2.2
33–40 per cent	1.6	1.3	1.0
Over 40 per cent	0.2	0.2	0.2
Used cars:			
Under 33 per cent	1.4	1.4	1.3
33–40 per cent	1.2	1.1	1.1
Over 40 per cent	0.4	0.5	0.5

Source: A large sales finance company, NBER Consumer Credit Quality Study.

[a]Computed by dividing the percentage distribution of repossessions in January by the corresponding percentage distribution of all accounts purchased during the preceding calendar year.

losses on loans with longer maturities were higher (Table 26). More recent evidence is shown in Chart 8 and Table 27. These materials indicate some of the complications which ensue from a consideration of maturities. Chart 8 shows bad-loan relatives and repossession and loss rates for various samples ranging from signature loans to automobile loans. Each of the samples pertaining to loans on new cars and appliances shows that collection difficulties increase as the maturity of the contract is lengthened. On the other hand, the loans on used cars exhibit more favorable experience on the longer maturities, and the evidence on personal or unsecured loans is mixed.[4]

Interviews with lenders suggest that the reason for the poor ex-

[4] Some further evidence on maturities in relation to loan experience which broadly supports the above results for new and used cars and personal loans is presented for 1958–59 by McCracken, Mao, and Fricke, *Consumer Instalment Credit*, p. 139, and for 1952–58 by Paul Smith, "Measuring Risk on Instalment Credit," *Management Science*, November 1964.

TABLE 26

*The Relation of Loan Maturity and Repossession Losses,
Automobile Contracts, 1925–30*

Length of Contract	1925	1926	1927	1928	1929	1930
	Average Direct Loss Per Repossessed Car, In Dollars					
12 or fewer equal monthly payments	50	65	43	56	60	61
13 to 18 equal monthly payments	78	94	58	75	n.a.	n.a.
Over 18 monthly payments or balloon note	220	158	n.a.	n.a.	n.a.	n.a.

Source: "Composite Experience of Finance Companies and Automobile Dealers," a mimeographed statement of the National Association of Finance Companies, April 13, 1931.

n.a. Not available.

perience on used-car loans of extremely short maturities is that the short-maturity loans are generally on the cheapest cars, purchased usually by the poorest credit risks. This is to some extent borne out by Durand's findings, which indicated very little difference in collection experience on new cars of different price ranges up to $1,500 (1938 price levels), but that the incidence of collection difficulty for used cars selling for under $200 was about three times that for cars selling for over $600. In order to establish the point definitely, however, loans should be cross-classified by maturity, selling price, down payment percentages, and so on. An experiment of this sort has been made with the limited data available and is considered below.

THE 1954–55 SURVEY OF NEW-CAR PURCHASES

The results described above can now be supplemented by special tabulations from the Federal Reserve survey of new-car purchases in

CHART 8

The Relation of Length of Contract to Subsequent Repossession and Loss Experience

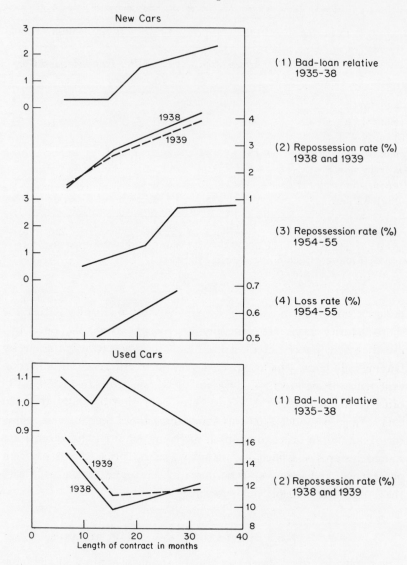

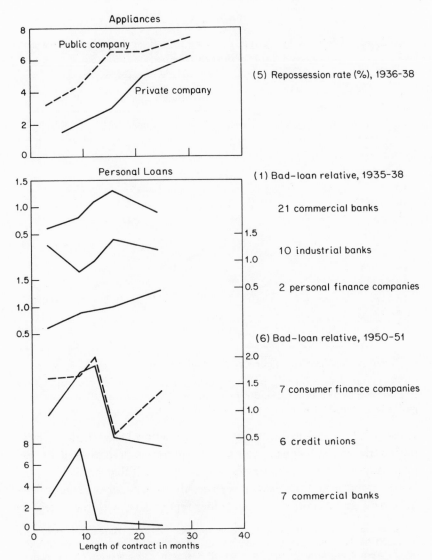

Appliances

(5) Repossession rate (%), 1936-38

Public company

Private company

Personal Loans

(1) Bad-loan relative, 1935-38

21 commercial banks

10 industrial banks

2 personal finance companies

(6) Bad-loan relative, 1950-51

7 consumer finance companies

6 credit unions

7 commercial banks

Length of contract in months

SOURCE: (1) *Risk Elements*, Table 6, p. 54. (2) Ames, "Our Responsibility to Consumer Credit." (3) See Table D-4. Unpublished lender report data from National Analysts Survey of New Car Purchases for Federal Reserve Board, 1954–55. (4) Wonderlic, "Control of Losses in Instalment Credit." (5) Plummer and Young, *Sales Finance Companies*, Table 47, p. 186. (6) W. David Robbins, *Consumer Instalment Loans*, Columbus, Ohio, 1955, Table 34, p. 106.

Quality of Consumer Instalment Credit

TABLE 27

Bad-Loan Relatives by Length of Contract, Based on Repossessions
by a Large Sales Finance Company, 1954–56

Length of Contract (months)	Bad-Loan Relative[a]		
	Jan. 1954	Jan. 1955	Jan. 1956
New cars:			
12 or less	.9	.7	.7
13–18	.9		
19–24	1.0	1.1	.8
25–30	1.2	1.1	1.2
Over 30		1.2	1.2
Used cars:			
12 or less	1.3	1.3	1.3
13–18	1.0	.9	1.0
19–24	.6	.6	.6
Over 24	1.0	.8	.7

Source: NBER Consumer Credit Quality Study.

[a]Computed by dividing the percentage distribution of repossessions in January by the corresponding percentage distribution of all accounts purchased during the preceding calendar year.

1954–55.[5] Two independent tests of the relation between down payment ratio and subsequent collection experience, as measured by delinquency and repossession rates, are shown in Table 28, cols. 3 and 5—one using data from lender reports; the other, personal interviews of borrowers.[6] According to the lender report data, with the exception

    [5] Some of the tabulations were made for the National Bureau of Economic Research by National Analysts, Inc., the concern that conducted the survey. For others we are indebted to the Division of Research and Statistics of the Federal Reserve Board. The tabulations are based on what was termed the "replicated sample" of loans, as explained in the Appendix to Part IV of *Consumer Instalment Credit*. Briefly, the individual loan cards were replicated to allow for changes in the ratio of the sample (550 loans every month) to total loan volume (which, of course, varied) and also for nonresponse items. The replication rate was 1.9; that is, the replicated number of loans was nearly twice the actual number.
    [6] This important feature of the survey not only permitted validation of the findings from both the lender and the borrower but also provided information from the borrower that the lender did not have and vice versa. Many of the data used in this study have been derived from the personal interview materials,

TABLE 28

Credit Terms and Collection Experience on New-Car Loans, 1954–55

Contract Down-Payment Ratio (%)	Lender Report Sample — No. of Contracts (1)	Bad Loan Rate (%) (2)	Personal Interview Sample — No. of Contracts (3)	Bad Loan Rate (%) (4)	Effective Down-Payment Ratio (%) (5)	Personal Interview Sample — No. of Contracts (6)	Bad Loan Rate (%) (7)	Original Maturity (mos.) (8)	Lender Report Sample — No. of Contracts (9)	Bad Loan Rate (%) (10)	Personal Interview Sample — No. of Contracts (11)	Bad Loan Rate (%) (12)
Under 20.0	346	8.4	311	3.5	Under 20.0	1,382	4.2	Less than 18	856	1.3	556	2.3
20.0–24.9	429	13.8	275	6.2	20.0–24.9	659	1.7	18–23	687	2.4	492	2.2
25.0–29.9	1,084	11.9	533	3.2	25.0–29.9	581	2.9	24–29	3,021	4.9	1,674	2.3
30.0–34.9	1,797	6.7	991	3.7	30.0–34.9	615	1.8	30–35	3,080	7.8	1,597	3.3
35.0–39.9	1,127	5.8	695	1.9	35.0–39.9	413	2.4	36 & over	1,232	7.9	728	1.3
40.0–49.9	1,438	2.4	920	1.5	40.0–49.9	562	0.9	Total	8,876	5.8	5,047	2.5
50.0 & over	1,793	1.8	1,322	0.8	50.0 & over	822	1.0					
Total	8,014	5.8	5,047	2.4	Total	5,034	2.4					

Source: Unpublished data from the National Analysts New Automobile Purchase Survey for the Federal Reserve Board.

Note: The bad-loan rate is total number of delinquencies and repossessions expressed as a percentage of the number of contracts in the group. Contracts that could not be classified because information was lacking are excluded.

of the smallest down payment group, the repossession and delinquency rate falls steadily as the contract down payment ratio increases. The personal interview data (col. 5) present a similar though weaker pattern.[7]

In both cases it is clear that loans on which the contract down payment ratio fell below 35 per cent had markedly inferior collection experience. The broad relationships are similar despite the fact that the frequency of collection difficulty disclosed by personal interview was substantially less than that reported by lenders.

The Federal Reserve survey adopted a special method for handling the difficult problem mentioned above of estimating the degree to which stated down payment percentages are altered by the large variation in trade-in allowances given on new-automobile instalment contracts. The method, which involved an effort by the interviewers themselves to estimate the degree of overallowance on trade-ins, is admittedly subject to considerable error.[8] Both the size of the contract

because the lender reports included few questions on borrower characteristics. For a detailed account of the survey method, definitions, and sampling procedure see Volume VI of the Federal Reserve Board's report.

In Table 28 and subsequent text tables the number of loans reported delinquent and the number on which repossession had occurred are combined to produce a bad-loan rate. The separate data for the two categories, which are given in Appendix D, provide more information by distinguishing a more serious from a less serious form of credit difficulty. However, the combined data are less subject to erratic sampling variations and also eliminate the tendency, in this survey, for offsetting variations to occur between contracts classified as repossessed and as delinquent. This occurs because contracts recorded as repossessed undoubtedly were delinquent at an earlier date but are not so recorded (except in a very few instances). Hence the repossessions in effect remove an equivalent number of contracts from the delinquent category. Another way to regard the combined repossession and delinquency rate, therefore, is to say that it represents a more comprehensive delinquency rate (assuming all repossessions were initially delinquent).

[7] If, therefore, it is true, as the credit industry has long maintained, that it scrutinizes carefully the credit records and other pertinent characteristics of the borrowers to whom it grants loans involving the lowest initial equity, the effects show up only in the lowest (under 20 per cent) down payment class, where in fact the collection experience is somewhat better than in the next higher class. The explanation for this deviation from the over-all pattern might lie, at least partially, in the compensatory screening of these prospective borrowers. However, the general pattern suggests that the credit industry does not, as a rule, offset liberal loan terms with stricter borrower standards. Cf. Chapter 5, especially Table 36, which also suggests that the notion of offsetting the risks attendant on easy terms with higher standards for borrowers does not generally hold.

[8] For a detailed discussion of the method, see *Consumer Instalment Credit*, Part IV, pp. 136–137.

down payment and the contract price were adjusted by the estimated amount of overallowance on trade-ins. The result gave what the Federal Reserve termed the "effective" down payment and the "effective" price. Since the overallowance on trade-ins is subtracted from both the contract price and the contract down payment to obtain the effective ratio, the effective down payment ratios are substantially smaller than the contract ratios (compare the distribution of loans in Table 28, cols. 4 and 7).

The analysis, available only for the personal interview data, suggests that the highest incidence of repossession and delinquency occurs among loans involving smaller effective down payment ratios. However, there is no evidence here that "effective down payment" is more consistently related to collection experience than is the "contract down payment." Indeed, in these data, the contract down payment is the more effective discriminator. Apparently the overallowance on trade-in can be included without adversely affecting the relation between down payment and subsequent collection experience.

Columns 11 and 13 in Table 28 pertain to the relation between loan maturity and subsequent collection experience as revealed by lender reports and personal interviews, respectively. From the data on lender reports it appears that loans with shorter maturities have significantly lower risk of delinquency or repossession. This relation is less clear in the personal interview sample. Indeed, in the personal interview data, the longest maturity group (thirty-six months and over) had lower than average repossession and delinquency rates. How can this be accounted for?

Incomplete coverage of collection difficulties in the personal interview sample may be partly responsible. The lender reports were evidently much more complete on this score, and hence probably provide more dependable estimates of the relation of collection experience to credit terms. Another factor to be considered in evaluating the performance of the long maturity loans in this survey is that loan experience was measured only up to the date of the survey and not through the full life of the loan (unless it had already terminated). The loans were made in 1954 and 1955, and the survey was taken in June and July 1956. Thus loans issued in the last month of 1954 were only eighteen months old at the time of the survey, and loans made in the last month of 1955 were only six months old. Since during this period the proportion of loans made at longer maturities was rising

TABLE 29

Distribution of Instalment Contracts by Maturity and Date of Origination, Federal Reserve Survey of New-Car Purchases, 1954–55

Date When Contract Originated	Total Number of Contracts[a] (1)	Percentage Distribution Within Each Period, by Maturity				Percentage Distribution Within Each Maturity Class, by Period			
		Under 30 Mos. (2)	30–35 Mos. (3)	36 Mos. and Over (4)	Total (5)	Under 30 Mos. (6)	30–35 Mos. (7)	36 Mos. and Over (8)	Total (9)
A. Lender Report Sample									
1954, first half	1,683	66	27	7	100	27	14	8	19
1954, second half	1,858	52	35	13	100	23	20	16	21
1955, first half	2,517	43	39	18	100	26	30	30	28
1955, second half	2,863	34	41	25	100	24	36	47	32
Total	8,921	46	37	17	100	100	100	100	100
B. Personal Interview Sample									
1954	2,027	64	28	8	100	48	35	22	40
1955	3,042	47	34	19	100	52	65	78	60
Total	5,069	54	32	15	100	100	100	100	100

Source: *Consumer Instalment Credit*, Part IV, "Financing New Car Purchases," Tables 33 and 38, pp. 59 and 63, Board of Governors of the Federal Reserve System, 1957.

[a]From special tabulations. Lender report sample includes forty-five cases that did not report maturity; personal interview sample includes twenty two such cases.

rapidly (see Table 29, cols. 3–5), the long loans in general would have been outstanding for a shorter period than the short loans at the date of the survey. Hence the experience record on long loans would not only fail to cover their full life but would actually cover a shorter interval than many of the shorter loans made early in the period. Table 29 (cols. 7–9) shows that 47 per cent of all loans for thirty-six months and over originated within the last six months of the survey period, according to the lender report sample, while this was true of only 24 per cent of the shortest maturities. This difference might, therefore, tend to produce fewer cases of delinquency or repossession on the longer loans.

This inference must be qualified, however, because most collection difficulties appear in the first few months of the life of a loan, and all the loans in the survey were at least six months old at the time of the survey. It may be that delinquency takes longer to develop in long-maturity as compared with short-maturity loans, but we have no evidence on this point. Moreover, the distribution of long-maturity loans within the survey period, according to column 9 of the table, seems to be about the same for both the lender report and personal interview samples, whereas the low delinquency rates on these loans appeared only in the personal interview data.

Another possible explanation is that loan experience generally improved between 1954 and 1955 in the course of the recovery from the 1953–54 recession. Since the long-maturity loans were granted chiefly in 1955, they were less affected by adverse economic conditions than the short loans. Again, however, this consideration would apply to both the lender report and personal interview samples. The upshot is that we are unable to account for the sharp divergence between the two samples with respect to the relation between length of maturity and collection experience, but the pattern revealed by the lender report data is consistent with that shown by all other samples utilized in this study, namely, poorer collection experience on longer maturity loans for new cars.

Apart from these considerations having to do with the survey itself, the relation between repayment experience and loan maturity is complicated by the operation of several factors that have different effects. One is that longer maturities for a given size loan imply smaller monthly payments, which, being easier to pay, make delinquency less

TABLE 30

Frequency of Refinancing to Reduce Monthly Payments,
New-Car Loans, Classified by Original Maturity, 1954-55

Original Maturity (months)	Number of Loans		Refinancing Rate (per cent)
	All	Refinanced to Reduce Monthly Payments	
Lender Report Sample			
Less than 18	856	12	1.4
18–23	687	21	3.1
24–29	3,021	111	3.7
30–35	3,080	97	3.1
36 and over	1,232	20	1.6
All loans	8,876	261	2.9
Personal Interview Sample			
Less than 18	556	11	2.0
18–23	492	11	2.2
24–29	1,674	59	3.5
30–35	1,597	43	2.7
36 and over	728	6	0.8
All loans	5,047	130	2.6

Source: Unpublished data from the National Analysts Survey of New Car Purchases for the Federal Reserve Board.

likely. However, as noted earlier and again below, long maturities and low down payments typically go together, so that the effect of the longer period in reducing monthly payments is mitigated. Another factor is that longer maturities mean a longer time for the financial position of the borrower to change, increasing the possibility of delinquency at some time during the life of the loan. Such shifts in financial circumstances are indicated by the frequency with which loans are refinanced to reduce monthly payments, which tends to increase, up to a point, with length of maturity (Table 30). A third factor is that longer maturities mean that it takes longer for the borrower to build up his equity by any given date, making his stake in fulfilling his contract correspondingly smaller.[9] Apparently these last two factors generally dominate the result in new-car lending, so that the longer maturities typically represent greater credit risk.

The Federal Reserve survey of new-car purchases enables us to determine, for the first time, the joint relationship between down payments and maturities, on the one hand, and subsequent collection experience, on the other. Unfortunately this can be done only for the personal interview data, which appear to be less reliable, especially with respect to maturities, than the lender reports. Nevertheless, it is clear from Table 31 that within each maturity group, collection experience improves consistently as the effective down payment percentage increases. Also, within a given down payment group, maturities of thirty to thirty-five months experience higher repossession and delinquency rates than do shorter maturities. The abnormally low repossession and delinquency rates on loans of thirty-six months or more also appear consistently, but this result must be heavily discounted for the reasons alluded to earlier.

Table 31 brings out the fact that loans with long maturities are predominantly low down payment loans, while short maturities much more frequently involve high down payments. As a result, when only one of these characteristics is taken into account at a time, its relationship to collection experience is apt to be exaggerated. To illustrate the point, in Table 31 the largest number of contracts is in the group with maturity "under 30 months" and down payment "40 and over," and the next largest is in the group with maturity "30–35 months" and down payment "under 29." Hence the low delinquency and repossession rate for the first group (1.0 per cent) dominates the weighted average rate for all loans with maturities under 30 months and the high rate for the second group (3.4 per cent) dominates the average for all loans of 30–35 months. Similarly, the average rate for all high down payment loans is heavily influenced by the low rate in

TABLE 31

Collection Experience on Loans Cross-Classified
by Effective Down Payment and Original Maturity, 1954-55

Original Maturity (mos.)	Effective Down Payment (per cent)			Total
	Under 30	30–39	40 and over	

1. Number Of Contracts

Under 30	991	592	1,119	2,702
30–35	1,060	343	187	1,590
36 and over	564	86	72	722
Total	2,615	1,021	1,378	5,014

2. Bad Loan Rate

				Average	
				Unwtd.	Wtd.
Under 30	3.1	1.6	1.0	1.9	2.1
30–35	3.4	3.2	1.1	2.6	3.1
36 and over	1.8	0	0	0.6	1.3
Average, unwtd.	2.8	1.6	0.7	1.7	––
wtd.	3.0	2.1	1.0	––	2.2

Source: Unpublished data from the National Analysts
New Automobile Purchase Survey for the Federal Reserve
Board.

Note: Contracts that could not be classified because information
was lacking are excluded. The bad loan rate is the total number of
delinquencies and repossessions expressed as a percentage of the
number of contracts in the group. The unweighted averages are based
on the rates in each row (or column) without taking into account the
number of contracts in the respective row (or column).

the shortest maturity class, and the average for all low down payment loans is more influenced by the high rate in the 30–35-month class. The unweighted averages shown in the table represent a crude way of eliminating much of this joint effect and more nearly approximate the relationship between each characteristic separately and the measure of lending experience.

INTERAREA ANALYSIS, 1953–56

The relation between changes in loan terms and subsequent collection experience can be further studied by means of data provided by a large sales finance company for twelve metropolitan areas for every third month from 1953 to April 1956. In this analysis we have concentrated on the repossession rate related to the date the loan was made as the best single measure of collection experience.[10]

Chart 9 shows how the repossession rate varied with the proportion of loans with down payments under 33 per cent in each of the years 1953, 1954, and 1955. In each area, for each year, the ultimate repossession rates are estimated for the same loans to which the down payment percentages apply. First, it is fairly clear from the over-all pattern that between 1953 and 1955 the easing of down payments in most areas was accompanied by an increase in repossession rates on the loans made. Second, *within* each of the three years 1953, 1954, and 1955, the areas with the most liberal down payment requirements had the poorest repossession experience. Viewed either way, the association of low down payments with high repossession rates is moderately close.

We have observed previously that while down payments and maturities tend to move together, by and large, down payments seem to be a clearer indicator of what subsequent collection experience will be. Chart 10, comparable with Chart 9, relates the percentage of new automobile loans with maturities of twenty-five months or more to the estimated repossession rates on the same loans. The over-all positive association for the three years is clearly visible, but the interarea association within each of the three periods is considerably less pro-

[10] Other measures of collection experience are considered in Appendix C. The consequences of using repossession figures arranged by date of repossession instead of by date loan was made are discussed in Appendix F.

CHART 9

New-Automobile Contracts with Down Payments Under 33 Per
Cent and Estimated Repossession Rate as of Year of Purchase,
Twelve Metropolitan Areas, 1953–55

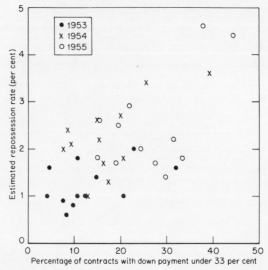

SOURCE: Tables F-2 and F-5. Data from a large sales finance company; 1955 based
on January and April.

CHART 10

New-Automobile Contracts with Maturities 25 Months or Longer
and Estimated Repossession Rate as of Year of Purchase,
Twelve Metropolitan Areas, 1953–55

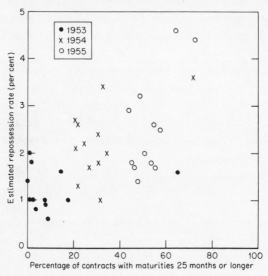

SOURCE: Tables F-3 and F-5. Data from a large sales finance company; 1955
based on January and April.

CHART 11

Used-Automobile Contracts with Down Payments Under 33 Per Cent and Estimated Repossession Rate as of Year of Purchase, Twelve Metropolitan Areas, 1953–55

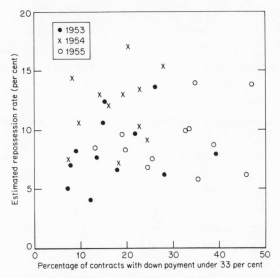

SOURCE: Tables F-6 and F-8. Data from a large sales finance company.

CHART 12

Used-Automobile Contracts with Maturities 25 Months or Longer and Estimated Repossession Rate as of Year of Purchase, Twelve Metropolitan Areas, 1953–55

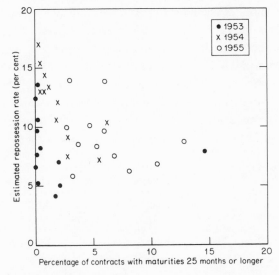

SOURCE: Tables F-7 and F-8. Data from a large sales finance company.

nounced than with down payments in Chart 9. In short, differences among areas in loan-maturity distribution in a given year are scarcely associated at all with differences in their repossession experience on these loans. This may be due to the fact that the differences in the maturity distributions within a year were relatively small. In 1953 and 1954, the one area in which terms were spectacularly easier than in the other eleven areas did have one of the higher repossession rates. In 1955, the two areas that were much more lenient than the rest in the matter of maturities had high repossession rates.

The data just considered were also analyzed on a quarterly basis (see Tables F-1, F-2, and F-3). That the general relations between down payments and ultimate repossession rates, and between maturities and ultimate repossession rates, are pervasive and fairly consistent was borne out by the quarterly analysis, although the results were striking only for those areas with very liberal terms.

Study of the quarterly data suggests that the general lowering of down payment requirements and lengthening of maturities during the 1953–55 period tended to raise repossession rates, and also that, as a consequence of the business recession of 1954, repossession rates tended to go up even without any change in loan terms. Chapter 6 will examine these materials from the latter point of view.

Another facet of the relation between loan terms and ultimate repossession experience on automobiles is revealed by examining loans on used automobiles made by the same sales finance company's branch offices in the same twelve metropolitan areas (Charts 11, 12, and 13).[11] Despite the fact that down payment percentages are about the same and maturities much shorter on used than on new cars, the estimated repossession rates on used-auto loans are far higher than those on new-auto loans (compare Chart 9 with 11, and 10 with 12). Other factors than credit terms evidently account for these differences in collection experience—differences that also appear in the other loan samples

---

[11] The data on down payment and maturities were available separately for late-model used automobiles and older-model used automobiles, whereas the repossession rate data apply to all used autos. Since the late-model used automobiles made up the bulk of the volume involved and hence are likely to be the major contributor to the used-automobile repossessions, the terms on late models are used here. Inclusion of the older model figures would tend to make the terms less liberal since more liberal provisions prevail on the higher-priced more recent models.

considered in the section "Conspectus of Evidence from the 1920's to the 1950's" in this chapter.

Chart 11 shows a modest tendency for the highest repossession rates to be associated with the greatest percentage of low-down-payment loans on used autos. But many areas with a high percentage of low-down-payment paper experienced repossession rates no higher than those with a low percentage.

Chart 12 reveals, like the national data considered earlier, that longer maturities in used-automobile loans are associated with lower repossession rates. This appears clearly in the 1954 figures and to some extent in 1955. In 1953, so few loans were made for twenty-five months or longer that the figures are not very meaningful. However, when a different grouping, eighteen months and over, is used for that year (Chart 13), the inverse relation between maturities and repossessions appears clearly. Thus the area data do not suggest that a lengthening of maturities on used-automobile loans typically leads to higher repossession rates, as in the case of new-automobile loans. In used-automobile loans other factors evidently offset the greater risks that longer maturities usually entail.

CHART 13

Late Model Used-Automobile Contracts with Maturity over 18 Months and Estimated Repossession Rate as of Year of Purchase, Twelve Metropolitan Areas, 1953

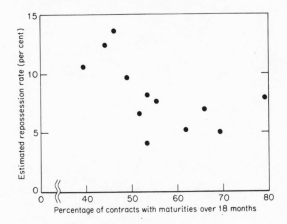

SOURCE: Tables F-7 and F-8. Data from a large sales finance company.

In sum, a partial answer is possible to the question posed at the beginning of this chapter. Credit terms do seem to be significantly related to subsequent collection experience. Utilizing data covering in
varying degree the period since 1925, we can conclude that high down
payment ratios have been consistently associated with a smaller degree
of subsequent collection difficulty on both new- and used-automobile
credit. Shorter maturities on new automobile paper also have been associated with better subsequent collection experience, though somewhat less strongly than down payments. In the case of contracts on
used automobiles the maturity relationship is reversed.

Moreover, we find these general tendencies strikingly visible when
collection experience is recorded for loans cross-classified by both
down payment ratio and by maturity. This enables us to consider the
effect of each aspect of the credit contract, holding the other constant,
as well as the combined effect of an easing or tightening in both. We
find that down payments and maturities typically reinforce rather than
offset each other in their effects on subsequent collection experience.

4. Borrower Characteristics and Subsequent Collection Experience

The question whether quality, or credit risk, is measurable at the time the loan is made involves not only the terms on which loans are made but also the characteristics of the borrowers who obtain these terms. The same credit terms offered to different groups of borrowers can represent different degrees of risk exposure to the lender. Having previously considered the terms, we now examine borrower characteristics and their relation to loan quality.

REVIEW OF EARLIER EVIDENCE

A major contribution toward the analysis of borrower characteristics was David Durand's study for the National Bureau, published in 1941.[1] Durand based his study on data provided by banks and sales finance companies, classified loans by various characteristics of the borrowers on which the lenders had information, and compared the collection experience on loans in the various classes. His findings, together with certain other evidence from previous studies, may be summarized as follows:

1. The higher income groups appear to be moderately better loan risks than the lower income groups according to most of the distributions shown in Table 32. The results are not beyond dispute, however, because for several of the samples the bad-loan relatives behave irregularly and do not show progressively lower figures as higher income groups are reached. For example, the sample of Title I loans shows progressively higher bad-loan relatives as higher income groups

[1] David Durand, *Risk Elements in Consumer Instalment Financing*, New York, National Bureau of Economic Research, 1941.

TABLE 32

Relationship of Loan Experience to Borrower's Income, Bad Loan Relatives

Borrower's Annual Income (dollars)	A. 1935–38 Commercial Banks	A. 1935–38 Industrial Banks	A. 1935–38 Personal Finance Companies	Auto Finance Companies New Cars	Auto Finance Companies Used Cars	B. 1938 Electric Home and Farm Authority	C. 1939–41 Title I Loans	D. 1950–51 Commercial Banks	D. 1950–51 Consumer Finance Companies	D. 1950–51 Credit Unions
Under 600						1.4				
600–899	0.9	1.1	1.3		1.5	2.2	1.0	9.9	3.2	—
900–1,999				1.7		1.8				
1,200–1,499	1.2	1.1	1.1		1.4	1.3	.9			
1,500–1,799						.7		2.4	2.4	5.0
1,800–2,399	1.0	.9	.9	1.1	.8	.8		2.1	1.8	1.6
2,400–2,999	1.0	1.1	.7	1.2	.5			1.3	1.1	1.2
3,000–3,599	.8	.8	.8	.7	.9		1.1	.8	.8	1.1
3,600–4,799	.8	1.1		.6			1.2	.7	.6	.2
4,800–5,999						.5				
6,000–7,199	.7	.7	1.2	.6	.4		1.3	.8	.5	.2
7,200 and over							1.6	.8	.3	.9

Source: A. — Durand, *Risk Elements*, Table 4, pp. 46-47; B. — Plummer and Young, *Sales Finance Companies*, computed from Table 44, p. 181; C. — unpublished data from a large New York bank, based on sample of 16,000 Title I FHA repair and modernization loans; D. — Robbins, *Consumer Instalment Loans*, compiled from Table 36, p. 110.

Note: Bad loan relatives for Durand material obtained by dividing the percentage each income group contributes to all loans with collection difficulty by the percentage contributed to all good loans. Relatives for other data obtained by using outstanding loans, rather than good loans as denominator.

are considered, the opposite tendency from that observed in the other samples. Durand also noted the conflicting evidence on the relation of borrower income to quality and the doubtful statistical significance of most of the findings. In part, this may be due to a failure to take into account the size of the borrower's obligation. Two available samples of loans classified by the ratio of monthly payments to income show increasing collection difficulties as the burden of payments increases, one of them being the sample of Title I loans that shows inconsistent results when income alone is considered.[2]

2. Ownership of certain assets, such as bank accounts and insurance, is another characteristic closely associated with loan quality.

3. Stability of job and stability of residence both seem to be consistently important factors in determining lender risk exposure.

4. Durand found that persons in professional occupations as a group produce the most favorable repayment experience, and other bits of evidence, summarized in Table 33, are consistent with this result. The clerical and sales group ranked next in Durand's study, but other evidence is less clear cut. This group ranked well in some of the samples studied and not so well in others. It seems clear that wage earners constitute the group with the least favorable experience generally, although there are several samples in which proprietors occupied this position.

It is therefore difficult to summarize the findings of previous efforts to evaluate the risk exposure associated with various occupations. The evidence is sparse, and has been acquired from diverse lenders. Some occupations (for example, the professions) are quite consistently as-

[2] One sample, provided by a large New York bank, applies to Title I repair and modernization loans; the other, given in Plummer and Young, *Sales Finance Companies and Their Credit Practices*, Table 45, is based on Electric Home and Farm Authority experience on appliance loans:

Title I Loans		EHFA Loans	
Ratio of Fixed Charges to Income (%)	Delinquency Rate (%)	Ratio of Monthly Payment to Income (%)	Repossession Rate (%)
Less than 10	5.7	Under 2.5	2.4
10–20	6.0	2.5 to 5	3.3
20–30	5.2	5 to 7.5	5.3
30–40	6.9	7.5 to 10	6.5
40–50	6.8	10 to 22.5	4.0
Over 50	8.0		

TABLE 33

Relationship of Loan Experience to Borrower's Occupation

Occupational Classification	A. 1935–38					B. 1939–41	C. 1950–51		
	Commercial Banks	Industrial Banks	Personal Finance Companies	Auto Finance Companies		Title I Loans	Commercial Banks	Consumer Finance Companies	Credit Unions
				New Cars	Used Cars				
Bad-Loan Relatives									
Professions	0.6	0.7	0.7	0.6	0.4	0.8	0.7	0.9	0
Clerical and sales	0.8	1.0	0.9	1.0	0.8	0.9	0.8	1.2	0.2
Proprietors	1.0	1.1	1.5	1.3	1.3	1.2	0.1	1.2	0
Managers and officials	1.3	1.1	1.1	0.7	1.2	1.1	0.9	1.5	0
Wage earners	1.4	1.2	1.1	1.2	1.3	1.0	1.3	0.9	1.0
Rank									
Professions	1	1	1	1	1	1	2	2	2
Clerical and sales	2	2	2	3	2	2	3	3	5
Proprietors	3	3	5	5	4	5	1	4	2
Managers and officials	4	4	4	2	3	4	4	5	2
Wage earners	5	5	3	4	5	3	5	1	4

Source: A. — Durand, *Risk Elements*, Table 13, pp. 70–71. B. — Unpublished data from a large New York bank relating to Title I FHA repair and modernization loans made July 1939 to July 1941. C. — Robbins, *Consumer Instalment Loans*, Table 35, p. 108.

Note: Bad loan relatives for Durand material obtained by dividing the percentage each occupational group contributes to all loans with collection difficulty by the percentage contributed to all good loans. Relatives for other data obtained by using total loans rather than good loans as denominator. Rank is based on bad-loan relatives carried to two decimals.

sociated with good experience and others with less favorable experience (wage earners), but these generalizations are not universally valid and for several occupational groups the evidence is conflicting.

5. With respect to other personal characteristics, Durand found that women seemed to be better risks than men, but he could find no significant difference between married and single people. By age, he found a "slight" tendency for older borrowers to be better risks, though even this failed to show up in the commercial bank samples. The number of dependents he found to be "virtually unimportant."

THE 1954–55 SURVEY OF NEW-CAR PURCHASES

As noted earlier, the most recent large-scale study giving attention to borrower characteristics was the Federal Reserve Board's survey of new-car financing in 1954–55. The published report provides information on cash in contrast to credit purchases classified according to various borrower characteristics, but no attempt was made to relate them to collection experience.[3] New computations made for the present study make this possible. Not only does this information permit us to test with recent data the relationship between many of the borrower characteristics previously considered and collection experience, but there is information, albeit scanty, on several other relevant characteristics. Furthermore, it is possible for the first time, to our knowledge, to take borrower characteristics and loan terms jointly into account (see Chapter 5).

These data have been classified in order to group, by borrower characteristics, the number of loans in the sample that were delinquent at the time of the interview, and the number that had resulted in repossession of the automobile by the time of the interview. This information, when related to the total number of loans in the same class, provides the measure of collection experience used in Table 34.

Because of the limitations of the sample, the number in each class is sometimes too small to give reliable results. Moreover, the information on borrower characteristics is provided only by the personal interview sample, and, as noted earlier, the personal interviews disclosed fewer cases of collection difficulty than the lender reports. A number

[3] *Consumer Instalment Credit*, Part IV, p. 33.

TABLE 34

Borrower Characteristics and Collection Experience
on New-Car Loans, Personal Interview Sample, 1954-55

1. Borrower's Income in Year of Purchase	No. of Contracts	Bad-Loan Rate (per cent)	2. Borrower's 1955 Income	No. of Contracts	Bad-Loan Rate (per cent)
Under $3,000	325	3.4	Under $3,000	287	4.5
3,000—3,999	502	4.4	3,000—3,999	463	4.1
4,000—4,999	812	2.7	4,000—4,999	789	2.2
5,000—9,999	2,636	1.9	5,000—9,999	2,685	2.1
10,000 and over	610	1.5	10,000 and over	662	1.7
Total	4,885	2.4	Total	4,886	2.4

3. Borrower's 1955 Disposable Income	No. of Contracts	Bad-Loan Rate (per cent)	4. Net Worth of Borrower	No. of Contracts	Bad-Loan Rate (per cent)
Under $3,000	455	4.6	Negative	186	5.4
3,000—3,999	690	3.5	Zero	35	17.1
4,000—4,999	1,058	2.6	$1—999	351	4.3
5,000—9,999	2,320	1.7	1,000—2,999	626	1.0
10,000 and over	363	0.8	3,000—4,999	440	3.0
Total	4,886	2.4	5,000—9,999	743	2.3
			10,000—24,999	1,024	1.3
			25,000 and over	615	2.3
			Total	4,020	2.3

Source: Unpublished data from the National Analysts New Automobile Purchase Survey for the Federal Reserve Board.

Note: The bad-loan rate is the total number of deliquencies and repossessions expressed as a percentage of the number of contracts in the group. Contracts that could not be classified because information was lacking are excluded.

TABLE 34 (concluded)

5. Liquid Asset Holdings of Borrower	No. of Con- tracts	Bad- Loan Rate (per cent)	6. Occupation of Borrower	No. of Con- tracts	Bad- Loan Rate (per cent)
Zero	687	8.0	Professional and technical	623	1.8
$1−199	747	3.2	Clerical and sales	738	0.9
200−499	767	1.0	Skilled, semi- skilled, unskilled	2,267	3.3
500−999	650	0.9	Self-employed, nonfarm	521	2.7
1,000−1,999	564	1.2	Managers, officials proprietors	645	1.2
2,000−4,999	518	0.8	Farm operators	74	0
5,000−9,999	155	1.3	Housewives	127	1.6
10,000 and over	72	0	Unemployed	52	5.8
Total	4,160	2.5	Total	5,047	2.4

7. Life Cycle Status of Borrower	No. of Con- tracts	Bad- Loan Rate (per cent)	8. Age of Borrower	No. of Con- tracts	Bad- Loan Rate (per cent)
Under 45 years					
Single	512	2.7	18−29	966	3.0
Married, no children	563	0.4	30−39	1,648	2.6
Married, with children	2,231	3.0	40−49	1,395	2.2
45 Years and over			50 and over	1,041	2.1
Single	163	1.8	Total	5,050	2.5
Married, no children	887	1.5			
Married, with children	617	3.6			
Total	4,973	2.4			

of the inconsistencies in the patterns considered below can no doubt be thus explained.

The first three panels in the table pertain to loans in groups classified by income. They differ with respect to the definition of income used, but they are alike in showing that collection difficulties occur relatively more frequently with low-income than with high-income borrowers. Hence these data support the general tendencies shown by earlier surveys. It appears, too, that income as of a given year (1955) discriminates among risks better than income in year of purchase (1954 or 1955), and that disposable income does this somewhat better than total income.

When income is used as the measure of ability to meet financial responsibility it appears to be related to loan quality, but Durand found another type of measure, the possession of a bank account, to be more important. Measures of the borrower's asset position available in the 1954–55 survey data support this finding.

The fourth panel in Table 34 presents the relevant information concerning the significance of the borrower's net worth in relation to collection experience on automobile loans. Individuals with a net worth under $1,000 represent considerably greater risk than those with net worth above this figure.

A more immediate indication of a borrower's ability to meet his financial obligations is his liquid-asset holdings (panel 5). The results are striking. Borrowers without liquid assets experienced much higher delinquency and repossession rates than those with such assets. Only about one-third of the borrowers had liquid assets of less than $200, but they accounted for three-fourths of all the repossessions and delinquencies.

It must be observed, however, that the implications of these relationships are not as clear-cut as they might be, because the net worth and liquid-asset holdings were recorded as of the time the car buyer was interviewed in the survey, rather than as of the date the loan was originated. Hence the results do not necessarily mean that low net worth or a weak liquid-asset position at the time of borrowing leads to repayment difficulty, though they may mean that. Of course, it is precisely the people with little or no liquid assets to whom instalment purchasing offers the greatest appeal. Waiving the difficulty just noticed, it appears that information on liquid-asset holdings can be of great importance in evaluating credit quality.

It will be recalled from our summary of earlier studies that borrowers in professional occupations usually had a better, and wage earners a worse, repayment record than those in other occupations. Our new data (panel 6) are generally consistent with this. Clerical and sales groups also turned in a relatively good performance in both the earlier samples and the present one.

The survey data enable consideration of marital status in conjunction with age and the presence or absence of children, a combination of characteristics that may be called the "life cycle status" of the borrower. Whereas Durand found marital status to be of little significance in determining risk, panel 7 suggests that the life cycle status of the borrower may affect significantly the collection experience history of automobile loans. Married couples without children show generally the best collection experience in both age groups. Married couples with children, where the bulk of the loans were concentrated, generally exhibited the poorest experience in both age groups. Among single individuals, the younger group had a poorer record than the older. The association between the borrower's age and credit risk is examined further in panel 8. The results confirm Durand's earlier finding that older borrowers are apt to have the better payment record.

Considering the results of the 1954–55 survey for the several types of borrower characteristics in relation to one another, it appears that the highest rates of collection difficulty are those for borrowers with zero or negative net worth at the time of the survey, for borrowers with no liquid assets, and for borrowers with incomes under $3,000 (and the unemployed). The lowest rates are for married borrowers under 45 with no children, for farm operators and clerical and sales personnel, and for borrowers with high income and substantial liquid assets. Each of the characteristics investigated appears capable of distinguishing classes of borrowers that differ considerably in their propensity to avoid repayment problems.

INTERRELATIONS AMONG BORROWER CHARACTERISTICS

All the data just examined take up borrower characteristics one by one and relate them to loan experience. This does not necessarily mean, of course, that each characteristic independently has some bearing on risk. Several may be reflecting their association with each other, or with some unobserved factor. For example, the relatively high delinquency

TABLE 35

Median Ratio of Monthly Payment to Monthly Income,
by Income, Occupation, Marital Status, and Age of
Borrower, New Automobile Sales Contracts, 1953 and 1957

	Number of Contracts		Median Ratio, Payment to Income (per cent)	
	June 1953	July 1957	June 1953	July 1957
Monthly Income at Annual Rate ($)				
Under 3,000	484	503	29.5	33.6[a]
3,000–4,199	1,229	1,572	20.6	26.0
4,200–5,999	1,458	3,272	16.1	19.5
6,000–11,999	975	2,441	12.3	14.2
12,000 and over	120	269	6.0	6.9
Occupation				
Farm				
Operator	96	142	19.4	19.6
Wage earner	41	69	21.2	24.4
Nonfarm				
Proprietor	424	567	14.8	15.5
Professional	246	423	14.9	16.7
Salaried	1,475	2,700	17.1	19.4
Wage earner	1,655	3,685	17.1	19.1
Miscellaneous	309	453	19.0	21.4
Marital Status				
Single	740	1,195	20.5	23.7
Married	3,501	6,836	16.4	18.5
Divorced-widowed	13	––	18.1	––
Age (years)				
30 and under	1,386	2,562	19.1	21.5
31–40	1,343	2,657	15.7	18.2
41–50	963	1,834	16.1	17.8
Over 50	551	984	16.1	18.8
All contracts (including incomplete questionnaires)	4,266	8,057	17.0	19.0

Source: A large sales finance company. Separate groups do not add
to total because contracts with incomplete information have been eliminated. For results of a chi-square test of association see Appendix
Tables B-13, B-14, B-15, B-16.
[a]Median value falls in open-end class.

rates for younger borrowers may reflect the influence of their lower incomes, or the easier terms they typically obtain. In the next chapter, we will examine some evidence that ties borrower characteristics, credit terms, and risk together, so that the separate influence of each can be tested. Before turning to it, however, we will consider data relating the borrower characteristics we have examined to a measure of the burden of monthly instalment payments (Table 35).

It is not surprising, of course, that the ratio of monthly payments to monthly income is lower for the higher income groups. Some association of this sort would be expected since income is the denominator of the ratio. Nevertheless, this does not render insignificant the fact that in the very lowest income group the instalment payment absorbs nearly a third of the monthly income, whereas in the highest group the payment takes no more than one-fifteenth of income. Differences of this magnitude seem likely to be a significant cause of greater repayment difficulty on the part of low income groups.

The payment-to-income ratio also is higher for the younger age groups, single persons, farmers, and wage earners. With the exception of some of the occupational groups, the differences in payment burden are similar to those in collection experience, with the groups having a greater burden generally showing less satisfactory experience. All of this suggests, though it does not definitely establish the point, that variation in the ratio of instalment payments to income is one of the factors that explain the association between certain borrower characteristics and risk of delinquency or default.

SUMMARY

The answer to the question posed in this and the preceding chapter, i.e., whether credit terms and borrower characteristics are related to collection difficulties and loss experience, seems clear. Examination of the evidence has shown that credit terms such as maturity and especially down payment are importantly related to the ultimate outcome of the loan, while borrower characteristics such as income, liquid-asset holdings, and life cycle status also bear a relationship—in some cases a striking relationship—to repayment experience.[4] The results sug-

---

[4] Three recent studies provide some additional evidence. In a sample of direct instalment loans made during 1952–58 by a commercial bank, Paul Smith derived

gest that, by observing terms of credit or relevant characteristics of borrowers, one can determine in advance certain broad variations in credit risk.

delinquency rates associated with each of some twenty loan and borrower characteristics. The rates were found to vary inversely with the maturity of the loan and with the borrower's income, age, length of time in last residence, and time on last job. Higher delinquency rates were also found for renters than for homeowners, for those without a telephone, for those without a bank account, and for men than for women borrowers. See "Measuring Risk on Instalment Credit," *Management Science*, November 1964, pp. 327–340.

Broadly similar results with respect to repossession rates on new-car contracts written by a large sales finance company during 1957–58 are reported by Paul W. McCracken, James C. T. Mao, and Cedric V. Fricke in *Consumer Instalment Credit and Public Policy*, Ann Arbor, Mich., 1965, pp. 134–140. As in earlier studies, repossession rates were found to vary positively with maturity on new-car contracts and inversely on used-car contracts. They also varied positively with the percentage of dealer cost (new cars) or wholesale value (used cars) financed. The results for income, age, length of residence and of employment, homeownership, occupation, and marital status correspond to those reported above.

Finally, the preliminary results of a new Federal Reserve survey also are generally consistent with the above findings. See *Monthly Review*, Federal Reserve Bank of Atlanta, November 1966, pp. 85–88.

5. The Relations Among Credit Terms, Borrower Characteristics, and Collection Experience

In the three preceding chapters we have examined the relations between credit terms and borrower characteristics, between credit terms and collection experience, and between borrower characteristics and collection experience. In each case there is a measurably large area of association, but an as yet unanswered question concerns the independent impact of terms and borrower characteristics on collection experience. To what extent do credit terms and borrower characteristics reinforce each other in regard to variations in collection experience? Are credit terms associated with collection experience merely because easy terms go to low income borrowers? Do low income borrowers occasion greater risk simply because they get easy terms?

In this chapter we utilize the Federal Reserve's 1954–55 Survey of New-Car Purchases to cross-classify loans by borrower characteristics and by credit terms, computing repossession and delinquency rates for the resulting groups. Hence it is possible for the first time to approach directly the question whether loans with liberal terms tend to be riskier than other loans *to the same type of borrower*. A considerable controversy has revolved around this issue, with some observers contending that borrower characteristics are fundamental, and terms incidental to quality. The analysis in preceding chapters of these relationships considered separately does not settle the matter, but the evidence which we will now consider supports the view that both aspects of the lending situation have an independent bearing on ultimate collection experience.

DOWN PAYMENTS AND BORROWER CHARACTERISTICS

We begin by examining repossession and delinquency rates for loans cross-classified by effective down payment and age of borrower (Table 36). It will be recalled from the earlier analysis that collection experience tended to improve with the down payment percentage and with the age of the borrower, considered separately. Both of these conclusions are corroborated in this table, but in addition it shows to what extent each factor is related to collection experience when the other is held substantially constant.

Within each age group, there is a fairly regular tendency for the repossession and delinquency rate to decline as down payments increase. The result is that, in all but one age group, bad-loan rates (repossession and delinquency) are more than four times as high when the effective down payment is less than 30 per cent than when it is 40 per cent or more.

The relationship of the borrower's age to repayment experience, holding down payment constant, seems clear only for the lowest down payment class. That is, when down payments are less than 30 per cent, there is a fairly steady decline in the bad-loan rate as age increases. When down payments are higher, age seems to make little difference—a not unreasonable result.

The effect of both factors taken together is shown by comparing the bad-loan rates in the upper left cells of the table with those in the lower right cells. The incidence of repayment difficulty for the youngest age group making the smallest down payment was six times as high as that for the oldest group making the largest down payment. The simultaneous consideration of the relation of both down payments and age to collection experience confirms, therefore, what the previous analysis of each led us to expect.

It should be noted that the present analysis is based on effective down payment rather than on contract down payment. The former is generally smaller than the latter, because it adjusts for the practice of overallowing on autos traded-in. In general, delinquency and repossession rates are higher in the latter case for the same percentage down payment. For example, collection experience with a 30 per cent contract down payment could be expected to be worse than that with a 30 per cent effective down payment. However, since the analysis in

TABLE 36

Collection Experience on Loans Cross-Classified by
Effective Down Payment and Borrower Characteristics, 1954-55

| | Number of Contracts | | | | Bad Loan Rate | | | | |
| | Effective Down Payment (per cent) | | | | Effective Down Payment (per cent) | | | Average | |
	Under 30	30-39	40 & over	Total	Under 30	30-39	40 & over	Un-wtd.	Wtd.
Age (years)									
Under 30	537	179	246	962	3.8	1.1	0.8	1.9	2.5
30–39	879	331	420	1,630	3.1	3.0	0.5	2.2	2.4
40–49	678	325	386	1,389	2.4	2.2	1.8	2.1	2.2
50 & over	518	190	326	1,034	2.7	1.1	0.6	1.5	1.8
Total	2,612	1,025	1,378	5,015					
Average, unwtd.					3.0	1.9	0.9	1.9	——
wtd.					3.0	2.1	1.0	——	2.2
Income in Year of Purchase ($)									
Under 3,000	192	55	76	323	3.7	3.6	2.6	3.3	3.4
3,000–4,999	717	250	340	1,307	4.1	2.4	0	2.2	2.7
5,000–7,499	977	417	457	1,851	2.6	2.4	1.3	2.1	2.2
7,500 & over	658	272	443	1,373	1.4	0.4	0.7	0.9	1.0
Total	2,544	994	1,316	4,854					
Average, unwtd.					2.9	2.2	1.2	2.1	——
wtd.					2.9	1.9	0.8	——	2.1
Liquid-Asset Holdings ($)									
None	441	118	118	677	8.6	5.1	1.7	5.1	6.8
1–499	904	323	284	1,511	2.6	1.8	0.7	1.7	2.2
500–1,999	587	244	377	1,208	0.5	2.0	0.8	1.1	0.9
2,000 or more	256	177	308	741	0.8	1.1	0.6	0.8	0.8
Total	2,188	862	1,087	4,137					
Average, unwtd.					3.2	2.5	1.0	2.1	——
wtd.					3.0	2.2	0.9	——	2.3

Source: Unpublished data from the National Analysts New Automobile Purchase Survey for the Federal Reserve Board.

Note: Contracts that could not be classified because information was lacking are excluded. The bad loan rate is the total number of delinquencies and repossessions expressed as a percentage of the number of contracts in the group. The unweighted averages are based on the rates in each row (or column) without taking into account the number of contracts in the respective row (or column).

Chapter 3 indicated that both methods of measuring down payments clearly distinguished the poorer from the better credit risks, the analysis here is limited to the effective down payment.

In the middle section of Table 36 we have the relevant information for assessing the effect of down payment percentages and the borrowers' income in the year of purchase on subsequent repossession and delinquency rates. Repayment experience tends to be more favorable the higher the income, within a given down payment class. Similarly, within a given income class, repossession and delinquency rates are generally lower when the effective down payment is large than when it is small.

The combined effect of low income and small down payment is strong indeed. The percentage of borrowers experiencing repayment difficulty (delinquency or repossession) is more than five times as high for those earning low incomes (under $3,000) and making small down payments (under 30 per cent) as for those earning high incomes ($7,500 and over) and making large down payments (40 per cent and over). The bad-loan rate for the former group is 3.7 per cent; for the latter, 0.7 per cent.

The bottom section of the table attests to the importance of liquid assets held by the borrower, independently of the down payment percentage, and vice versa. The decline in repossession and delinquency rates for borrowers without liquid assets in successively higher down payment groups is most striking. The decline is sharpest in the under 30 per cent down payment class, though still present in the higher classes. This is not unlike what was found in assessing the importance of age, and suggests that borrower characteristics may be more important in determining collection experience when down payments are low than when they are high, although down payments affect subsequent collection experience most when borrowers are in a less secure financial position.

Once again, the combined effect of both factors considered simultaneously can be seen by comparing the delinquency and repossession rates in the upper left cells with those in the lower right cells. The combined effect is such as to make the bad-loan rates on contracts with low down payments to borrowers with no liquid assets more than fourteen times as high as those to borrowers with large liquid-asset holdings who made substantial down payments.

It is important to recall that the Federal Reserve survey determined the borrower's liquid asset position as of the time of the interview, rather than as of the time the automobile was purchased. While there is undoubtedly some correlation between borrower's liquid asset positions at these two dates, we have no way of knowing how high it may be.[1] Hence, we have no way of knowing how frequently the circumstances which led to repayment difficulty also led to depletion of liquid assets.

MATURITIES AND BORROWER CHARACTERISTICS

The information on maturities available from the Federal Reserve's 1954–1955 Survey of New Car Purchases can be cross-classified with the borrower's age, income, and liquid-asset holdings in the same way that down payments were treated in the previous section (Table 37). The difficulties described in Chapter 3 in interpreting the survey data on the relationship of maturities to loan experience need to be kept in mind. In particular, the low incidence of collection difficulty on the longest-maturity loans, which shows up throughout, may be spurious, and our discussion of this problem in Chapter 3 is relevant. This problem is especially important in the personal interview sample, which we must rely on here since information on borrower characteristics was not available from the lender reports. The results *within* maturity groups are not affected by the difficulties mentioned and are therefore more firmly established.

Since, in general, the maturity tables reveal the same pattern as those pertaining to experience within down payment groups, we can be brief. The relationship of repayment difficulty to age of borrower is plain only for the longer maturities, a result consistent with that observed for down payments, where the effect of age appeared clearly only in the lowest down payment class. In the case of income and liquid assets, however, a strong relationship appears within each maturity class, as indeed it did within each down payment class. The

---

[1] Some evidence of the correlation is provided by the fact that among those who made large down payments the proportion who had substantial liquid assets was much larger than among those who made small down payments, which is what one would expect if the liquid assets were reported as of the time the loans were made.

TABLE 37

Collection Experience on Loans Cross-Classified by Original Maturity and Borrower Characteristics, 1954-55

| | Number Of Contracts | | | | Bad Loan Rate | | | | |
| | Original Maturity (mos.) | | | | Original Maturity (mos.) | | | Average | |
	Under 30	30-35	36 & over	Total	Under 30	30-35	36 & over	Un-wtd.	Wtd.
Age (years)									
Under 30	467	359	136	962	1.9	3.6	1.5	2.3	2.5
30-39	842	540	260	1,642	2.1	3.9	1.9	2.6	2.7
40-49	807	412	173	1,392	2.3	2.4	0.6	1.7	2.2
50 & over	600	277	155	1,032	1.8	1.8	1.3	1.6	1.8
Total	2,716	1,588	724	5,028					
Average, unwtd.					2.1	2.9	1.3	2.1	—
wtd.					2.1	3.1	1.4	—	2.3
Income in Year of Purchase ($)									
Under 3,000	166	120	39	325	3.0	4.2	2.6	3.2	3.3
3,000-4,999	614	488	210	1,312	2.3	4.5	2.0	3.0	3.0
5,000-7,499	969	594	291	1,854	2.1	2.6	1.7	2.1	2.2
7,500 & over	864	349	162	1,375	1.2	0.6	0	0.6	1.0
Total	2,613	1,551	702	4,866					
Average, unwtd.					2.1	3.0	1.6	2.3	—
wtd.					1.9	2.9	1.5	—	2.2
Liquid Asset Holdings ($)									
None	278	300	107	685	7.9	7.7	4.7	6.7	7.3
1-499	669	567	273	1,509	2.2	2.1	1.8	2.0	2.2
500-1,999	679	375	158	1,212	0.9	1.3	0	0.7	0.9
2,000 or more	545	123	75	743	1.1	0	0	0.3	0.8
Total	2,171	1,365	613	4,149					
Average, unwtd.					3.0	2.8	1.6	2.5	—
wtd.					2.2	2.9	1.7	—	2.3

Source: Unpublished data from the National Analysts New Automobile Purchase Survey for the Federal Reserve Board.

Note: Contracts that could not be classified because information was lacking are excluded. The bad-loan rate is the total number of delinquencies and repossessions expressed as a percentage of the number of contracts in the group. The unweighted averages are based on the rates in each row (or column) without taking into account the number of contracts in the respective row (or column).

influence of maturity itself, however, is much less apparent, partly because of the peculiarities of this survey which were discussed in Chapter 3.

SUMMARY

The evidence points to the conclusion that both loan terms and borrower characteristics are independently related to ultimate collection experience, and that both should be considered in estimating the prospective quality of consumer instalment credit. When loan terms are sufficiently restrictive, they can largely compensate for borrower characteristics that are associated with less favorable credit experience. On the other hand, the granting of easier terms to borrowers with less satisfactory characteristics can produce less favorable collection experience than either factor alone. This is particularly true of the combined effects of borrower characteristics and down payment ratios. The effect of lengthening maturities is apparently less significant, but a firm conclusion on this point is impossible because of deficiencies in the data available for analysis.

6. Credit Experience and the Business Cycle

From the preceding analysis, it appears that both loan terms and certain borrower characteristics are capable of distinguishing broad groups of high-risk loans from low-risk loans at a given time. This suggests that a shift over time to easier terms or to less qualified borrowers would increase risk and produce less favorable repayment experience. Does this actually happen? It is one thing to infer that it must occur in view of the preceding evidence and quite another to show that it really does occur on a significant scale. For this, we need to examine changes in experience with respect to credit repayment and determine to what extent they are associated with prior changes in loan terms or borrower characteristics.

Here, however, we run up against the fact that changes in credit experience are related also to changes in business conditions, apart from any prior changes in the terms or types of borrowers financed. Hard times naturally bring more repayment difficulty. We need then to know something about the direct influence of the business cycle on credit experience, and that is taken up in this chapter. The next will attempt to trace the impact on credit experience of changes in the terms or in the characteristics of the borrowers, changes that may or may not also be associated with the business cycle. Both chapters are concerned with changes over the short run (periods of a year or two or three), not with the long-run changes of the kind considered briefly in Chapter 1.

THE SEQUENCE OF CHANGE IN DELINQUENCY, REPOSSESSION, AND LOSS

Differences in measurement methods can be the source of much confusion concerning the behavior of repayment difficulties during the business cycle. The absolute volume of delinquencies, for example, might begin to rise as a business recovery gets under way simply because the recovery brings with it an increase in the volume of consumer lending. Accordingly, one is likely to shift attention from absolute measures such as the number of delinquent loans, the number of repossessions, or the dollar amount of losses to relative measures of such difficulties—i.e., the percentage of loans delinquent, the percentage of articles financed that were repossessed, or the loss rate. Such measures of the relative incidence of unfavorable loan experience may also be deceptive, however. A sharp decline in the volume of new lending may cause the relative measures to rise for a time even though there has been little change or even a decline in the level of unfavorable experience.

Further complications arise as a result of the use of different bases to measure relative collection experience. For example, the behavior of repossessions taken as a percentage of loans made during the period may be different from the measure relating repossessions to outstandings or repossessions to collections or liquidations. Since the repossessions made during a given month, for the most part, come from a different (older) loan population than the loans made during the month, the propriety of using the latter as the base may be questioned. The question is less serious when the time unit is a year rather than a month, because a large proportion of repossessions occur within the first few months after a loan is made. Furthermore, since the cyclical behavior of loan volume differs from that of outstandings, the cyclical behavior of the repossession rate will depend on which is used as the base. The measure used, therefore, must be carefully specified if confusion is to be avoided, and the use of several measures instead of a single one is a valuable safeguard. (Cf. Appendix C for more detailed consideration of measures of collection difficulty.)

It is obvious, of course, that collection difficulties are likely to show a decided relationship to changes in the level of business activity, increasing when overtime pay is eliminated, hours of work reduced, wages cut, and some employees lose their jobs, and diminishing when prosperity reverses these developments. The sequence of collection difficulties is well demonstrated in Charts 14 and 15, which show moving averages of volume of automotive loans, delinquent accounts, repossessions, and losses monthly (1952–56) for two samples, one of

CHART 14

Delinquencies, Repossessions, and Losses on Automobile Loans, in Relation to Unemployment and Volume of Loans, Three Banks, 1952–56

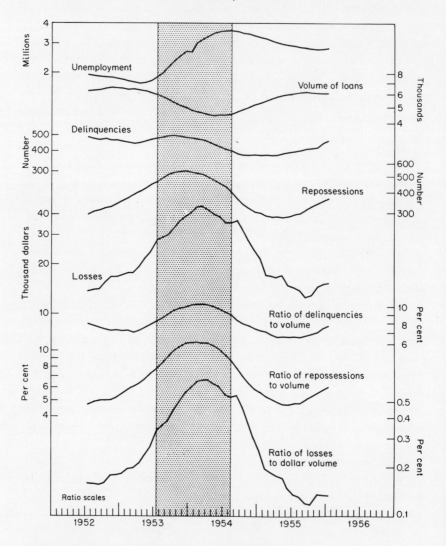

SOURCE: Unpublished data supplied to the NBER.
NOTE: Shaded area represents business cycle contraction.

CHART 15

Delinquencies, Repossessions, and Losses on Automobile Loans, in
Relation to Unemployment and Volume of Loans,
Three Sales Finance Companies, 1952–55

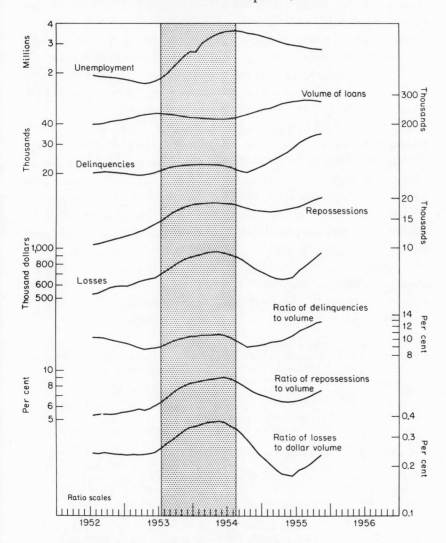

SOURCE: Unpublished data supplied to the NBER.
NOTE: Shaded area represents business cycle contraction.

three banks, the other of three finance companies. In quite regular fashion peaks were reached during the mild business contraction of 1953–54, first in the number of delinquent accounts, next in the number of repossessions, and last in the dollar amount of losses. The timing sequence at the troughs in 1954–55 is the same. The logic of this sequence is clear: it follows from the process by which collection difficulties first manifest themselves when monthly payments become overdue, which may then lead to voluntary or involuntary repossession of the article securing the loan, its eventual sale in a market characterized perhaps by falling prices of used durable goods, and the ultimate write-off of losses on the books of the lending institution.[1]

The timing of the troughs and peaks of each of the measures of collection difficulty at the business cycle peak of July 1953 and trough of August 1954 is given in Table 38. All of the entries for this small sample are leads. More persuasive evidence that delinquency rates tend to turn up some months prior to the onset of a business recession and to turn down before a recovery starts is provided by the monthly series compiled by the American Bankers Association subsequent to 1948. Seasonally adjusted data for delinquencies of various durations on direct and indirect (purchased) automobile loans are shown in Chart 16. The rates are based on the number of delinquent accounts relative to the total number outstanding. The timing of cyclical peaks and troughs in these rates relative to business cycle

---

[1] The movements of and relations among the measures of collection difficulty are subject to shifts in administrative procedure. For example, part of the sharp rise in the spring of 1955 in both the absolute and relative measures of delinquencies for sales finance companies (Chart 15) is attributable to a change in the administrative practices of one company included in the sample. According to this company, "In March 1955, a policy change was made in . . . collection procedure under which less intensive collection effort was given to those accounts which had accumulated a sufficiently large customer equity to indicate the probability of assured payment."

A more subtle difficulty encountered in analyzing collection difficulties arises as a result of recourse arrangements between the ultimate lender and the retailer whereby the latter agrees to absorb all or part of the loss encountered on loans he originates. The result is that while delinquency and repossession figures of banks and sales finance companies as shown in Charts 14 and 15 usually include collection difficulties arising in the case of both recourse and nonrecourse contracts (see, however, footnote 3), measures of losses shown in the charts include only losses on nonrecourse paper. It is possible that the timing of losses charged to dealers under recourse agreements would not differ significantly from those arising from nonrecourse contracts, although the level and trend of the reported (nonrecourse) losses would be affected by shifts in the proportion of business done on a nonrecourse basis.

TABLE 38

Cyclical Highs and Lows in Delinquencies, Repossessions, and Losses, Automobile Contracts, 1953-55

Item	Low Corresponding to July 1953 Business Cycle Peak		High Corresponding to August 1954 Business Cycle Trough		Subsequent Low, to End of 1955
	Date	Lead (months)	Date	Lead (months)	
			3 Banks		
Delinquencies	March 1953	4	October 1953	10	October 1954
Repossessions	Before July 1952	--	December 1953	8	May 1955
Losses	Before July 1952	--	March 1954	5	September 1955
			3 Sales Finance Companies		
Delinquencies	March 1953	4	February 1954	6	October 1954
Repossessions	Before July 1952	--	May 1954	3	February 1955
Losses	Before July 1952	--	May 1954	3	April 1955

Source: Based on National Bureau data for three banks and three sales finance companies, each of which reported monthly volume, delinquency, repossession, and losses on automotive loans. Data were smoothed by a twelve-month moving average centered on the seventh month.

CHART 16

Unemployment Rate and Delinquency Rates on Automobile Loans by Banks, 1948–66

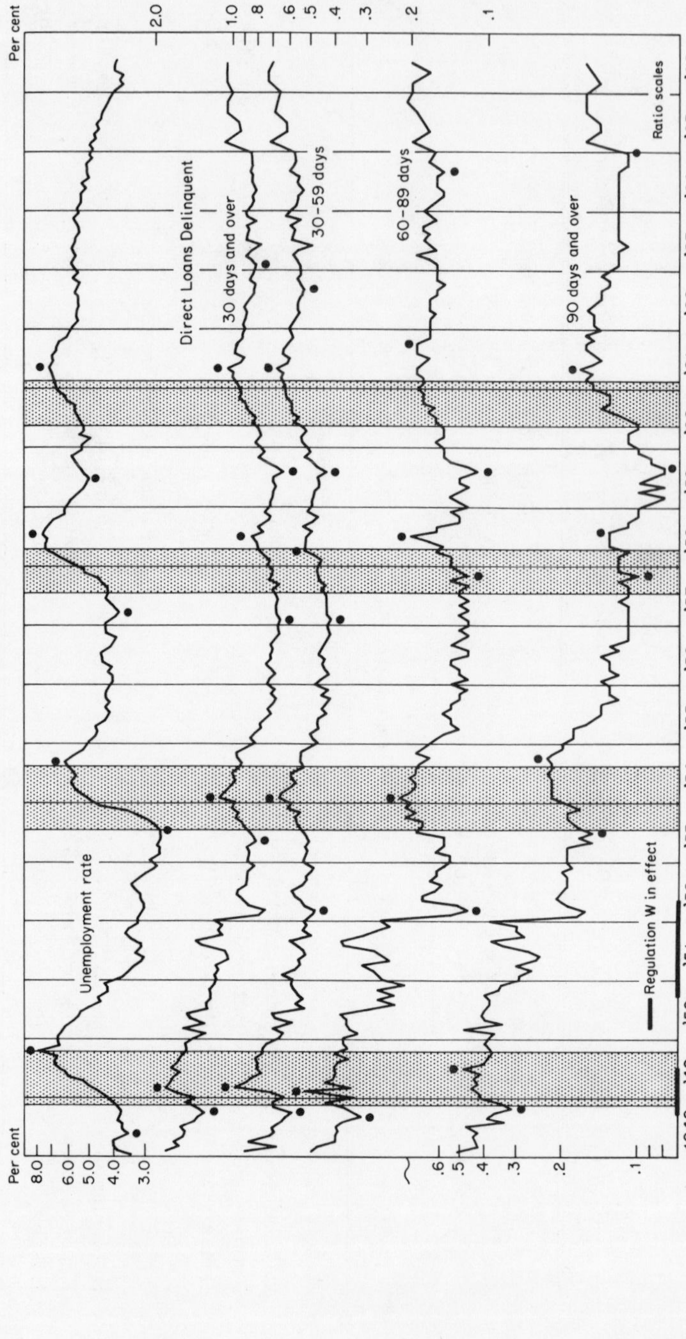

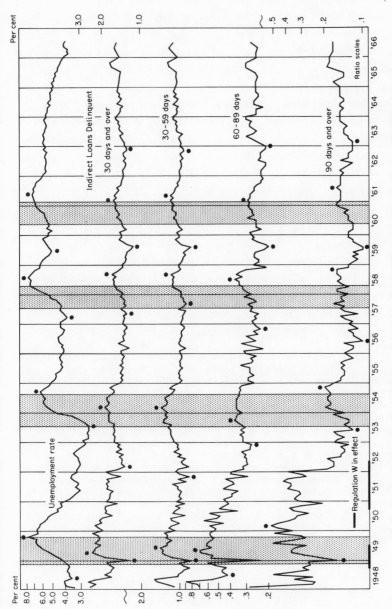

SOURCE: Unemployment rate, Bureau of Labor Statistics; delinquency rates, adjusted to level of currently published data and issued bimonthly after October 1964 by American Bankers Association.

NOTE: All series adjusted for seasonal variations by NBER. Shaded areas represent business cycle contractions. Dots identify specific cycle peaks and troughs.

troughs and peaks is entered in Table 39, together with similar data for the unemployment rate. The table suggests that the leads in the delinquency rates may be somewhat longer at business cycle peaks than at troughs; that is, the rise in delinquencies usually begins well before business activity turns down, whereas the decline in delinquencies usually begins only a short time before business begins to improve. In this respect, delinquencies resemble the unemployment rate at business cycle peaks since they both tend to lead, but at troughs delinquency rates have nearly always preceded the corresponding turns in the unemployment rate.[2] On the average, too, the turns in delinquencies of short duration have preceded those of longer duration, though this has not happened at every turn.

As for the differences between direct and indirect loans, the short-duration delinquency rates on direct loans have been consistently lower than those on indirect loans, while the more serious delinquencies, those of ninety days and over, have been at substantially the same rate on both types. That is, at any given time, about the same proportion of direct and of indirect loans have been delinquent ninety days or over, but a larger proportion of the indirect loans have been delinquent less than ninety days.[3] Despite these differences in level, the cyclical move-

[2] If the leads or lags in delinquencies are measured with respect to the turns in the unemployment rate rather than (as in Table 39) the business cycle turns, the difference between peak and trough timing which shows up in the table largely disappears. The variability of the timing of delinquencies about the turns in the unemployment rate is as great, however, as it is about the business cycle turns. The distinctive timing of the unemployment rate, Arthur F. Burns has suggested, can be understood in terms of the following model: Assume that the labor force grows at a constant rate throughout the business cycle, but that employment rises at a diminishing rate toward the end of a cyclical expansion. Then the unemployment rate will reach its trough before employment reaches its peak. Similarly, if employment rises slowly at the beginning of a cyclical expansion, the unemployment rate will reach its peak after the low point in employment. To put it differently, the employment *rate* (employment divided by labor force) will, under the assumed conditions, reach its peaks earlier and its troughs later than the corresponding turns in the number employed; turns in the unemployment rate will occur, of course, at the same time as the opposite turns in the employment rate.

[3] Apparently the similarity of the ninety day delinquency rates for direct and indirect loans has to do with a common practice with regard to recourse on indirect loans, whereby the banks agree to repossess within ninety days of the onset of delinquency if the loan is to be returned to the dealer. The result is, in effect, a reduction in indirect loans delinquent more than ninety days to approximately the levels for direct loans, since no recourse is to be had on either. We are indebted to J. Howard Craven of the Bank of America for this explanation.

TABLE 39

Timing of Delinquency Rates on Automobile Loans by Banks, and the Unemployment Rate, at Business Cycle Turns, 1948-61

Lead (−) Or Lag (+), In Months, Of Corresponding Turn In

	Unemployment Rate	Delinquency Rate on Direct Loans				Delinquency Rate on Indirect Loans			
		30-59 Days	60-89 Days	90 Days & Over	30 Days & Over	30-59 Days	60-89 Days	90 Days & Over	30 Days & Over
Business Cycle Peak									
November 1948	−6	−2	−2	0	−2	+2	−4	+2	+2
July 1953	0	−16	−16	0	−2	−20	−8	−2	−16
July 1957	−4	−6	+4	+4	−6	+2	−8	−14	−2
May 1960	−11	−10	−10	−8	−10	−10	−10	−10	−10
Median, at peaks	−5	−8	−6	0	−4	−4	−8	−6	−6
Business Cycle Trough									
October 1949	0	−8	−8	−4	−8	−4	−6	+4	−6
August 1954	+1	−6	−6	+2	−6	−6	−10	+2	−6
April 1958	+3	0	+2	+4	+2	+4	+2	+6	+4
February 1961	+3	+2	+8	+2	+2	+2	0	+6	0
Median, at troughs	+2	−3	−2	+2	−2	−1	−3	+5	−3
Peaks and Troughs									
Median	0	−6	−4	+1	−4	−1	−7	+2	−4
Average deviation	3.5	4.2	6.5	3.0	3.8	6.2	3.5	5.2	5.2

Source: Unemployment rate, BLS; Delinquency rates, ABA, *Delinquency Survey*. Series are adjusted for seasonal variation and the delinquency rates are raised to the level of currently published data.

Note: Troughs in the unemployment and delinquency rates are matched with business cycle peaks, and peaks with business cycle troughs. For delinquency rates the leads and lags are computed from end-of-month data; the resulting entries expressed in half months are rounded to the nearest even number. The median is the middle item in the array, or the mean of the two middle items. The average deviation is computed from the median.

ments and the timing of the direct and indirect rates have been very much alike. Leads predominate over lags, and the leads of the short-duration delinquencies are longer, on the average, than those of the longer duration.[4]

While it is evident from Charts 14 and 15 that on a monthly basis loss rates on automotive loans do not necessarily reach their peak precisely at the business trough, on a yearly basis there is likely to be considerably greater agreement between peaks in loss rates and business cycle troughs (Chart 17). Table 40 shows that since 1929 the loss rates of sales finance companies reached their peak in the same year as business reached its trough on four out of seven occasions. One exception occurred in 1953–54, one immediately after World War II, the third during the Great Depression, when loss rates were apparently higher shortly after the depression began (i.e., in 1930), rather than when it reached its ultimate depth (in 1932). Possibly significant is the fact that two of these are the only business contractions that, on an annual basis, lasted more than one year. That is to say, another way of looking at the evidence is to say that the highest loss rates invariably occurred one year after a business contraction began; improvement thereafter was the rule.

This way of viewing the matter corresponds to the characteristic pattern at business cycle peaks: loss rates reach their lowest point prior to the business peak and rise in the later stages of the expansion. This happened in no less than five out of seven occasions and may have occurred in one of the remaining two (1929), but data are not available to determine it.

The evidence is, then, that delinquency and loss rates are likely to be high at or near the bottom of a depression, and conversely, low at or before the peak of prosperity. This inverse conformity is surely

[4] Annual data on instalment loan delinquencies of ninety days or more on auto loans outstanding at approximately 4,000 national banks, published in the Annual Report of the Comptroller of the Currency, are as follows: 1956, 0.33 per cent; 1957, 0.20 per cent; 1958, 0.28 per cent. Data are not shown for later years. These figures, which represent the ratio of unpaid balances of delinquent loans to total outstanding for banks examined during the year, are substantially higher than those reported by the ABA for the same periods (cf. Chart 16). Since the ABA data are ratios of the number of loans delinquent to number outstanding, this suggests a greater frequency of delinquency among the larger loans, which seems unlikely. A more likely explanation is that it is due to differences in the samples of banks, with the comptroller's sample including more small banks with higher delinquency rates.

CHART 17

Loss Rates, 1929–65

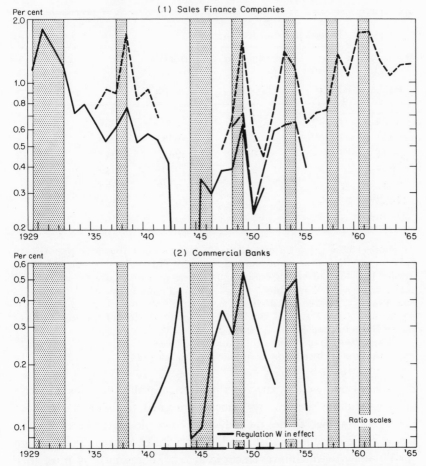

SOURCE: (1) Sales finance companies—1929–51: James F. Winchester, *Consumer Installment Loan Losses and Valuation Reserves*, Cambridge, Mass., 1955, Table 10, p. 33; five sales finance companies, loss rates based on average outstandings for the year. 1948–55: NBER Consumer Credit Quality Study, five sales finance companies, 1935–41. 1947–65: First National Bank of Chicago sample of nineteen sales finance companies. (2) Banks—1940–52: Winchester, *Consumer Installment Loan Losses*, Table 12, p. 39; five banks, loss rates based on average outstandings for the year. 1952–55: NBER Consumer Credit Quality Study, five banks; loss rates are on direct loans only.

NOTE: Shaded areas represent business cycle contractions; 1943 and 1944 are not shown because there were net recoveries instead of net losses.

TABLE 40

Timing of Loss Rates at Business Cycle Turns,
Sales Finance Companies, 1929-61

	Trough in Loss Rates			Peak in Loss Rates	
Business Cycle Peak	Date	Lead (-) or Lag (+), in Years	Business Cycle Trough	Date	Lead (-) or Lag (+), in Years
1929	1929[a]	0	1932	1930	-2
1937	1935[b]	-2	1938	1938	0
1944	1944	0	1946	1945	-1
1948	1946	-2	1949	1949	0
1953	1951[b]	-2	1954	1953	-1
1957	1955	-2	1958	1958	0
1960	1959	-1	1961	1961	0

Source: For 1929-35 and 1941-47, losses on automobile paper as a percentage of average outstandings of five sales finance companies, James P. Winchester, "Consumer Installment Loan Losses and Valuation Reserves," Cambridge, Mass., 1955, Table 10, p. 33. For 1935-41 and 1947-61, losses on all instalment receivables as a per cent of repayments, First National Bank of Chicago, "Ratios of the Instalment Sales Finance and Small Loan Companies.

[a]Tentative. Data prior to 1929 not available.
[b]Winchester data show troughs in 1936 and 1950.

the pattern one would expect if the average quality of loans, in terms of the standards applied by lenders, remained the same throughout the cycle. In that event, the difficulties occasioned by a depression would cause some loans that would otherwise have been "good" to go "bad"; similarly, the improvement in incomes occasioned by prosperity would cause some loans to remain good that might otherwise have gone bad. Losses would mount as income or employment declined, and would diminish as income or employment improved. But what if the quality of lending varies over the cycle? Suppose that lenders and borrowers alike are induced to take greater risks in prosperous times—risks that might lead to trouble even though conditions remained prosperous and to more trouble if they changed for the worse. And suppose, on the other hand, that risk taking becomes less popular in depression, so that only the very safest loans are entered into. How would the pattern of losses be altered?

Taken by itself, the pattern of risk taking just described should lead to a pattern of loss rates that would move *with* the business cycle with some lag. The length of the lag would depend on the period of time it took for losses to develop on loans. In the case of instalment credit this is not very long; a substantial fraction of repossessions, for example, occurs before the first half-dozen monthly payments have been made. One would expect, therefore, that losses would become more and more frequent as prosperity advanced and riskier loans were entered into. Conversely, as depression deepened and more and more conservative attitudes prevailed, losses would diminish.

The direct influence of income, unemployment, and associated factors on losses obviously dominates their behavior in fact. But if the pattern of quality change described above actually occurred, one would not expect losses to be a perfect counterpart of unemployment. Rather, toward the end of a contraction in income, losses might begin to diminish because of the preceding improvement in quality and despite the continued decline in income; and toward the end of an expansion in income, losses might begin to increase because of the preceding deterioration in quality and despite the continued improvement in income. Thus the combined effect of the change in income and the change in quality might be to make the peak in losses come earlier than the trough in income, and the trough in losses earlier than the peak in income. This would be especially likely if income were to decline more slowly as it reached its trough, and to rise more slowly when it neared its peak, while risk-taking propensities varied in opposite fashion, accelerating in the later stages of prosperity and dropping off more rapidly in the later stages of business contraction. This hypothesis might explain the pattern of delinquency rates and losses on auto loans that emerges from the data presented. However, the monthly estimates of delinquency risk developed in Chapter 7 from information on the quality characteristics of commercial bank loans do not, in fact, provide much, if any, support for it (see Chart 27, below). The cyclical movements in these data are slight, and it is difficult to discern any trace of the pattern hypothesized. Another possibility is that delinquency may be especially sensitive to certain developments that typically occur prior to downturns in general business activity, such as reductions in overtime earnings. We need much fuller data than we possess at present to test these propositions adequately.

REGIONAL AND LOCAL VARIATIONS IN LOAN EXPERIENCE DURING BUSINESS CYCLES

The preceding section considered the process of change in delinquency, repossession, and loss in terms of countrywide data, or samples undifferentiated with respect to geographic origin. Regional or local data can extend this analysis in two ways. First, time series for each of a number of regions can be treated in the same way as national data, thus multiplying the number of observations of this type. Second, variations among regions at a given time can be considered. Here, for example, we can direct our attention to the question whether those areas that experience the sharpest changes in income and employment also experience the sharpest (inverse) changes in credit collection experience. If for the country as a whole variations in loan experience are attributable to variations in the severity of economic fluctuations, we should be able to substantiate this by examining more restricted sections of the economy and determining whether those areas most depressed or those experiencing especially prosperous conditions exhibit the expected differences in repayment experience. Regional and local analyses can thus serve to measure the strength of the relationship between changes in income and employment, on the one hand, and changes in credit experience, on the other, and perhaps to suggest the effects of recessions more severe than those of the postwar period.

This method of analysis is important also for another reason. Whether or not we can assume that sharp economic contractions have been banished at the national level, it is clear from experience in recent recessions that they remain at the local level. In each of these recessions, some areas experienced severe drops in employment or income. If the relationship under discussion is substantiated, these areas may have experienced more serious credit difficulty as well, creating a problem of concern both to the areas themselves and to those who do business with them.

Two types of geographically differentiated data are available, one

covering broad regions of the country, the other the twelve metropolitan areas referred to earlier. The regional data include the American Bankers Association's delinquency series, data on losses and
repossessions which we have developed on the basis of our own
sample of reporting banks, and employment and personal income
for the corresponding regions. The metropolitan areas were selected
from those for which the Bureau of Labor Statistics reports labor market
conditions, and included some with a balanced labor supply (in 1954)
and some with a substantial labor surplus (high unemployment). To
employment data for these areas we have attempted to relate information on delinquency, repossessions, and losses obtained from individual banks and sales finance company offices located in the same places.

Regional Variations. We begin by examining the regional employment and income patterns for the period 1948–64. The annual data
gathered in Appendix E do not give as precise a picture of cyclical
movements as would monthly or quarterly data. The latter would no
doubt reveal more widespread and larger declines than the annual data
show. Nevertheless, eight of the nine regions experienced year-to-
year declines in nonfarm employment in the 1948–49 recession. The
sharpest declines occurred in the East South Central, East North
Central, Middle Atlantic, and New England regions. In the 1953–54
recession, the four regions in the industrialized eastern section of the
country again revealed their cyclical sensitivity, though there was a
decline in all nine regions. In the 1957–58 recession, all but one region
experienced a decline in employment, but the sharpest declines were
in the same four regions as before. In the 1960–61 recession, declines
in employment occurred in only three regions. This time the East
North Central and Middle Atlantic were joined by the West North
Central states.

The regional changes in personal income are, of course, correlated
with those in employment. As a rule, however, personal income either
did not decline or declined less than employment in each of the four
postwar recessions, and income usually increased faster than employment in the years between.

The range of variation among the regions in respect of change in
income or employment is considerable. For example, in each recession,
the region with the largest percentage decline in employment ex-

perienced roughly twice as large a decline as that shown by the countrywide totals. Moreover, if we take as a standard of comparison the
decline in nonfarm employment in the country as a whole in 1937–38
(5.9 per cent), which was one of the sharpest contractions on record,
the largest regional declines in employment are quite substantial.
They reached 4.1 per cent in the New England states in 1948–49, 4.4
per cent in the East North Central states in 1953–54, and 5.6 per cent
in the same region in 1957–58. In terms of income, on the other hand,
even the largest regional declines in the 1954 or 1958 recessions (1.3
and 0.7 per cent respectively) were small compared with the 7.3 per
cent nationwide drop in 1937–38. Income has become much more
stable than employment.

CHART 18

Year-to-Year Change in Income and in Delinquency Rates on
Direct Automobile Loans, Nine Regions, 1948–64

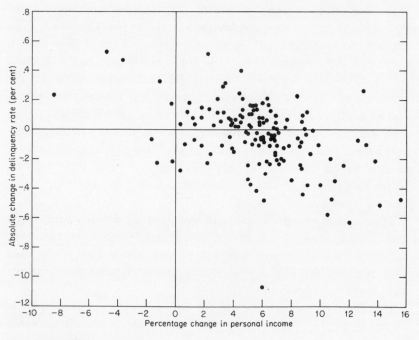

SOURCE: Tables E-1 and E-3.

CHART 19

Year-to-Year Change in Income and in Delinquency Rates on
Indirect Automobile Loans, Nine Regions, 1948–64

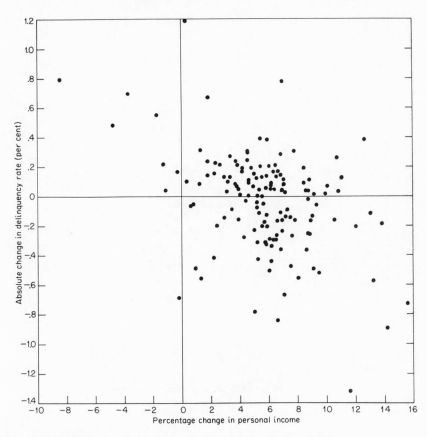

SOURCE: Tables E-1 and E-3.

What happened to credit collection experience in these regions
during this period? Appendix E shows the levels and year-to-year
changes in delinquency rates for both direct and indirect automobile
loans by commercial banks in each of the nine regions, and Charts 18,
19, 20, and 21 depict the relation between the change in income or
employment and the change in delinquency.

Obviously, there is a decided tendency for delinquency rates on
both direct and indirect loans to increase when income or employment

CHART 20

Year-to-Year Change in Employment and in Delinquency Rates on
Direct Automobile Loans, Nine Regions, 1948–64

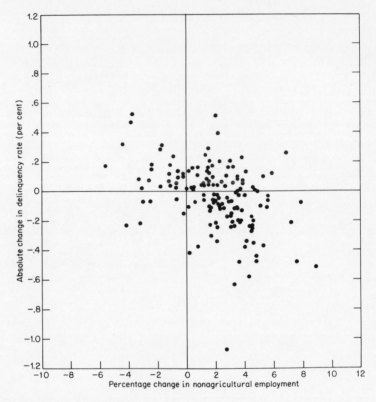

SOURCE: Tables E-2 and E-3.

drops and to decrease when they rise. Table 41 summarizes the relationship. It indicates, for example, that a year-to-year decline in
income of about 6 per cent has raised delinquency rates about half of
one per cent. Such a drop in income and rise in delinquency rates
greatly exceeds any year-to-year change that has occurred on a countrywide basis since 1948.

However, the wide scatter of points in Charts 18–21 indicates that
many other factors besides the contemporary change in income or
employment affect delinquency rates. The persistence of depressed

conditions in an area, variations in lending terms and standards, and the efforts of different lending institutions to reduce delinquency by increased collection effort or refinancing must all be taken into account.

Does the relationship we have observed between delinquency rates and income and employment changes hold also for the repossession and loss rates? Table 42 presents regional repossession and loss rates based on our own bank sample. It must be emphasized that this sample

CHART 21

Year-to-Year Change in Employment and in Delinquency Rates on Indirect Automobile Loans, Nine Regions, 1948–64

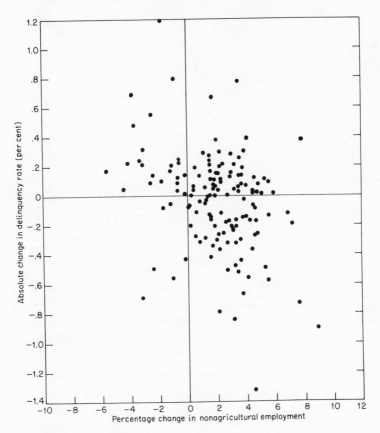

SOURCE: Tables E-2 and E-3.

TABLE 41

Regional Changes in Income and Employment and
Associated Changes in Delinquency Rates on Auto Loans, 1948-64

	Average Change in Delinquency Rates		
Class Interval	On Direct Loans	On Indirect Loans	Number of Observations
Percentage Change in Personal Income			
−11.9 to −8.0	+.236	+.794	1
−7.9 to −4.0	+.525	+.479	1
−3.9 to 0.0	+.074	+.161	6
+0.1 to +4.0	+.039	+.081	30
+4.1 to +8.0	−.042	−.058	77
+8.1 to +12.0	−.187	−.132	23
+12.1 to +16.0	−.191	−.356	6
Percentage Change in Non-agricultural Employment			
−7.9 to −4.0	+.089	+.140	3
−3.9 to 0.0	+.079	+.133	27
+0.1 to +4.0	−.043	−.045	87
+4.1 to +8.0	−.170	−.163	26
+8.1 to +12.0	−.517	−.898	1

Source: Tables E-1, E-2, E-3.

is very small for each region and the results must be considered merely suggestive of the relationship more extensive data and analysis might reveal. In 1954, when employment fell in all regions and income either fell or rose at a much slower rate, the repossession rate went up in every case, and it went down in 1955 as income and employment resumed their advance. The loss-rate picture is fairly similar, although two regions show higher loss rates in 1953 than in 1954.

Local Variations. Our analysis of metropolitan area data differs from that for the regions in three respects. First, we have included delinquency rates on all instalment loans which are reported to the American Bankers Association, as well as on automobile loans separately. Second, we consider sales finance company as well as bank experience. Third, we utilize quarterly data to examine the sequence of change in delinquency, repossession, and loss.

The most significant conclusion reached on the basis of the regional analysis is again the most striking fact revealed by the local data. In the 1954 contraction, when nonagricultural employment declined in ten of the eleven cities examined, the delinquency rate rose in eight

TABLE 42

Repossession and Loss Rates on Auto Loans Reported by Banks, Six Regions, 1953-55

Region	Number of Banks Reporting	1953	1954	1955
	Repossession Rates (per cent)			
Pacific	4	6.45	8.73	4.05
West North Central	2	6.67	7.71	5.74
East North Central	3	1.03	2.05	.36
South Atlantic	2	9.08	12.41	8.24
Middle Atlantic	4	1.34	2.27	1.79
	Loss Rates (per cent)			
Pacific	2	.190[a]	.507	.072
Mountain	2	.398	.328	.079
West North Central	2	.206	.274	.169
East North Central	3	.591	.459	.219
South Atlantic	1	n.a.	.389	.064
Middle Atlantic	2	.185	.329	.233

Source: National Bureau Consumer Credit Quality Study. Repossession rates are based on number of loans made, loss rates on dollar volume of loans made. The 1955 coverage ratio for banks reporting repossessions is 16.1 per cent; for banks reporting losses, 7.9 per cent. The coverage ratio compares the 1955 dollar volume of automobile paper reported by banks in the sample with that for all commercial banks as estimated by the Federal Reserve Board.

n.a. = not available.

[a]One bank only.

TABLE 43

Changes in Nonagricultural Employment and in Delinquency on
Direct Automobile Loans by Banks, 11 Cities, 1953-55

City and Number of Banks	Percentage Change in Nonagricultural Employment (1)	Percentage Change in Number of Delinquent Loans (2)	Percentage Change in Number of Loans Outstanding (3)	Delinquency Rate (per cent) (4)	(5)	Change in Delinquency Rate (6)
	1953-54	1953-54	1953-54	1953	1954	1953-54
Detroit (3)	-11.4	+147.7	+14.8	.64	1.38	+.74
Pittsburgh (1)	-9.2	0.0	-17.8	.17	.21	+0.4
Denver (4)	-5.7	-11.1	-1.6	.89	.81	-.08
Indianapolis (3)	-4.6	+40.9	+11.4	.27	.34	+.07
Philadelphia (5)	-4.5	+68.6	+45.4	1.33	1.54	+.21
St. Louis (3)	-4.5	+5.8	+12.0	1.84	1.74	-.10
Chicago (3)	-3.8	+37.2	+.2	1.11	1.52	+.41
Atlanta (2)	-3.4	-39.0	-4.9	1.97	1.26	-.71
New York (3)	-1.8	-6.3	-10.5	.45	.47	+.02
Los Angeles (3)	-.8	+101.9	+72.8	.77	.90	+.13
Dallas (1)	+.1	+100.0	-23.8	.17	.46	+.29
	1954-55	1954-55	1954-55	1954	1955	1954-55
New York (3)	-.3	-45.7	-.6	.47	.26	-.21
Philadelphia (5)	+.3	-12.7	-.7	1.54	1.36	-.18
St. Louis (3)	+2.1	-31.0	+9.7	1.74	1.09	-.65
Chicago (3)	+2.5	-55.8	+2.1	1.52	.66	-.86
Dallas (1)	+2.7	-40.0	-.2	.46	.27	-.19
Pittsburgh	+3.6	+27.8	+25.6	.21	.22	+.01
Indianapolis (3)	+5.1	+54.8	+56.3	.34	.34	0
Denver (4)	+5.5	+31.2	+27.2	.81	.83	+.02
Los Angeles (3)	+6.2	-13.9	+22.4	.90	.64	-.26
Atlanta (2)	+8.2	-37.2	-5.0	1.26	.84	-.42
Detroit (3)	+8.5	-49.5	+5.1	1.38	.66	-.72

Source: U.S. Bureau of Employment Security and unpublished ABA data.

Note: Data refer to July of each year. Delinquency figures are for loans delinquent over thirty days; rates are percentage of loans outstanding.

TABLE 44

Changes in Nonagricultural Employment and in Delinquency on All Instalment Loans Reported by Banks, 9 Cities, 1953-55

City and Number of Banks	Percentage Change in Nonagricultural Employment (1)	Percentage Change in Number of Delinquent Loans (2)	Percentage Change in Number of Loans Outstanding (3)	Delinquency Rate (per cent) (4) (5)		Change in Delinquency Rate (6)
	1953-54	1953-54	1953-54	1953	1954	1953-54
Detroit (3)	-11.4	+80.5	-.2	1.36	2.46	+1.10
Denver (4)	-5.7	-21.9	-6.8	2.13	1.79	-.34
Indianapolis (3)	-4.6	+32.8	+23.0	1.55	1.67	+.12
Philadelphia (5)	-4.5	-5.0	-3.2	3.11	3.05	-.06
St. Louis (3)	-4.5	+4.7	+.1	3.61	3.77	+.16
Chicago (3)	-3.8	-17.4	+1.3	2.00	1.63	-.37
Atlanta (2)	-3.4	-16.4	-2.4	3.72	3.18	-.54
New York (3)	-1.8	-18.1	-7.8	1.27	1.13	-.14
Los Angeles (3)	-.8	+8.6	+2.1	1.53	1.63	+.10
	1954-55	1954-55	1954-55	1954	1955	1954-55
New York (3)	-.3	-36.8	-1.9	1.13	.73	-.40
Philadelphia (5)	+.3	-39.0	-6.8	3.05	2.00	-1.05
St. Louis (3)	+2.1	-30.3	0	3.77	2.62	-1.15
Chicago (3)	+2.5	-29.6	-11.4	1.63	1.29	-.34
Indianapolis (3)	+5.1	-11.7	+30.7	1.67	1.13	-.54
Denver (4)	+5.5	-26.5	-1.5	1.79	1.33	-.46
Los Angeles (3)	+6.2	-18.8	+5.0	1.63	1.26	-.37
Atlanta (2)	+8.2	-46.1	-5.2	3.18	1.81	-1.37
Detroit (3)	+8.5	-54.7	-7.4	2.46	1.20	-1.26

Source: U.S. Bureau of Employment Security and unpublished ABA data.

Note: Data refer to July of each year. Delinquency figures are for loans delinquent over thirty days; rates are percentage of loans outstanding. Types of loans included are personal, auto (direct and indirect), FHA Title I, home appliance, property improvement-own plan.

of the eleven cities (Table 43). When recovery came in the following
year, employment rose in ten of the eleven cities and the delinquency
rate declined in eight.

Table 44 and Chart 22 show that a similar negative correlation prevailed between changes in employment and delinquency on all instalment loans. That correlation is considerably increased by the inclusion of Detroit, which is the most extreme point in the scatter
diagram (in the upper left and lower right quadrants). This supports
the hypothesis mentioned earlier; some local areas undergo cyclical
fluctuations far more intense than those experienced by the nation as
a whole, with the result that lenders with business concentrated in
these areas experience high delinquencies, repossessions, and losses,
even though conditions for the country as a whole are only moderately
depressed, as was the case in 1954.

CHART 22

Change in Employment and in Delinquency Rates on Instalment
Loans by Banks, Nine Cities, 1953–55

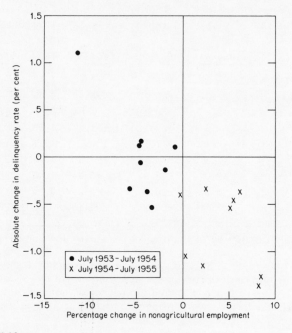

SOURCE: Table 44.

Our sales finance company data are for the local offices of one large sales finance company located in twelve metropolitan areas. Chart 23 demonstrates the relationship between changes in repossession rates and employment. Not only is the difference between the situation in the recession period of 1953–54 and the recovery period of 1954–55 pointed up in striking fashion, but there is also considerable—though far from perfect—association between the magnitudes of change within each period. The changes in collection experience for this company and the banks are also utilized in Table 45, which gives the rank correlation coefficients between the changes in non-

CHART 23

Change in Employment and in Repossession Rates on New-
Automobile Loans by a Large Sales Finance Company,
Twelve Metropolitan Areas, 1953–55

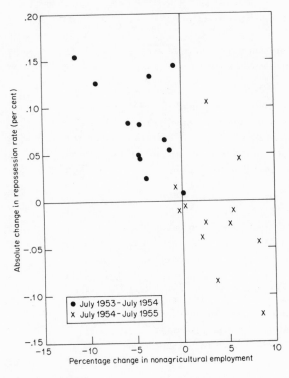

SOURCE: Tables 43 and F-4.

TABLE 45

*Relation Between Nonagricultural Employment and Delinquency,
Repossession, and Loss Rates in Metropolitan Areas, 1953-55*

	Rank Correlation Coefficient		
	1953-54	1954-55	Both Periods
Correlation between percentage change in nonagricultural employment and:			
Delinquency (direct auto loans, banks, 11 cities)			
a. Percentage change in number of delinquencies	+.04	+.10	-.42
b. Absolute change in delinquency rate	-.03	-.07	-.55
c. Delinquency rate in second year	+.01	+.03	-.25
Delinquency (all instalment loans, banks, 9 cities)			
a. Percentage change in number of delinquencies	-.25	-.13	-.42
b. Absolute change in delinquency rate	-.42	-.37	-.75
c. Delinquency rate in second year	-.38	-.07	-.25
Delinquency (automotive accounts, a large sales finance company, 12 areas)[a]			
a. Percentage change in number of delinquencies	-.06	-.66	+.41
b. Absolute change in delinquency rate	-.34	-.54	+.45
c. Delinquency rate in second year	-.31	-.30	+.47
Repossession (new cars, a large sales finance company, 12 areas)			
a. Percentage change in number of repossessions	-.29	-.34	-.75
b. Absolute change in repossession rate	-.36	-.42	-.74
c. Repossession rate in second year	+.05	+.17	-.14
Loss (all instalment loans, a large sales finance company, 12 areas)			
a. Percentage change in volume of net losses[b]	-.14	+.06	-.71
b. Absolute change in loss rate	-.28	-.21	-.68
c. Loss rate in second year	-.35	+.64	-.24

Notes to Table 45

Source: A large sales finance company and American Bankers Association (see Tables 43 and 44). All data are for the month of July only in each year. A negative coefficient signifies that large decreases in employment are associated with large increases in the credit variable. Definition of terms:

(1) Delinquency rate is ratio of number of delinquent loans to accounts outstanding at end of month.

(2) Repossession rate is ratio of number of repossessions during month to average number of accounts purchased for twelve preceding months.

(3) Loss rate is ratio of net losses charged to income and reserves to average receivables at beginning and end of month.

aSee text, footnote 5.

bAreas that show no net losses in any year were omitted.

agricultural employment by local areas and measures of delinquency, repossession, and loss, respectively. The coefficients are not high, but most are negative, indicating the tendency for collection experience, whether manifested in delinquencies, repossessions, or losses, to vary with the severity of economic contractions as measured by employment.[5]

Chart 24 displays the collection of delinquency, repossession, and loss rates for each area, expressed in terms of a four-quarter moving average (to eliminate seasonal fluctuations) from the middle of 1953 to the end of 1955. The chart, together with Table 46, reveals that the sequence of change in delinquency, repossession, and loss that the national figures showed (Charts 14 and 15) is repeated in virtually every area. Furthermore, downturns in the delinquency rates typically appeared well before the nationwide recession was over. (The business cycle trough was reached in the third quarter of 1954.) Even the repossession and loss rates generally reached their peaks early in this

[5] There is an anomaly in the section of the table on delinquency rates for the large sales finance company in twelve areas: the 1953–55 correlation coefficients are positive, but those for 1953–54 and 1954–55 are negative. The reason is the relatively early cyclical decline in delinquency rates in many areas, antedating the 1954–55 recovery in employment by nearly a year (cf. Chart 24 and Table 46). The result was that delinquency rates fell in many areas while employment was still declining in 1953–54, and that they rose in 1954–55 just as employment was starting to recover. Within each period, however, the areas with less favorable changes in employment tended to have greater increases or smaller declines in delinquency.

CHART 24

Delinquency, Repossession, and Loss Rates on Instalment Contracts, Twelve Metropolitan Areas, A Large Sales Finance Company, 1953–55

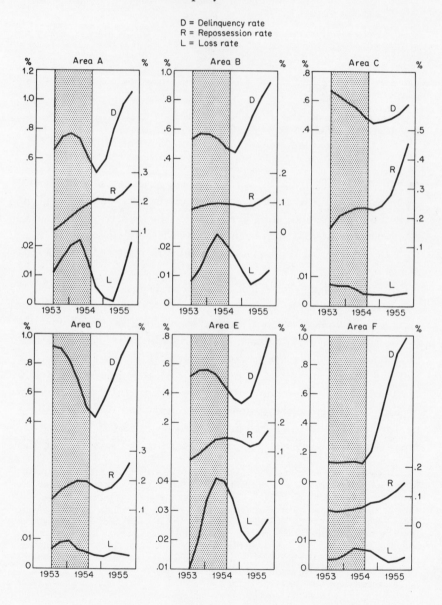

D = Delinquency rate
R = Repossession rate
L = Loss rate

D = Delinquency rate
R = Repossession rate
L = Loss rate

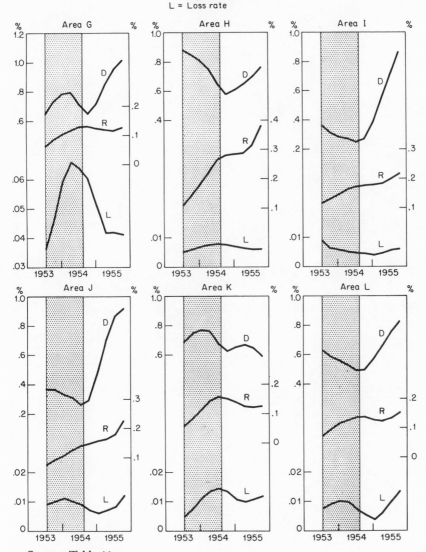

SOURCE: Table 46.
NOTE: Data are centered four-quarter moving averages of figures for every third month. Shaded area represents the business cycle contraction.

TABLE 46

Timing of Cyclical Turns in Delinquency, Repossession, and Loss Rates, on Instalment Contracts, Twelve Metropolitan Areas, 1953-55

	Areas Reaching Peak in			Areas Reaching Trough in		
	Delinquency Rate[a]	Repossession Rate[b]	Loss Rate	Delinquency Rate	Repossession Rate[b]	Loss Rate
1953						
July	C*,D*,H*,I*,J*,L*					
Oct.	B		C*,I*			
1954						
Jan.	A,E,K		D,J,L			
Apr.	G	B,D	A,B,C,E,F,G			
July		E,K	H,K	F,I,J,L		
Oct.		A,G,L		A,B,D,G,H		
1955						
Jan.				E	B,D	D,I,J,L
Apr.					A,E,L	A,B,C,E,F,K
July					G,K	
Oct.				K*		G*,H*

Notes to Table 46

Source: A large sales finance company. Data are centered four-quarter moving averages of figures for every third month, January 1953, April 1953, etc. through April 1956. Hence the initial moving average is centered on July 1953, the terminal one on October 1955. The delinquency rate is the ratio of the number of retail automotive accounts delinquent over thirty days to number outstanding at end of month; the repossession rate is the ratio of number of new-auto repossessions during month to new-auto accounts purchased during twelve preceding months; the loss rate is the ratio of net losses of auto and other financing charged to income and reserves to average receivables at beginning and end of month. For a list of the twelve areas, see App. F, headnote.

*Tentative peak (initial figure is high) or tentative trough (terminal figure is low).

aArea F: no peak recognized.

bAreas C, F, H, I, J rise throughout the period.

instance. But the improvement in economic conditions that began in 1954 and continued on into 1957 did not prevent an upturn in delinquency in the latter part of 1954 and in repossession and loss rates in 1955, possibly as a result of the easing of credit terms in 1954–55 (see Chapter 7).

Our review of credit experience at the national, regional, and local levels points to two conclusions. First, there is ample evidence of an inverse relationship between general economic conditions (as measured by changes in income or employment) and collection experience. During a boom it is to be expected that repayment problems will be minimal, though they may increase somewhat before the boom has run its course. The real difficulties, however, come when the economy begins to contract, and our regional studies show that there is a definite tendency for credit experience to be least favorable in those areas where economic contraction is most severe.

Second, although the general economic health of the country is probably the most important variable affecting loan experience, there are sizable variations, both over time and among areas, that remain to be explained by other factors. Variations in lending terms and standards, as we have seen in earlier chapters, may be one of these factors. How significant a role they play in causing changes in lending experience over time will be explored in the next chapter.

7. The Influence of Credit Quality and the Business Cycle on Credit Experience

The preceding chapters suggest that certain features of instalment credit terms and certain characteristics of the borrowers are directly related to subsequent performance. Since substantial changes have occurred from time to time in both credit terms and borrower characteristics, it should be possible to demonstrate that some of the changes in delinquency, repossession, and loss experience described earlier are attributable to the alterations in terms granted or in characteristics of credit users. But it is also clear from our analysis that due allowance must be made for the economic conditions prevailing in the periods being compared, for changes in such conditions themselves exert a powerful influence on credit experience.

We shall restrict ourselves to an examination of the effect of changes in credit terms because of the lack of adequate time series data on borrower characteristics that can be related to subsequent credit experience. Moreover, even the analysis of credit terms, which we further restrict to automobile paper, poses difficulties that can be surmounted only by rather arbitrary expedients, as will be seen. These are conditions that need not persist, however, if attention is given to the need for appropriate statistics.

To begin with, one inference is plain from the materials presented above. When loans made at about the same time are compared with one another, the longer-maturity contracts on new cars generally experience higher repossession and loss rates. This was true in the 1920's and 1930's as well as in the 1950's. Since maturities in the 1950's were substantially longer than in the 1920's and 1930's, one might expect to find higher repossession or loss rates in the later period. But there is no evidence that this is the case. Over-all loss rates show little change in level over this period (see Chapter 1, Table 15). Apparently the risk associated with a given length of maturity has diminished. A two- or three-year sales contract is not the hazard it was in the twenties. A variety of factors may account for this, one of them being the fact that autos have become more essential to the earning of income. We must, therefore, be aware that long-term changes of this sort do occur, and that a risk relationship that seems valid now will not necessarily remain so indefinitely.

Nevertheless, the relationships shown above between loan terms and collection experience on different groups of loans made at about the same time, especially those between down payment percentages and repossession or loss rates, have persisted over many years, and it would be surprising indeed to find that a substantial shift *within a short period* in the proportion of cars sold on low down payments or long maturities was not reflected in repossession or loss rates. Let us look, then, at the period since 1948, for which better statistics are available and during which substantial changes in credit terms did take place, in connection both with the imposition and expiration of Regulation W (in effect from September 1948 to June 1949, and from September 1950 to May 1952) and with the general relaxation of terms since 1954–55.

Our specific objective is to derive, from information on the maturity or down payment provisions of new-automobile credit contracts, an estimate of the risk of delinquency, repossession, or loss. That is, what rate of repayment difficulty is implied by the distribution of contracts according to maturity, down payment, or both? Further, we wish to compare this implicit risk with the rate of repayment difficulty that actually developed, and to make the comparison over a period of time in order to show whether the change in risk is similar to that in the actual rates. If the calculation passes this test, we can have some confidence that the method of translating data on contract terms into an index of credit quality is reliable. The available data, while lacking a desirable degree of comparability, do permit two independent sets of calculations, one for sales finance companies and the other for commercial banks.

REPOSSESSION RISK, SALES FINANCE COMPANIES, 1948–65

The following annual data on contract terms of sales finance companies can be used for the first calculation:

1. Percentage distribution of new-car contracts by maturity, reported for a group of nineteen companies by the First National
Bank of Chicago, can be utilized for this purpose. Two maturity
groups are reported, but the dividing line between them changed from
eighteen months (1953–57) to twenty-four months (1955–60) to thirty
months (1957–65). The data can be extended back to 1948 by figures
for two large companies, compiled by the National Bureau.

2. Percentage distribution of new-car contracts by down payment
ratio, 1953–57, and by ratio of contract balance to dealer cost since
1957, reported by the First National Bank of Chicago, can also be
used. Down payment data for five companies have been extended
back to 1950 by the National Bureau.

To convert the maturity, down payment, and dealer cost ratio distributions into estimates of the risk of repayment difficulty, we rely
upon the lender report sample of the Federal Reserve new-car purchases survey for 1954–55, despite the fact that this covers all lenders,
not just sales finance companies. As noted in Chapter 3, this shows
repossession rates on new-car contracts classified by original maturity
and by contract down payment. The lender report is used instead of
the personal interview sample because it appears to provide fuller
coverage of loan difficulty and a more accurate picture of the relation of loan difficulty to maturities and down payments. The same
materials can be used, by a more devious route, to estimate repossession risk on contracts classified by the ratio of contract balance to
dealer cost. The method of making all these calculations is described
in Appendix H. Since the maturity distributions provide one set of
estimates of risk and the down payment and dealer cost ratio distributions another, we combine the two by a simple average. This takes into
account both types of available information on contract terms of sales
finance companies and presumably provides the best estimate of repossession risk.

The annual estimates of repossession risk can be compared with
three annual series on the actual credit experience of sales finance
companies. The ratio of losses to retail paper liquidated is reported by
the First National Bank of Chicago for the same group of companies
that provide the data on new-auto contract terms. The loss rates, however, are not confined to new-auto credit. Another series measuring a
slightly different type of loss rate, the ratio of losses to total credit

TABLE 47

Actual Loss and Repossession Rates, and Estimated Repossession Risk, Sales Finance Companies, 1947-65

| | Actual Loss Rate, All Retail Paper | | | | Actual Repossession Rate, New-& Used-Auto Contracts, NBER Sample | | Estimated Repossession Risk, New-Auto Contracts | | | |
| | FNBC Sample | | NBER Sample | | | | Based on Maturity Distribution | Based on Down Payment and Dealer Cost Ratio Distribution | Average | |
Year	Per Cent (1)	Index, 1954-55:100 (2)	Per Cent (3)	Index, 1954-55:100 (4)	Per Cent (5)	Index, 1954-55:100 (6)	(per cent) (7)	(per cent) (8)	Per Cent (9)	Index, 1954-55:100 (10)
1947	.48	53	--	--	--	--	--	--	--	--
1948	.66	73	--	--	3.4	42	1.0	--	0.8a	43
1949	1.57	173	1.16	113	4.8	60	1.4	--	1.2a	65
1950	.58	64	.73	71	5.2	65	1.4	1.0	1.2	65
1951	.44	48	.88	85	4.8	60	0.6	0.8	0.7	38
1952	.76	84	1.17	114	6.1	76	1.4	1.0	1.2	65
1953	1.40	154	1.41	137	7.1	88	1.8	1.2	1.5	81
1954	1.18	130	1.23	119	9.3	116	1.9	1.5	1.7	92
1955	.64	70	.83	81	6.8	84	2.0	1.9	2.0	108
1956	.72	79	.97	94	10.7b	133	2.1	2.1	2.1	114
1957	.74	81	.95	92	--	--	2.2	2.2	2.2	119
1958	1.35	148	1.77	172	--	--	2.4	2.0	2.2	119
1959	1.07	118	1.11	108	--	--	2.5	2.2	2.4	130
1960	1.71	188	--	--	--	--	2.6	2.2	2.4	130
1961	1.73	190	--	--	--	--	2.6	2.2	2.4	130
1962	1.28	141	--	--	--	--	2.6	2.3	2.4	130
1963	1.08	119	--	--	--	--	2.6	2.4	2.5	135
1964	1.21	133	--	--	--	--	2.6	2.4	2.5	135
1965	1.22	134	--	--	--	--	2.6	2.4	2.5	135

Notes to Table 47

Source: Column 1 –– First National Bank of Chicago, *Ratios of the Instalment Sales Finance and Consumer Finance Companies, February 1961* and current issues. 1947-59; loss (charge-offs) to retail paper liquidated; since 1960: losses (charge-offs net of recoveries) to instalment receivables liquidated.

Column 3 –– Paul F. Smith, *Consumer Credit Costs, 1949-59* (Princeton University Press for NBER, 1964), Table C-4, p. 141. Losses net of recoveries per $100 of loans outstanding, ten companies.

Column 5 –– Moore, Atkinson, and Klein, *"Changes in the Quality of Consumer Instalment Credit,"* Table 29. Repossessions as a per cent of number of contracts purchased, five companies.

Columns 7-10 –– Appendix F, Tables F-3 and F-4.

aBased on maturity distribution only, adjusted to level of 1950 average.

bFirst six months.

outstanding, has been compiled by Paul F. Smith for the National Bureau's study of consumer finance. Its coverage also extends beyond new autos. Both series reflect losses in the year charged off, some of which may pertain to credits originating in the current year, but many of which must relate to contracts made a year or two earlier. Finally, there is a series on repossession rates for new and used autos. This comes closest in concept to the estimates of new-auto repossession risk, but covers a different group of companies and ends in 1956. Like the loss rates, the repossession rates refer to the year in which the auto was repossessed, whereas the risk estimates pertain to the year in which the contract originated. Ideally, one would like to have repossession or loss rates compiled for all contracts that originated in a given year. A substantial portion of repossessions do occur within the same year, however.

The three series on sales finance company loss and repossession rates are shown in Table 47, together with the average estimates of repossession risk computed from the maturity, down payment, and dealer-cost-ratio distributions.

Chart 25 compares the average index of repossession risk with the longer of the two actual loss rate indexes and with the actual repossession rate index, all indexes being expressed as relatives to the 1954–55 average. The results suggest the following conclusions:

1. Repossession risk increased generally during 1948–65 as a result both of longer maturities and lower down payments. The only ap-

CHART 25

Actual Loss and Repossession Rates, and Estimated Repossession Risk, Sales Finance Companies, 1947–65

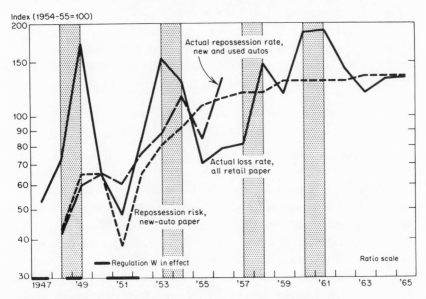

Index (1954-55=100)

Actual repossession rate, new and used autos

Actual loss rate, all retail paper

Repossession risk, new-auto paper

Regulation W in effect

Ratio scale

1947   '49   '51   '53   '55   '57   '59   '61   '63   '65

SOURCE: Table 47.
NOTE: Shaded areas represent business cycle contractions.

preciable decline in the risk index occurred in 1951, when terms stiffened in accordance with Regulation W. The increase in risk position was rapid from 1952 to 1955, but gradual since 1955. By 1965, the risk of repossession on new autos was more than three times what it was in 1948.

2. Actual loss and repossession rates have experienced an upward trend since 1948 that is broadly parallel to the risk index, though somewhat less steep. Loss rates on all retail paper in 1965 were nearly double their 1948 level.[1]

[1] The actual repossession rates for new and used autos (Table 47, col. 6) are substantially higher than the risk rates estimated from contract terms for new autos (col. 10). The 1954-55 average for the former was 8.05 per cent; for the latter, 1.85 per cent. The difference may be partly due to the inclusion of used autos in the former, since used-auto contracts have higher repossession rates than those for new autos. But it may also be due to differences in methods of computing the rate. The 1954-55 Federal Reserve survey, on which the estimated rates for new autos were based, gives the number of repossessions up to the date of

3. Actual loss and repossession rates fluctuate much more widely than the risk index, largely because of the effects of recession and prosperity. Loss rates were high in the recession years 1949, 1954, 1958, and 1961 and generally low in the other years (except 1953 and 1960, where recession effects may have occurred earlier than in most economic series). There is little or no evidence of cyclical sensitivity in the risk index. Hence in a recession year actual repossessions and losses are likely to be higher than indicated by the risk index, whereas in a more than normally prosperous year they are likely to be lower.

DELINQUENCY RISK, COMMERCIAL BANKS, 1954–65

For commercial banks we can compare monthly as well as annual estimates of delinquency risk with actual delinquency rates. Monthly distributions of new-auto paper cross-classified by maturity and by ratio of contract balance to dealer cost have been compiled for a sample of commercial banks by the Federal Reserve Board since 1957. Data for purchased paper and direct loans are reported separately.[2] We convert these distributions into estimates of delinquency risk by using the delinquency rates on new-auto contracts cross-classified by maturity and dealer cost ratio, derived from the lender report sample of the 1954–55 Federal Reserve new-car purchases survey. The method of deriving these 1954–55 rates, which were not reported in terms of this cross-classification, is described in Appendix H, together with the details of their application to the monthly distributions. Finally, the delinquency rates actually experienced monthly are provided by the American Bankers Association, separately for purchased paper and direct loans, but covering both new and used autos. The

the survey for contracts originating during 1954–55; repossessions that occurred after the survey data are, of course, not included. The series of actual repossession rates, on the other hand, is the number of repossessions during a calendar year relative to the number of contracts originating during the year; hence it includes repossessions on contracts originating prior to that year and yields a better approximation to the true repossession rate over the life of the contracts. Our estimated rate evidently underestimates the true level. See, however, note 3, below.

[2] Data for used cars also are reported, but are not employed in our risk calculation since estimates of delinquency rates in relation to maturity and down payment, comparable with those we use for new cars, are not available. This omission is unfortunate, since the actual delinquency rates with which our risk estimates are to be compared include loans on both new and used cars.

actual rates were adjusted for seasonal variations by the National Bureau; the risk estimates seemed to require no seasonal adjustment.

The results of these calculations (Table 48 and Charts 26 and 27) support the following conclusions:

1. Delinquency risk is substantially higher on new-car paper purchased by banks than on their own direct auto loans. However, the differential has diminished since 1957, with risks on direct paper rising more rapidly than on purchased paper. Actual delinquency rates are similar in both respects: rates on purchased paper are higher, but those on direct loans have advanced more rapidly since 1957, reducing the differential between them.[3]

2. The actual delinquency rates are sensitive to the business cycle, reaching relatively high levels during the recession years 1954, 1958, and 1961 and falling during the subsequent recovery periods. The risk estimates show no such cyclical sensitivity, but move in fairly smooth trends superimposed on short (monthly) irregular movements that may be due to sampling variations.

3. The movements in delinquency risk on bank-purchased paper since 1954 are similar to those in repossession risk for sales finance companies. (The latter also purchase their paper from dealers.) Both estimates rise from 1954 to 1959, remain relatively stable from 1959 to 1961 or 1962, and rise again to 1965. By 1965, delinquency risk on bank purchased paper had risen 58 per cent above the 1954–55 level, while repossession risk on sales finance company paper had risen 35 per cent.

4. The actual delinquency rates on bank-purchased paper do not show the marked upward trend since 1954 shown by the delinquency risk estimates for such paper. The trends in risk and actual rates for direct paper are more alike, especially since 1957. Higher delinquency rates on purchased paper may have been prevented by the recourse practice described in footnote 3 in Chapter 6.

Our experimental attempts to translate changes in credit terms into estimates of credit quality express in quantitative fashion the effects

---

[3] The estimated delinquency risks based on contract terms are at a substantially higher level than the actual delinquency rates (see Table 48). The reason probably lies in the fact that the actual rate is the percentage of loans delinquent on a given date, whereas the risk estimate refers to the percentage of loans that became delinquent at any time during their life, in so far as this was covered by the 1954–55 survey.

TABLE 48

Actual Delinquency Rates and Estimated Delinquency Risk,
Auto Loans, Commercial Banks, 1954-65

| | Actual Delinquency Rate, New-And Used-Auto Loans | | | | Estimated Delinquency Risk, New-Auto Loans | | | |
| | Purchased Paper | | Direct Loans | | Purchased Paper | | Direct Loans | |
Year	Per Cent (1)	Index, 1954-55:100 (2)	Per Cent (3)	Index, 1954-55:100 (4)	Per Cent (5)	Index, 1954-55:100 (6)	Per Cent (7)	Index, 1954-55:100 (8)
1954	1.71	110	1.05	112	3.8	94	3.3	99
1955	1.41	90	.82	88	4.3	106	3.4	101
1956	1.36	87	.76	81	n.a.	n.a.	n.a.	n.a.
1957	1.35	87	.75	80	5.1[a]	126	3.1[a]	93
1958	1.53	98	.84	90	5.4[b]	133	3.4[b]	101
1959	1.31	84	.78	83	5.7	141	3.6	107
1960	1.46	94	.94	101	5.8	143	3.9	116
1961	1.49	96	1.05	112	5.8	143	4.2	125
1962	1.33	85	.95	102	5.9	146	4.5	134
1963	1.42	91	.94	101	6.2	153	4.6	137
1964	1.50	96	.94	101	6.3	156	4.8	143
1965	1.57	101	1.14	122	6.4	158	4.9	146

Source: Columns 1, 3 — Table 14 above. Rates refer to percentage of loans outstanding that are delinquent thirty days or more.

Columns 5, 7 — 1954 and 1955, computed from data on contract maturities and dealer-cost ratios in Federal Reserve New-Car Purchases survey. 1957-64, annual averages of monthly estimates, computed from data on contract maturities and dealer cost ratios in Federal Reserve survey of commercial bank credit terms. Estimates refer to percentage of contracts becoming delinquent at any time during their life. See Appendix H, Section 2, and Tables H-5 and H-6.

n.a. = not available.

[a]June, July, October, November, December.

[b]February through December.

CHART 26

Actual Delinquency Rates and Estimated Delinquency Risk, Auto
Loans, Commercial Banks, 1954–65

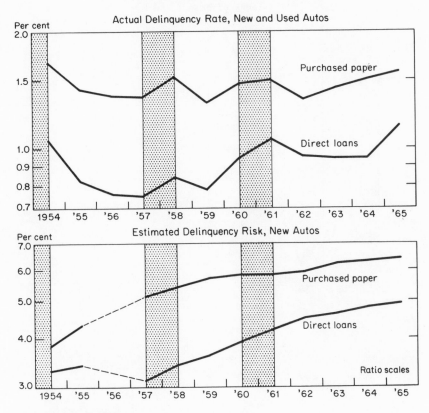

SOURCE: Table 48.
NOTE: Shaded areas represent business cycle contractions. Data for 1956 not
available.

on risk position of the longer maturities and smaller equities that
have characterized consumer credit transactions in recent years. Lenders and borrowers alike have assumed riskier positions—positions that
in the event of recession are likely to involve wider delinquency and
larger losses to both borrowers and lenders than would otherwise be
the case. We do not find that these changes in risk position reverse
themselves promptly and easily with the swings in the business cycle,
at least not in the relatively mild and brief recessions experienced since

CHART 27

Actual Delinquency Rates and Estimated Delinquency Risk, Auto Loans, Commercial Banks, 1957–66, Monthly

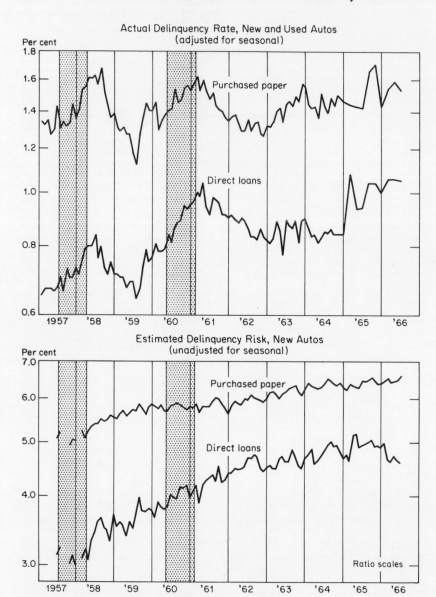

SOURCE: American Bankers Association and Table H-6.

NOTE: Estimated data on delinquency, no data available for August, September 1957 and January 1958. Actual delinquency rates adjusted to level of currently published data, issued bimonthly after October 1964.

1948. Instead, the movement so far has been mostly in one direction—toward the assumption of greater risk. The pace that this trend has taken has not accelerated—indeed, it has become less rapid—but neither has it come to a halt. Since the trend has consequences for the stability as well as the growth of the economy, its development over the years ahead should be well worth observing and evaluating.

8. Findings of the Study: A Conspectus and a Program

Anyone seeking to describe the transformation and growth of the United States economy during the past fifty years could not fail to stress the spectacular increase in the use of consumer credit. From its modest beginnings in aiding the purchase of pianos and sewing machines, credit has spread to automobiles, the many appliances which loom so large in modern living, and more recently to services such as travel and education. From a $3-billion level in 1920, consumer debt (exclusive of mortgage debt) had grown to $88 billion by 1965. Of this total, instalment debt accounted for $69 billion in 1965, compared with only $1 billion forty-five years earlier.

As total instalment debt has grown, the terms on which it has been extended and the kind of borrowers to whom it has been offered have changed, too. In the 1920's more than 80 per cent of all instalment contracts issued for the purchase of new automobiles matured in twelve months or less. By 1965, 86 per cent of all new-car loans were extended for periods of more than two and a half years. Almost 80 per cent of loans on used cars had maturities of more than two years.

Moreover, as the maturities on instalment loans lengthened secularly, the down payments tended to become smaller. While more than 80 per cent of all instalment contracts for automobiles provided for down payments of one-third or more of the purchase price in 1925, by the late 1950's only about 40 per cent of such contracts provided for down payments of as much as one-third. The evidence suggests that down payments have continued to ease since then.

As the terms have become less restrictive, the characteristics of the borrowers who enter into instalment credit contracts have changed as well. Debt holding has increased throughout the population, but it has increased disproportionately among younger people and among those with higher real incomes. The stability of the incomes of the population as a whole, and no doubt of the borrowing population, has improved markedly.

In short, extensive changes in lending and borrowing standards or requirements—i.e., credit quality—have accompanied the growth in the volume of instalment credit. Thus far there has been, at most, only a moderate increase in the incidence of collection difficulties, but there remains the important question whether it is reasonable to expect this record to continue. We have attempted to investigate the possibilities in several ways. First, we have endeavored to establish whether loans extended on terms involving either lower down payments or longer maturities increase the risk of subsequent repayment difficulties. We have, similarly, sought to determine whether loans to certain types of borrowers are more likely to encounter trouble. Second, we have considered the question whether easing in one dimension is typically offset or reinforced by the lending standards imposed on loans in some other dimension. Thus we have investigated whether loans with low down payments generally have short maturities, or the reverse. We have, moreover, tried to find out whether loans with easy terms tend to be offered to borrowers with characteristics associated with poorer or better-than-average collection experience.

In considering the problem of predicting the degree of risk which attaches to loans of given characteristics at the time they are extended, it is necessary to take into account the effect of subsequent economic conditions on actual collection experience. We have examined the evidence on this point. Finally, we have attempted to compare the collection experience estimated in advance on the basis of various kinds of lending standards with that actually experienced later.

Our purpose in thus marshaling the evidence on the quality of consumer credit is a broad one. Lenders, of course, are continually evaluating credit quality in deciding whether to make individual loans and in setting up guidelines for the conduct of their business. Heretofore, however, the results of all these individual evaluations and decisions have not been widely known or generally considered on a broad scale. Yet shifts in the risk position of consumers and their creditors have become of great potential importance to the economic prosperity of the nation. It was in order to contribute to a better understanding of this subject that this study was undertaken.

CONCLUSIONS

Our conclusions, which pertain almost exclusively to automobile credit, may be summarized as follows:

1. While there are many exceptions, for the most part loans granted with low down payments are generally loans with long maturities. This is true not only nationally but at regional and local levels also. Those parts of the country which have the lowest average down payment requirements are usually those with the longest average maturities.

2. Terms tend to vary systematically with certain borrower characteristics. Specifically, younger borrowers, wage and salary earners, and lower-income groups generally obtain longer maturities and make smaller down payments. Shorter maturities and larger down payments prevail among borrowers over 40; farmers, proprietors, and professional people; and higher-income groups.

3. Credit terms are significantly related to subsequent collection or repayment experience. Utilizing various kinds of data from the 1920's to the 1950's, we find that higher down payment requirements were quite consistently associated with lower delinquency, repossession, and loss rates. Shorter maturities were associated with smaller risk of credit difficulty in the case of new-auto loans, though less strongly than was the case with high down payments. In the case of used cars, short maturities typically have been associated with poorer performance. All these tendencies appear in national data, but are corroborated by regional and local analysis showing that those areas with the highest average down payments had the fewest credit difficulties.

4. Similarly, we find that certain borrower characteristics have been quite closely associated with credit risk, while others seem to have little or no bearing on the prospective risk. Characteristics which are closely related to subsequent experience include income, liquid-asset holdings, and life-cycle status.

5. By considering variations in the terms of loans obtained by the same type of borrower (i.e., those with similar characteristics), we

find that credit risk is not associated with one factor alone. Typically, the degree of risk is affected by both terms and some borrower characteristics, notably age, income, and liquid-asset holdings. The combined effect, on the average, for example, of low down payments granted to borrowers with characteristics associated with poor repayment experience makes the subsequent experience worse than either factor alone. On the other hand, restrictive terms can largely compensate for borrower characteristics associated with high risk, although this does not, in fact, appear to be typical practice.

6. The above conclusions suggest that one can, by careful consideration of the terms on which loans are offered and the characteristics of the borrowers to whom they are offered, determine broadly, at the time a given volume of loans is made, the degree of credit risk associated with this group of loans. Actual collection or repayment experience, however, is importantly affected by the business cycle as well—that is, by the changing fortunes of the economy in the period after the loans are granted. Viewed in the aggregate, delinquency, repossession, and loss rates rise during recessions and fall during business expansions. Moreover, we find that a pattern in the cyclical turning point of these rates appears quite consistently not alone in the national data but also in regional and local series. As the peak in the business cycle approaches, delinquency rates begin to rise first (often before the business downturn itself), while repossession and loss rates turn up later. A similar sequence appears at business cycle troughs, although the downturn in delinquencies has led the upturn in business less frequently.

7. Finally, we have attempted to discover how much of the variation in credit experience in recent years could be accounted for by the changes in lending standards considered earlier in our study. By taking into consideration what was found concerning the degree of potential risk attaching to groups of loans with different terms, an index of credit risk was constructed. The long-term trend in the index turns out to be similar to that in actual credit experience, but the wide fluctuations in the latter, largely attributable to the effects of prosperity and recession, are not reflected. The results suggest, therefore, that one can explain a considerable part of the change in credit experience by careful consideration and evaluation of the

average terms and borrower characteristics of a given volume of loans.

8. Our findings and their limitations point up sharply the need for better continuing statistical information concerning consumer credit terms and borrower characteristics, as well as the related credit risks. With more adequate information the relationships we have found could not only be tested periodically but more fully elaborated. Our ability to understand contemporaneous changes in the quality of consumer credit and their implications for borrowers, lenders, and the public generally hinges on the provision of such information.

A NEEDED STATISTICAL PROGRAM

From time to time in this report we have observed that the limitations of the data, both in translating characteristics of the credit transaction into estimates of risk and in comparing such risk estimates with actual credit experience, constitute a severe handicap. The risk indexes in Chapter 7 are limited especially by the fact that they do not take into account changes in borrower characteristics. Indexes of credit quality in whose validity one could place a higher degree of confidence, therefore, await the provision of data explicitly designed and developed for the purpose. Hence it is fitting to conclude this exploration of the problem with a brief list of the chief data requirements in this field.

1. *Periodic surveys, perhaps every three or four years, designed to relate (a) specific characteristics of credit contracts and the borrower's income and liquid asset position to (b) credit experience in terms of delinquency, repossession, or loss.* Such surveys can be most effective for the purpose if they sample "bad loans" at a high rate and "good loans" at a much lower rate, since the latter far outnumber the former. The results should be compiled in the form of cross-tabulations of several variables against credit experience rather than one variable at a time. Such a survey program would prevent the kind of situation that presently exists in which the most recent comprehensive information of this type is ten years old, and at least one important credit indicator (the dealer cost ratio) has been in existence for nearly ten years with no comprehensive test of its efficacy.

2. *Continuing monthly or quarterly surveys of new credit contracts which would report the terms of the contract and the borrower's*

income, liquid asset position, and other characteristics. It is important that the basic data obtained from these surveys and the tabulations made from them match precisely in concept and coverage those obtained from the periodic surveys mentioned in point (1) above. Otherwise the latter cannot be used effectively to interpret the current surveys.

3. *Continuing statistical analyses that would translate the results of (2) into quarterly estimates of credit risk on new credit contracts using the results of the most recent periodic survey described in (1).* This can be done from cross-tabulations in the manner described earlier in Chapter 7. In addition, experiments should be undertaken to utilize, by means of multiple regression techniques and computer programs, information on each individual credit contract in the continuing survey sample in order to translate that information into estimates of credit risk.[1] These techniques might eventually supplant the estimates based on cross-tabulations, since they are potentially more efficient in their use of the available information.

4. *Regular monthly or quarterly surveys of actual delinquency, repossession, and loss rates.* The number and dollar volume of contracts delinquent, repossessed, or charged off should be tabulated both by date when the delinquency, etc., occurred and by date when the contract originated. The coverage and other aspects of this survey should be such that the results are comparable with the estimate of credit risk obtained in (3). In this way a continuing evaluation of risk and credit experience can be carried out in the manner developed in Chapter 7.

5. *In all of the above, separate analyses for each of the major credit sources (sales finance companies, banks, consumer finance companies, credit unions) and for each of the several types of credit (automobile, appliance, personal loans).* Consideration should be given as well to the provision of regional as well as national information.

This is a large program. It can, however, be attacked in stages, if carefully planned. Moreover, a considerable effort is already being made, by individual companies, trade associations, and government

[1] Note Paul Smith's recent proposal along these lines utilizing lending terms and borrower characteristics for instalment loans made by a commercial bank ("Measuring Risk on Instalment Credit," *Management Science*, November 1964).

agencies, to obtain information of this type. But these efforts are largely uncoordinated and produce data that are difficult to compare and analyze.

Consumer credit has come of age. It involves the lending and repayment of enormous sums on a national scale. We hope that this volume has demonstrated both the need for and the potential value of dependable, up-to-date, and coordinated information on its quality.

APPENDIXES

Appendix A: Supplementary Tables on Financing Terms and Borrower Characteristics, 1925–66

TABLE A-1

Automobile Financing Terms, 1925–39, Composite Experience of Sales Finance Companies

Year	Number of Cars Financed		Dollar Volume of Notes Purchased		Average Size of Note Purchased	Percentage Distribution of Dollar Volume by Length of Contract (months)				Distribution of Dollar Volume by Percentage of Down Payment	
	In Thousands	Index, 1929:100	In Millions	Index, 1929:100		12 or Less	13–18	19–24	Over 24	Under 33 Per Cent	33 Per Cent and Over
					A. New Cars						
1925	—	—	—	—	$550						
1926	—	—	—	—	595						
1927	—	—	—	—	574						
1928	1,333	70	848	75	635						
1929	1,892	100	1,126	100	595						
1930	1,381	73	778	69	564						
1931	1,028	54	570	51	554						
1932	555	29	303	27	546						
1933	760	40	392	35	516						
1934	1,064	56	587	52	551	62		38		17	83
1935	1,334	71	734	65	550	38		62		29	71
1936	1,908	101	1,106	98	580	28	45	25	2	26	74
1937	1,747	92	1,035	92	593	22	34	39	5	23	77
1938	824	44	519	46	630	28	47	25	(a)	19	81
1939	1,159	61	748	66	643	24	35	40	1	29	71

(continued)

TABLE A-1 (continued)

Year	Number of Cars Financed		Dollar Volume of Notes Purchased		Average Size of Note Purchased	Percentage Distribution of Dollar Volume by Length of Contract (months)				Distribution of Dollar Volume by Percentage of Down Payment		
	In Thousands	Index, 1929:100	In Millions	Index, 1929:100		12 or Less	13–18	19–24	Over 24	Under 33 Per Cent	33–39 Per Cent	40 Per Cent & Over
					B. Used Cars							
1925	--	--	--	--	$280							
1926	--	--	--	--	277							
1927	--	--	--	--	286							
1928	1,133	68	348	71	307							
1929	1,656	100	491	100	297							
1930	1,609	97	450	92	280							
1931	1,420	86	380	77	268							
1932	967	58	233	47	241							
1933	1,068	64	235	48	220							
1934	1,355	82	307	63	226	85		15		21		79
1935	1,792	108	424	86	237	76		24		43		57
1936	2,356	142	610	124	258	65	32	3	a	27	73	
1937	2,453	148	686	140	279	47	48	4	1	24	76	
1938	1,793	108	492	100	275	49	49	2	a	23	77	
1939	2,196	133	615	125	280	42	51	7	a	30	70	

(continued)

TABLE A-1 (concluded)

C. All Cars

Year	Number of Cars Financed		Dollar Volume of Notes Purchased		Average Size of Note Purchased	Percentage Distribution of Dollar Volume by Length of Contract (months)				Distribution of Dollar Volume by Percentage of Down Payment	
	In Thousands	Index, 1929:100	In Millions	Index, 1929:100		12 or Less	13–18	19–24	Over 24	Under 33 Per Cent[b]	33 Per Cent and Over
1925						81		19		19	81
1926						87		13		9	91
1927						88		12		5	95
1928	2,466	70	1,196	74	$485	86		14		6	94
1929	3,548	100	1,617	100	456	85		15		8	92
1930	2,990	84	1,228	76	411	83		17		12	88
1931	2,448	69	950	59	388	82		18		11	89
1932	1,522	43	536	33	352	78		22		14	86
1933	1,828	52	627	39	343	87		13		12	88
1934	2,419	68	894	55	370	70		30		18	82
1935	3,126	88	1,158	72	370	52	| 48 |			34	66
1936	4,264	120	1,716	106	400	41	40	17	2	26	74
1937	4,200	118	1,721	106	410	32	40	25	3	23	77
1938	2,617	74	1,011	63	386	38	48	14	a	21	79
1939	3,335	94	1,363	84	409	32	42	26	a	30	70

Source: National Association of Sales Finance Companies, "Composite Experience of Sales Finance Companies and Automobile Dealers, 1939."   aLess than 0.5 per cent.   b1925–35 used-car paper with down payment under 40 per cent is included with new-car paper under 33 per cent; for later years, the under 33 per cent bracket applies to both used and new cars.

TABLE A-2

Financing Terms, 1935–41, 1947–65, Instalment Sales Finance Companies Based on Dollar Volume

Statement Date	Percentage of Retail Paper Maturing in:			Maturing in More than:			Percentage of New-Car Paper:		
	6 Months or Less (1)	7–12 Months (2)	Over 12 Months (3)	18 Months (4)	24 Months (5)	30 Months (6)	Balloon, Excluding Demonstrator Paper (7)	With Down Payment Less Than 33 Per Cent (8)	With Dealer Cost Ratio 1.01 and Over[a] (9)
Dec. 31, 1935	62.1	30.1	7.8	2.3			7.6	21.0	
Dec. 31, 1936	56.1	31.1	12.8	29.7			9.6	38.6	
Dec. 31, 1937	56.7	31.6	11.7	34.8			5.6	22.3	
Dec. 31, 1938	59.0	30.5	10.5	19.8			6.6	17.5	
Dec. 31, 1939	54.6	31.4	14.0	33.5			8.5	25.2	
Dec. 31, 1940	52.7	31.6	15.7	46.3			10.5	32.4	
Dec. 31, 1941	54.8	31.8	13.4	46.7			11.0	33.0	
Dec. 31, 1947	57.2	31.6	11.2						
Dec. 31, 1948	52.4	31.5	16.1						
Dec. 31, 1949	51.9	30.1	18.0						
Dec. 31, 1950	47.2	32.0	20.8						
Dec. 31, 1951	56.6	31.9	11.5						
Dec. 31, 1952	47.5	30.7	21.8						
June 30, 1953	—	—	—	81.1			13.4	31.9	
Dec. 31, 1953	47.1	31.2	21.7	83.3			10.8	29.9	
June 30, 1954	—	—	—	83.3			10.9	35.2	
Dec. 31, 1954	45.0	30.0	25.0	86.2			11.8	40.3	
June 30, 1955	41.6	29.5	28.9	89.2	67.9		14.0	50.0	
Dec. 31, 1955	39.4	28.8	31.8	90.9	n.a.		12.8	52.0	
June 30, 1956	39.4	28.6	32.0	92.5	78.1		7.8	56.1	
Dec. 31, 1956	38.6	28.3	33.1	93.3	n.a.		5.3	57.2	
June 30, 1957	38.1	28.8	33.1	93.4	n.a.	n.a.	5.1	60.3	
Dec. 31, 1957	37.7	28.3	34.0	93.8	79.7	43.9	5.3	60.4	32.1

(continued)

TABLE A-2 (continued)

Statement Date	Percentage of Retail Paper Maturing in:			Percentage Of New-Car Paper:					
	6 Months or Less (1)	7–12 Months (2)	Over 12 Months (3)	Maturing in More than			Balloon, Excluding Demonstrator Paper (7)	With Down Payment Less Than 33 Per Cent (8)	With Dealer Cost Ratio 1.01 and Over[a] (9)
				18 Months (4)	24 Months (5)	30 Months (6)			
June 30, 1958	38.3	28.6	33.1	n.a.	82.3	56.1	4.7	n.a.	31.4
Dec. 31, 1958	37.1	28.4	34.5		82.8	63.9	4.5		28.6
June 30, 1959	36.1	27.9	36.0		84.5	73.4	4.0		34.8
Dec. 31, 1959	35.0	26.5	38.5		86.6	76.8	4.1		33.0
June 30, 1960	35.1	27.5	37.4		86.3	79.4	4.3		35.6
Dec. 31, 1960	63.3		36.7			80.8	3.9		32.1
June 30, 1961	65.4		34.6			77.6	5.2		30.0
Dec. 31, 1961	63.7		36.3			78.0	3.5		33.0
June 30, 1962	63.3		36.7			80.9	3.2		33.0
Dec. 31, 1962	61.9		38.1			81.4	5.1		35.0
June 30, 1963	61.3		38.7			83.3	4.6		37.9
Dec. 31, 1963	59.5		40.5			84.7	5.4		38.4
June 30, 1964	59.3		40.7			85.0	5.1		38.9
Dec. 31, 1964	58.2		41.8			85.4	4.0		38.8
June 30, 1965	57.7		42.3			86.3	3.5		41.0
Dec. 31, 1965	58.5		41.5			86.3	3.3		40.0
June 30, 1966	58.2		41.8			86.8	3.8		42.6

(continued)

TABLE A-2 (continued)

Percentage of Used-Car Paper:

Statement Date	Maturing in More than			With Final Installment Larger Than Preceding Ones (13)	With Down Payment Less Than 33 Per Cent (14)	With Dealer Cost Ratio 1.01 and Over[a] (15)
	12 Months (10)	18 Months[b] (11)	24 Months[b] (12)			
Dec. 31, 1935	20.6			4.2	20.6	
Dec. 31, 1936	38.8			7.1	37.1	
Dec. 31, 1937	49.2			5.7	27.9	
Dec. 31, 1938	46.4			4.9	21.9	
Dec. 31, 1939	52.7			5.5	31.8	
Dec. 31, 1940	60.2			6.5	40.0	
Dec. 31, 1941	63.0			5.7	37.2	
Dec. 31, 1947						
Dec. 31, 1948						
Dec. 31, 1949						
Dec. 31, 1950						
Dec. 31, 1951						
Dec. 31, 1952						
June 30, 1953	86.3			3.2	29.9	
Dec. 31, 1953	86.0			2.8	31.0	
June 30, 1954	78.7			2.7	25.7	
Dec. 31, 1954	79.6			2.6	27.3	
June 30, 1955	82.2	83.7		3.3	35.9	
Dec. 31, 1955	82.8	---		3.2	38.1	
June 30, 1956	83.8	86.0		2.2	43.1	
Dec. 31, 1956	84.6	n.a.		2.1	45.6	
June 30, 1957	88.4	88.1		2.2	51.8	
Dec. 31, 1957	88.7		34.7	2.0	53.6	59.0[c]

(continued)

TABLE A-2 (concluded)

| Statement Date | Percentage Of Used-Car Paper: | | | | | |
| | Maturing in More than | | | With Final Instalment Larger Than Preceding Ones (13) | With Down Payment Less Than 33 Per Cent (14) | With Dealer Cost Ratio 1.01 and Over[a] (15) |
	12 Months (10)	18 Months[b] (11)	24 Months[b] (12)			
June 30, 1958	n.a.	90.8	47.6	2.0	n.a.	35.5
Dec. 31, 1958		90.8	50.0	1.5		34.8
June 30, 1959		92.9	63.1	1.2		40.8
Dec. 31, 1959		93.1	61.5	1.1		41.9
June 30, 1960		93.2	67.6	1.1		38.9
Dec. 31, 1960			66.9	0.9		38.9
June 30, 1961			67.1	1.5		45.1
Dec. 31, 1961			66.3	1.0		47.4
June 30, 1962			75.0	1.5		50.9
Dec. 31, 1962			72.2	1.1		47.7
June 30, 1963			78.7	1.8		50.6
Dec. 31, 1963			78.7	1.4		53.1
June 30, 1964			78.8	1.5		50.6
Dec. 31, 1964			77.2	1.4		51.4
June 30, 1965			78.1	1.5		48.3
Dec. 31, 1965			79.5	1.4		52.2
June 30, 1966			81.3	1.4		58.5

Source: First National Bank of Chicago, "Ratios of the Instalment Sales Finance and Small Loan Companies," and supplements. Sample of 19 companies; percentages are simple averages of the percentages reported by each company.

aRatio of the amount of credit advanced to the cost of the car to the dealer (for new cars) or to its wholesale value (for used cars).

bCovering current and two preceding years' models and not comparable, therefore, with entries in Column 10, which covers all used cars.

cRelated to low book value.

TABLE A-3

Automobile Financing Terms, Sales Finance Companies, 1948–56

Year	Index of Number of Cars Financed (1950:100) (1)	Index of Dollar Volume of Contracts (1930:100) (2)	Average Size of Note (dollars) (3)	Average Monthly Instalment (dollars) (4)	Average Length of Contract (months) (5)	Cos. Whose Av. Contract Length: Increased From Preceding Year (6)	Cos. Whose Av. Contract Length: Decreased From Preceding Year (7)	% of Contracts Maturing in Over: 18 Months (2 cos.) (8)	% of Contracts Maturing in Over: 24 Months (5 cos.) (9)
A. New Cars								18 Months (2 cos.) (8)	24 Months (5 cos.) (9)
1948	43	41	1,342	—	17.2a	—	—	22	
1949	79	79	1,414	—	19.6a	3d	0	47	5
1950	100	100	1,416	73	20.0a	2d	0	52	e
1951	87	84	1,375	88	15.8	0	6	3	10
1952	89	105	1,674	83	21.1	6	0	49	19
1953	117	147	1,776	79	23.1	6	0		39
1954	117	159	1,932	79	25.1	6	0		64
1955	168	260	2,190	81	28.1	6	0		70
1956 (1st 6 months)	—	—	2,322b	82	29.3c	5	0		
B. Used Cars								13 Months (2 cos.) (8)	24 Months (4 cos.) (9)
1948	55	62	830	—	15.2a	—	—	49	e
1949	84	82	724	—	16.0a	3	0	50	e
1950	100	100	739	48	16.6	3	0	50	1
1951	124	131	777	54	15.0	0	6	63	1
1952	131	166	939	54	18.2	6	0	71	2
1953	132	164	917	51	18.8	5	1	70	5
1954	119	135	836	49	18.5	1	5	63	8
1955	138	164	873	50	19.5	6	0	—	—
1956 (1st 6 months)	—	—	930b	52	20.4c	5	0	—	—
C. New and Used Cars									
Number of Companies	7	7	7	4	6			2	5
Coverage Ratio, 1955	57.8	57.8	57.8	56.5	57.6			47.1	57.1

Source: *Consumer Instalment Credit*, Part II, Vol. 1, pp. 120 and 123–124. aEstimated on basis of three companies. bEstimated on basis of data for first four to six months of 1956. cEstimated on basis of five companies. dOne company showed no change. eLess than 0.5 per cent.

TABLE A-4

Maturity Structure of Automobile Loans, Commercial Banks, 1956–65

Date of Loan	Purchased Paper			Direct Loans		
	Most Common Term	Average Term (months)	Range	Most Common Term	Average Term (months)	Range
		New Cars				
1956	30	28	24–36	30	26	24–36
1957	36	30	24–36	30	27	24–36
1958	36	30	24–36	36	28	24–36
1959	36	32	24–36	36	30	24–36
1960	36	32	30–36	36	30	24–36
1961	36	32	30–36	36	31	24–36
1962	36	33	30–48	36	31	24–48
1963	36	33	n.a.	36	32	n.a.
1964	36	33	n.a.	36	32	n.a.
1965	36	n.a.	n.a.	36	n.a.	n.a.
		Used Cars, One Year Old[a]				
1956	24	23	18–30	24	22	18–30
1957	24	24	18–36	24	23	18–36
1958	24	23	18–36	24	22	18–36
1959	30	26	24–36	24	24	18–36
1960	30	26	24–36	30	24	12–36
1961	30	26	24–36	30	25	18–36
1962	30	27	24–36	30	25	15–36
1963	30	28	n.a.	30	25	n.a.
1964	30	28	n.a.	30	26	n.a.
1965	30	n.a.	n.a.	30	n.a.	n.a.
		Used Cars, Three Years Old[a]				
1956	18	18	12–24	18	17	12–24
1957	24	19	12–30	18	17	12–30
1958	18	18	12–30	18	16	12–30
1959	24	20	12–36	24	19	12–36
1960	24	20	12–36	24	19	12–36
1961	24	21	12–30	24	19	12–30
1962	24	21	12–36	24	20	12–36
1963	24	22	n.a.	24	20	n.a.
1964	24	21		24	20	
1965	24	n.a.		24	n.a.	

(continued)

TABLE A-4 (concluded)

Date of Loan	Purchased Paper			Direct Loans		
	Most Common Term	Average Term (months)	Range	Most Common Term	Average Term (months)	Range
Used Cars, Five Years Old[a]						
1956	12	12	12−24	12	12	12−24
1957	18	14	12−24	12	12	12−24
1958	12	12	12−24	12	12	12−24
1959	18	15	12−24	18	14	12−24
1960	18	16	12−36	18	15	12−36
1961	18	16	12−24	18	15	12−24
1962	18	16	12−36	18	15	12−36
1963	18	17	n.a.	18	16	n.a.
1964	18	17	n.a.	18	16	n.a.
1965	18	n.a.	n.a.	18	n.a.	n.a.

Source: American Bankers Association. Composite results based on questionnaire sent to outstanding commercial banks (varying from 235 in 1956 to 445 in 1965).

[a]At date of loan.

n.a. No longer published.

Quality of Consumer Instalment Credit

TABLE A-5

Distribution of New-Automobile Loans by Five Borrower Characteristics, June 1953 and July 1957

Borrower Characteristic	June 1953	July 1957	Direction of Change
	(per cent)		
Income per month (dollars)			
Under 250	11.37	6.21	–
250 – 349	28.83	19.61	–
350 – 499	34.15	40.41	+
500 – 999	22.76	30.34	+
1,000 and over	2.89	3.43	+
Total	100.00	100.00	
Sex			
Male	91.46	92.70	+
Female	8.54	7.30	–
Total	100.00	100.00	
Marital Status			
Married	82.44	85.29	+
Single	17.23	14.71	–
Divorced-widowed	.33	n.a.	
Total	100.00	100.00	
Age (years)			
30 and under	31.79	31.62	–
31–40	31.65	32.76	+
41–50	23.16	23.19	+
Over 50	13.40	12.42	–
Total	100.00	99.99	
Occupation			
Farm operators	3.28	2.42	–
Wage earners	1.07	1.01	–
Nonfarm proprietors	10.77	7.45	–
Professional	5.88	5.45	–
Salaried	33.73	33.12	–
Wage earners	37.71	44.75	+
Miscellaneous	7.56	5.80	–
Total	100.00	100.00	

Source: Tables B-3, B-5, B-7, B-9, B-11.
Note: Totals may not add to 100 due to rounding.
n.a. Not collected.

Appendix B: Cross-Classification of New-Auto Contracts by Credit Terms and Borrower Characteristics, and Chi-Square Tests of Relationship

The data in Appendix B are based on new-automobile contracts purchased through branch offices of a large sales finance company. The company made available to the National Bureau three samples covering all contracts purchased during the first ten days of the months of June 1953, July 1956, and July 1957.

These data permit cross-classification of contracts by credit terms, borrower characteristics, and regions. The states included in each region are shown in Table B-1. The existence of a relationship is tested by means of chi-square analyses.[1] Basically the test determines whether a distribution of observed frequencies differs from a distribution of theoretical frequencies (calculated on the assumption of independence) more than might be expected from sampling errors alone. (The observed and theoretical frequencies are shown in Tables B-2–B-16.) In the application here it is essentially a test of the association of one variable with another, and it tests the hypothesis that they are independent, any discrepancies between the two distributions being attributable solely to chance. The following symbols are used:

f_0 = observed frequency

f = theoretical frequency based on the hypothesis that the two variables are unrelated

S = chi-square values significant at the .05 level

N = chi-square values not significant at the .05 level

Only contracts with complete information on credit terms and borrower characteristics were included in the computations of theoretical frequencies and chi-square values.

[1] For a detailed description of the chi-square test, see Frederick C. Mills, *Statistical Methods*, Third Edition, Chapter 15, pp. 512–540.

TABLE B-1

Regional Classification of States in Continental United States

Pacific	Mountain	West North Central	West South Central	East South Central
Washington	Montana	Minnesota	Arkansas	Kentucky
Oregon	Idaho	Iowa	Louisiana	Tennessee
California	Wyoming	Missouri	Oklahoma	Alabama
Nevada	Colorado	North Dakota	Texas	Mississippi
	New Mexico	South Dakota		
	Arizona	Nebraska		
	Utah	Kansas		

East North Central	South Atlantic	Middle Atlantic	New England
Ohio	Delaware	New York	Maine
Indiana	Maryland	New Jersey	New Hampshire
Illinois	District of Columbia	Pennsylvania	Vermont
Michigan	Virginia		Massachusetts
Wisconsin	West Virginia		Rhode Island
	North Carolina		Connecticut
	South Carolina		
	Georgia		
	Florida		

Note: The regional classification is derived from delinquency reports of the American Bankers Association. It agrees with the Census classification with one exception (Nevada is classed as a Mountain state by the Census).

TABLE B-2

Length of Maturity and Down Payment Percentage, by Regions, July 1956 [a]

Down Payment as a Percentage of Cash Selling Price	Length of Maturity									
	12 Mos. and Under		13–24 Mos.		25–35 Mos.		36 Mos. and Over		All Contracts	
	f_O	f	f_O	f	f_O	f	f_O	f	f_O	f
Total United States (S)										
Under 20	24	59.1	168	205.7	820	617.6	438	567.4	1,450	1,449.8
20–24	30	84.3	197	293.6	1,024	881.3	818	809.7	2,069	2,068.9
25–29	45	71.8	161	250.1	687	750.7	869	689.7	1,762	1,762.3
30–34	26	38.1	156	132.7	322	398.4	431	366.0	935	935.2
35–49	81	35.1	221	122.2	258	366.7	301	336.9	861	860.9
50 & over	100	17.7	163	61.7	89	185.3	83	170.2	435	434.9
All contracts	306	306.1	1,066	1,066.0	3,200	3,200.0	2,940	2,939.9	7,512	7,512.0
Pacific Region (S)										
Under 20	3	1.9	3	4.9	36	26.5	54	62.7	96	96.0
20–24	1	3.1	8	7.8	48	42.5	97	100.6	154	154.0
25–29	2	3.6	3	9.2	40	50.2	137	118.9	182	181.9
30–34	0	1.1	3	2.8	14	15.4	39	36.6	56	55.9
35–49	4	1.0	10	2.5	8	13.8	28	32.7	50	50.0
50 & over	1	.3	1	.7	6	3.6	5	8.5	13	13.1
All contracts	11	11.0	28	27.9	152	152.0	360	360.0	551	550.9

(continued)

TABLE B-2 (continued)

Length of Maturity

Down Payment as a Percentage of Cash Selling Price	12 Mos. and Under		13–24 Mos.		25–35 Mos.		36 Mos. and Over		All Contracts	
	t_O	t	t_O	t	t_O	t	t_O	t	t_O	t
Mountain Region (S)										
Under 20	0	1.7	7	4.9	28	22.0	0	6.3	35	34.9
20–24	1	2.6	2	7.5	43	33.3	7	9.6	53	53.0
25–29	1	2.8	8	8.2	36	36.5	13	10.5	58	58.0
30–34	1	1.8	3	5.2	22	23.3	11	6.7	37	37.0
35–49	2	2.1	8	6.1	21	27.1	12	7.8	43	43.1
50 & over	7	1.1	7	3.1	6	13.8	2	4.0	22	22.0
All contracts	12	12.1	35	35.0	156	156.0	45	44.9	248	248.0
West North Central Region (S)										
Under 20	1	5.3	14	20.4	43	38.3	91	85.0	149	149.0
20–24	5	7.7	18	29.7	61	55.8	133	123.8	217	217.0
25–29	2	5.3	17	20.4	39	38.3	91	85.0	149	149.0
30–34	3	2.8	14	10.9	15	20.6	48	45.6	80	79.9
35–49	6	1.8	14	7.0	14	13.1	17	29.1	51	51.0
50 & over	7	1.2	16	4.6	3	8.8	8	19.4	34	34.0
All contracts	24	24.1	93	93.0	175	174.9	388	387.9	680	679.9

(continued)

TABLE B-2 (continued)

Down Payment as a Percentage of Cash Selling Price	Length of Maturity									
	12 Mos. and Under		13–24 Mos.		25–35 Mos.		36 Mos. and Over		All Contracts	
	f_O	f	f_O	f	f_O	f	f_O	f	f_O	f
West South Central Region (S)										
Under 20	3	9.8	53	55.2	190	173.4	56	63.6	302	302.0
20–24	2	11.1	56	62.7	209	197.0	76	72.2	343	343.0
25–29	8	6.9	28	38.9	126	122.3	51	44.9	213	213.0
30–34	4	3.2	24	18.3	47	57.4	25	21.1	100	100.0
35–49	9	2.7	24	15.2	34	47.7	16	17.5	83	83.1
50 & over	9	1.2	12	6.8	13	21.2	3	7.8	37	37.0
All contracts	35	34.9	197	197.1	619	619.0	227	227.1	1,078	1,078.1
East South Central Region (S)										
Under 20	2	5.1	19	20.1	55	49.7	23	24.2	99	99.1
20–24	2	8.5	23	33.6	99	83.3	42	40.6	166	166.0
25–29	7	6.0	21	23.9	56	59.2	34	28.9	118	118.0
30–34	6	3.8	16	15.0	33	37.1	19	18.1	74	74.0
35–49	11	3.5	20	14.0	26	34.6	12	16.9	69	69.0
50 & over	0	1.1	12	4.5	6	11.0	4	5.4	22	22.0
All contracts	28	28.0	111	111.1	275	274.9	134	134.1	548	548.1

(continued)

TABLE B-2 (continued)

Length of Maturity

Down Payment as a Percentage of Cash Selling Price	12 Mos. and Under		13–24 Mos.		25–35 Mos.		36 Mos. and Over		All Contracts	
	f_O	f	f_O	f	f_O	f	f_O	f	f_O	f
East North Central Region (S)										
Under 20	4	17.1	42	51.6	318	250.3	64	108.9	428	427.9
20–24	5	20.8	32	62.7	346	304.2	137	132.3	520	520.0
25–29	11	15.9	36	48.0	202	232.8	149	101.2	398	397.9
30–34	5	8.0	36	24.0	88	116.4	70	50.6	199	199.0
35–49	18	7.8	49	23.4	88	113.5	39	49.4	194	194.1
50 & over	30	3.4	25	10.3	25	49.7	5	21.6	85	85.0
All contracts	73	73.0	220	220.0	1,067	1,066.9	464	464.0	1,824	1,823.9
South Atlantic Region (S)										
Under 20	10	10.6	20	30.3	119	93.4	19	33.6	168	167.9
20–24	12	19.2	39	54.8	182	169.1	71	60.9	304	304.0
25–29	12	16.7	28	47.6	162	146.8	62	52.9	264	264.0
30–34	4	8.7	30	24.9	70	76.7	34	27.6	138	137.9
35–49	16	7.9	48	22.5	42	69.5	19	25.0	125	124.9
50 & over	13	3.8	26	10.8	14	33.4	7	12.0	60	60.0
All contracts	67	66.9	191	190.9	589	588.9	212	212.0	1,059	1,058.7

(continued)

TABLE B-2 (concluded)

Length of Maturity

Down Payment as a Percentage of Cash Selling Price	12 Mos. and Under		13–24 Mos.		25–35 Mos.		36 Mos. and Over		All Contracts	
	f_o	f	f_o	f	f_o	f	f_o	f	f_o	f
Middle Atlantic Region (S)										
Under 20	0	3.9	8	17.7	24	14.4	107	103.1	139	139.1
20–24	1	7.0	15	31.8	28	25.8	206	185.3	250	249.9
25–29	0	8.5	15	38.4	19	31.2	268	224.0	302	302.1
30–34	2	5.6	22	25.4	26	20.6	150	148.3	200	199.9
35–49	12	5.6	44	25.3	18	20.5	125	147.5	199	198.9
50 & over	19	3.4	50	15.4	10	12.5	42	89.7	121	121.0
All contracts	34	34.0	154	154.0	125	125.0	898	897.9	1,211	1,210.9
New England Region (S)										
Under 20	1	2.4	2	4.0	7	4.6	24	23.0	34	34.0
20–24	1	4.4	4	7.3	8	8.3	49	42.0	62	62.0
25–29	2	5.5	5	9.2	7	10.5	64	52.8	78	78.0
30–34	1	3.6	8	6.0	7	6.8	35	34.5	51	50.9
35–49	3	3.3	4	5.6	7	6.3	33	31.8	47	47.0
50 & over	14	2.9	14	4.8	6	5.5	7	27.8	41	41.0
All contracts	22	22.1	37	36.9	42	42.0	212	211.9	313	312.9

TABLE B-3

Length of Maturity and Borrower's Income, June 1953 and July 1957

Income Per Month (dollars)	Length of Maturity									
	12 Mos. and Under		13–24 Mos.		25–35 Mos.		36 Mos. and Over		All Contracts	
	f_o	f	f_o	f	f_o	f	f_o	f	f_o	f
	June 1953 Sample (S)									
Under 250	48	45.5	336	308.6	95	127.6	12	9.3	491	491.0
250–349	100	115.6	772	782.4	354	323.5	19	23.6	1,245	1,245.1
350–499	125	136.9	898	926.8	426	383.2	26	28.0	1,475	1,474.9
500–999	111	91.3	626	617.7	225	255.4	21	18.7	983	983.1
1,000 & over	17	11.6	82	78.4	22	32.4	4	2.4	125	124.8
All contracts	401	400.9	2,714	2,713.9	1,122	1,122.1	82	82.0	4,319	4,318.9
	July 1957 Sample (S)									
Under 250	15	17.9	53	62.0	162	144.4	279	285.1	509	509.4
250–349	47	56.6	133	195.7	463	455.9	966	900.3	1,609	1,608.5
350–499	71	116.8	382	403.3	953	939.5	1,909	1,855.2	3,315	3,314.8
500–999	123	87.7	364	302.8	675	705.4	1,327	1,392.9	2,489	2,488.8
1,000 & over	33	9.9	66	34.2	72	79.7	110	157.5	281	281.3
All contracts	289	288.9	998	998.0	2,325	2,324.9	4,591	4,591.0	8,203	8,202.8

TABLE B-4

Down-Payment Percentage and Borrower's Income, June 1953 and July 1957

Income Per Month (dollars)	Down Payment As A Percentage Of Cash Selling Price												All Contracts	
	Under 20%		20–24%		25–29%		30–34%		35–49%		50% and Over			
	f_o	t	f_o	t	f_o	t	f_o	t	f_o	t	f_o	t	f_o	t
June 1953 Sample (N)														
Under 250	6	4.4	10	15.0	39	60.2	155	130.4	156	165.9	123	112.9	489	488.8
250–349	7	11.2	37	38.3	168	153.3	323	331.9	416	422.2	293	287.3	1,244	1,244.2
350–499	16	13.4	46	45.6	193	182.6	389	395.4	519	502.9	319	342.3	1,482	1,482.2
500–999	9	8.9	36	30.4	118	121.7	254	263.6	342	335.3	229	228.2	988	988.1
1,000 & over	1	1.1	4	3.8	15	15.1	33	32.8	35	41.7	35	28.4	123	122.9
All contracts	39	39.0	133	133.1	533	532.9	1,154	1,154.1	1,468	1,468.0	999	999.1	4,326	4,326.2
July 1957 Sample (N)														
Under 250	41	41.7	40	56.9	95	109.8	129	111.4	147	130.9	58	59.0	510	509.7
250–349	126	132.0	178	179.8	364	347.4	347	352.3	415	414.1	182	186.5	1,612	1,612.1
350–499	264	271.1	391	369.3	732	713.5	723	723.6	845	850.4	356	383.0	3,311	3,310.9
500–999	210	203.4	275	277.0	531	535.3	532	542.9	627	638.0	309	287.3	2,484	2,483.9
1,000 & over	30	22.7	30	31.0	44	59.9	60	60.7	71	71.4	43	32.1	278	277.8
All contracts	671	670.9	914	914.0	1,766	1,765.9	1,791	1,790.9	2,105	2,104.8	948	947.9	8,195	8,194.4

TABLE B-5

Length of Maturity and Borrower's Sex, June 1953 and July 1957

Sex	Length of Maturity									
	12 Mos. and Under		13–24 Mos.		25–35 Mos.		36 Mos. and Over		All Contracts	
	f_O	f	f_O	f	f_O	f	f_O	f	f_O	f
June 1953 Sample (N)										
Male	432	428.9	2,602	2,616.7	1,082	1,072.8	91	88.7	4,207	4,207.1
Female	37	40.1	259	244.3	91	100.2	6	8.3	393	392.9
All contracts	469	469.0	2,861	2,861	1,173	1,173.0	97	97.0	4,600	4,600.0
July 1957 Sample (N)										
Male	317	309.6	965	965.9	2,222	2,232.2	4,366	4,362.5	7,870	7,870.2
Female	17	24.4	77	76.1	186	175.8	340	343.5	620	619.8
All contracts	334	334.0	1,042	1,042.0	2,408	2,408.0	4,706	4,706.0	8,490	8,490.0

TABLE B-6

Down Payment Percentage and Borrower's Sex, June 1953 and July 1957

| | Down Payment As A Percentage Of Cash Selling Price | | | | | | | | | | | | | |
| | Under 20% | | 20–24% | | 25–29% | | 30–34% | | 35–49% | | 50% and Over | | All Contracts | |
Sex	f_o	f	f_o	f	f_o	f	f_o	f	f_o	f	f_o	f	f_o	f
						June 1953 Sample (N)								
Male	36	38.4	128	127.2	509	513.4	1,112	1,110.0	1,434	1,429.4	996	996.5	4,215	4,214.9
Female	6	3.6	11	11.8	52	47.6	101	103.0	128	132.6	93	92.5	391	391.1
All contracts	42	42.0	139	139.0	561	561.0	1,213	1,213.0	1,562	1,562.0	1,089	1,089.0	4,606	4,606.0
						July 1957 Sample (N)								
Male	647	650.4	858	861.6	1,686	1,680.7	1,694	1,702.9	2,041	2,036.4	927	920.9	7,853	7,852.9
Female	55	51.6	72	68.4	128	133.3	144	135.1	157	161.6	67	73.1	623	623.1
All contracts	702	702.0	930	930.0	1,814	1,814.0	1,838	1,838.0	2,198	2,198.0	994	994.0	8,476	8,476.0

TABLE B-7

Length of Maturity and Borrower's Marital Status, June 1953 and July 1957

Marital Status	Length Of Maturity									
	12 Mos. and Under		13–24 Mos.		25–35 Mos.		36 Mos. and Over		All Contracts	
	f_o	f	f_o	f	f_o	f	f_o	f	f_o	f
June 1953 Sample (S)										
Married	376	383.3	2,336	2,352.0	983	964.5	84	79.1	3,779	3,778.9
Single	89	80.1	512	491.6	178	201.6	11	16.5	790	789.8
Divorced-Widowed	0	1.5	5	9.4	9	3.9	1	.3	15	15.1
All contracts	465	464.9	2,853	2,853.0	1,170	1,170.0	96	95.9	4,584	4,583.8
July 1957 Sample[a] (S)										
Married	281	282.3	900	887.9	1,998	2,052.1	4,036	3,992.4	7,215	7,214.7
Single	50	48.7	141	153.1	408	353.9	645	688.6	1,244	1,244.3
All contracts	331	331.0	1,041	1,041.0	2,406	2,406.0	4,681	4,681.0	8,459	8,459.0

[a]The distribution for 1957 includes no category for 'divorced' status.

TABLE B-8

Down Payment Percentage and Borrower's Marital Status, June 1953 and July 1957

Marital Status	Down Payment As A Percentage Of Cash Selling Price													All Contracts	
	Under 20%		20–24%		25–29%		30–34%		35–49%		50% and Over				
	f_O	f	f_O	f	f_O	f	f_O	f	f_O	f	f_O	f		f_O	f
June 1953 Sample (S)															
Married	33	33.8	107	113.7	470	462.3	997	998.7	1,311	1,282.1	865	892.4		3,783	3,783.0
Single	8	7.1	30	23.8	87	96.8	211	209.1	240	268.4	216	186.8		792	792.0
Divorced–widowed	0	.1	1	.5	4	2.0	4	4.2	5	5.4	2	3.8		16	16.0
All contracts	41	41.0	138	138.0	561	561.1	1,212	1,212.0	1,556	1,555.9	1,083	1,083.0		4,591	4,591.0
July 1957 Sample[a] (S)															
Married	575	593.4	779	787.8	1,561	1,544.9	1,585	1,566.2	1,879	1,867.2	826	845.8		7,205	7,205.3
Single	121	102.6	145	136.2	251	267.1	252	270.8	311	322.8	166	146.2		1,246	1,245.7
All contracts	696	696.0	924	924.0	1,812	1,812.0	1,837	1,837.0	2,190	2,190.0	992	992.0		8,451	8,451.0

[a]The distribution for 1957 includes no category for 'divorced' status.

TABLE B-9

Length of Maturity and Borrower's Age, June 1953 and July 1957

Age (years)	Length Of Maturity									
	12 Mos. and Under		13–24 Mos.		25–35 Mos.		36 Mos. and Over		All Contracts	
	f_O	f	f_O	f	f_O	f	f_O	f	f_O	f
June 1953 Sample (S)										
30 & under	110	147.5	958	903.8	360	370.0	24	30.8	1,452	1,452.1
31–40	140	146.9	860	899.8	406	368.4	40	30.7	1,446	1,445.8
41–50	132	107.5	644	658.4	263	269.6	19	22.5	1,058	1,058.0
Over 50	82	62.2	381	381.0	135	156.0	14	13.0	612	612.2
All contracts	464	464.1	2,843	2,843.0	1,164	1,164.0	97	97.0	4,568	4,568.1
July 1957 Sample (S)										
30 & under	77	103.7	242	328.2	825	762.7	1,534	1,483.0	2,678	2,677.6
31–40	89	107.5	327	340.0	764	790.2	1,594	1,536.4	2,774	2,774.1
41–50	98	76.1	284	240.7	548	559.3	1,034	7,087.6	1,964	1,963.7
Over 50	64	40.7	185	128.9	275	299.6	528	582.5	1,052	1,051.7
All contracts	328	328.0	1,038	1,037.8	2,412	2,411.8	4,690	4,689.5	8,468	8,467.1

TABLE B-10

Down-Payment Percentage and Borrower's Age, June 1953 and July 1957

Down Payment As A Percentage Of Cash Selling Price

Age (years)	Under 20%		20–24%		25–29%		30–34%		35–49%		50% and Over		All Contracts	
	f_o	f	f_o	f	f_o	f	f_o	f	f_o	f	f_o	f	f_o	f
						June 1953 Sample (S)								
30 & under	15	12.7	59	43.7	216	176.5	414	382.8	453	492.5	293	341.9	1,450	1,450.1
31–40	13	12.7	44	43.7	149	176.5	386	382.8	504	492.5	354	341.9	1,450	1,450.1
41–50	9	9.3	23	32.0	126	129.1	273	280.0	392	360.2	238	250.1	1,061	1,060.7
Over 50	3	5.4	12	18.5	66	74.9	135	162.4	205	208.9	194	145.0	615	615.1
All contracts	40	40.1	138	137.9	557	557.0	1,208	1,208.0	1,554	1,554.1	1,079	1,078.9	4,576	4,576.0
						July 1957 Sample (S)								
30 & under	232	221.4	302	294.6	629	574.0	628	581.6	659	693.5	229	313.6	2,679	2,678.7
31–40	247	228.6	321	304.1	587	592.5	590	600.4	715	715.8	305	323.7	2,765	2,765.1
41–50	150	162.0	203	215.5	409	419.8	415	425.4	513	507.2	269	229.4	1,959	1,959.3
Over 50	70	87.0	104	115.8	187	225.6	203	228.6	302	272.5	187	123.3	1,053	1,052.8
All contracts	699	699.0	930	930.0	1,812	1,811.9	1,836	1,836.0	2,189	2,189.0	990	990.0	8,456	8,455.9

TABLE B-11

Length of Maturity and Borrower's Occupation, June 1953 and July 1957

| | Length of Maturity | | | | | | | | |
| | 12 Mos. and Under | | 13–24 Mos. | | 25–35 Mos. | | 36 Mos. and Over | | Total | |
Occupation	t_O	t	t_O	t	t_O	t	t_O	t	t_O	t
				June 1953 Sample (S)						
Farm										
Operators	65	15.3	78	93.4	6	38.2	1	3.2	150	150.1
Wage earners	12	5.0	30	30.5	7	12.5	0	1.0	49	49.0
Nonfarm										
Proprietors	78	50.2	312	306.8	94	125.5	9	10.4	493	492.9
Professional	27	27.4	179	167.5	58	68.5	5	5.7	269	269.1
Salaried	123	157.2	987	961.0	408	393.0	26	32.7	1,544	1,543.9
Wage earners	125	175.7	1,054	1,074.4	501	439.3	46	36.6	1,726	1,726.0
Miscellaneous	36	35.2	209	215.4	91	88.1	10	7.3	346	346.0
All contracts	466	466.0	2,849	2,849.0	1,165	1,165.1	97	96.9	4,577	4,577.0
				July 1957 Sample (S)						
Farm										
Operators	46	8.1	44	25.4	42	58.3	73	113.5	205	205.3
Wage earners	10	3.4	16	10.6	24	24.3	36	47.4	86	85.7
Nonfarm										
Proprietors	46	24.9	128	78.2	179	179.6	279	350.0	632	632.7
Professional	28	18.2	78	57.1	133	131.2	223	255.7	462	462.2
Salaried	89	110.6	336	347.0	785	797.3	1,599	553.5	2,809	2,808.4
Wage earners	93	149.5	386	469.2	1,115	1,078.1	2,202	2,100.6	3,796	3,797.4
Miscellaneous	22	19.3	60	60.7	130	139.4	280	271.7	492	491.1
All contracts	334	334.0	1,048	1,048.2	2,408	2,408.2	4,692	4,692.4	8,482	8,482.8

TABLE B-12
Down Payment Percentage and Borrower's Occupation, June 1953 and July 1957

Occupation	Down Payment As A Percentage Of Cash Selling Price													All Contracts	
	Under 20%		20–24%		25–29%		30–34%		35–49%		50% and Over			
	f_O	f	f_O	f	f_O	f	f_O	f	f_O	f	f_O	f	f_O	f
June 1953 Sample (S)														
Farm														
Operators	0	1.4	0	4.5	8	18.2	42	39.0	51	49.9	47	34.9	148	147.9
Wage earners	0	.5	0	1.4	3	5.9	15	12.7	15	16.2	15	11.4	48	48.1
Nonfarm														
Proprietors	6	4.6	9	14.9	60	60.8	124	130.6	165	167.1	131	117.0	495	495.0
Professional	1	2.5	8	8.1	24	33.2	73	71.3	106	91.2	58	63.8	270	270.1
Salaried	20	14.5	61	46.4	179	189.0	421	406.3	519	519.9	340	363.9	1,540	1,540.0
Wage earners	11	16.2	48	52.1	243	212.1	439	455.9	579	583.5	408	408.3	1,728	1,728.1
Miscellaneous	5	3.3	12	10.5	45	42.9	94	92.3	111	118.1	83	82.7	350	349.8
All contracts	43	43.0	138	137.9	562	562.1	1,208	1,208.1	1,546	1,545.9	1,082	1,082.0	4,579	4,579.0
July 1957 Sample (S)														
Farm														
Operators	8	17.6	15	23.4	30	45.6	38	46.4	78	55.3	44	25.0	213	213.3
Wage earners	9	7.3	3	9.6	15	18.8	17	19.2	35	22.8	9	10.3	88	88.0
Nonfarm														
Proprietors	46	52.0	62	69.0	111	134.7	133	137.0	178	163.4	100	73.9	630	630.0
Professional	47	38.0	38	50.4	90	98.5	97	100.2	128	119.5	61	54.0	461	460.6
Salaried	261	230.7	364	306.0	647	597.8	531	608.0	672	724.9	320	327.8	2,795	2,795.2
Wage earners	283	312.9	411	415.0	814	810.8	914	824.7	979	983.1	390	446.6	3,791	3,791.1
Miscellaneous	45	40.5	34	53.7	104	104.9	112	106.7	126	127.1	69	57.5	490	490.4
All contracts	699	699.0	927	927.1	1,811	1,811.1	1,842	1,842.2	2,196	2,196.1	993	993.1	8,468	8,468.6

TABLE B-13

Ratio of Monthly Payment to Monthly Income and Borrower's Income, June 1953 and July 1957

Income Per Month (dollars)	Ratio Of Monthly Payment To Monthly Income											All Contracts	
	Under 10%		10–14%		15–19%		20–29%		30% and Over				
	f_o	f	f_o	f	f_o	f	f_o	f	f_o	f		f_o	f
June 1953 Sample (S)													
Under 250	1	56.0	8	133.5	44	130.3	199	119.7	232	44.7		484	484.2
250–349	22	142.0	168	338.8	394	330.7	552	303.9	93	113.5		1,229	1,228.9
350–499	94	168.5	516	402.0	555	392.4	245	360.6	48	134.7		1,458	1,458.2
500–999	276	112.7	468	268.8	154	262.4	57	241.2	20	90.1		975	975.2
1,000 & over	100	13.9	16	33.0	1	32.3	2	29.6	1	11.1		120	119.9
All contracts	493	493.1	1,176	1,176.1	1,148	1,148.1	1,055	1,055.0	394	394.1		4,266	4,266.4
July 1957 Sample (S)													
Under 250	1	31.9	3	101.0	4	146.6	99	166.2	396	57.0		503	502.7
250–349	3	99.7	40	315.9	175	458.5	950	519.7	404	178.1		1,572	1,571.9
350–499	34	207.5	386	657.5	1,362	954.3	1,400	1,081.9	90	370.8		3,272	3,272.0
500–999	279	154.8	1,129	490.6	801	712.0	211	807.2	21	276.6		2,441	2,441.2
1,000 & over	194	17.1	61	54.1	8	78.5	4	89.0	2	30.5		269	269.2
All contracts	511	511.0	1,619	1,619.1	2,350	2,349.9	2,664	2,664.0	913	913.0		8,057	8,057.0

TABLE B-14

Ratio of Monthly Payment to Monthly Income and Borrower's Marital Status, June 1953 and July 1957

Marital Status	Ratio of Monthly Payment to Monthly Income											All Contracts	
	Under 10%		10–14%		15–19%		20–29%		30% and Over			All Contracts	
	f_o	f	f_o	f	f_o	f	f_o	f	f_o	f		f_o	f
June 1953 Sample (S)													
Married	449	403.3	1,044	966.2	950	941.5	789	866.6	269	323.4		3,501	3,501.0
Single	40	85.3	127	204.3	190	199.1	260	183.2	123	68.4		740	740.3
Divorced–widowed	1	1.5	3	3.6	4	3.5	4	3.3	1	1.2		13	13.1
All contracts	490	490.1	1,174	1,174.1	1,144	1,144.1	1,053	1,053.1	393	393.0		4,254	4,254.4
July 1957 Sample (S) [a]													
Married	484	434.1	1,482	1,373.0	2,103	1,996.9	2,119	2,259.1	648	772.9		6,836	6,836.0
Single	26	75.9	131	240.0	243	349.1	535	394.9	260	135.1		1,195	1,195.0
All contracts	510	510.0	1,613	1,613.0	2,346	2,346.0	2,654	2,654.0	908	908.0		8,031	8,031.0

[a]The distribution for 1957 does not include a category for divorced status.

TABLE B-15

Ratio of Monthly Payment to Monthly Income and Borrower's Age, June 1953 and July 1957

Age (years)	Ratio of Monthly Payment to Monthly Income										All Contracts	
	Under 10%		10–14%		15–19%		20–29%		30% and Over			
	f_o	f	f_o	f	f_o	f	f_o	f	f_o	f	f_o	f
June 1953 Sample (S)												
30 and under	81	159.4	291	382.2	396	373.7	433	343.0	185	127.7	1,386	1,386.0
31–40	191	154.5	431	370.3	331	362.1	300	332.3	90	123.8	1,343	1,343.0
41–50	141	110.8	281	265.6	264	259.7	196	238.4	81	88.8	963	963.3
Over 50	75	63.4	167	152.0	153	148.6	121	136.4	35	50.8	551	551.2
All contracts	488	488.1	1,170	1,170.1	1,144	1,144.1	1,050	1,050.1	391	391.1	4,243	4,243.5
July 1957 Sample (S)												
30 and under	68	162.6	351	514.9	707	747.3	1,057	847.1	379	290.4	2,562	2,562.3
31–40	185	168.6	613	533.9	834	774.9	785	878.4	240	301.2	2,657	2,657.0
41–50	169	116.4	450	368.5	533	534.9	514	606.3	168	207.9	1,834	1,834.0
Over 50	88	62.4	201	197.7	270	286.9	301	325.2	124	111.5	984	983.7
All contracts	510	510.0	1,615	1,615.0	2,344	2,344.0	2,657	2,657.0	911	911.0	8,037	8,037.0

TABLE B-16

Ratio of Monthly Payment to Monthly Income and Borrower's Occupation, June 1953 and July 1957

Occupation	Ratio of Monthly Payment to Monthly Income										All Contracts	
	Under 10%		10–14%		15–19%		20–29%		30% and Over			
	f_O	f	f_O	f	f_O	f	f_O	f	f_O	f	f_O	f
June 1953 Sample (S)												
Farm												
Operators	15	11.1	18	26.4	17	25.9	26	23.7	20	8.9	96	96.0
Wage earners	5	4.8	6	11.3	8	11.1	13	10.2	9	3.8	41	41.2
Nonfarm												
Proprietors	90	49.2	126	116.8	84	114.3	90	104.7	34	39.3	424	424.3
Professional	50	28.5	74	67.7	48	66.2	49	60.7	25	22.8	246	245.9
Salaried	169	170.9	395	406.1	410	397.4	373	364.1	128	136.5	1,475	1,475.0
Wage earners	131	191.8	485	455.7	506	445.9	424	408.5	109	153.2	1,655	1,655.1
Miscellaneous	32	35.8	65	85.1	71	83.3	73	76.3	68	28.6	309	309.1
All contracts	492	492.1	1,169	1,169.1	1,144	1,144.1	1,048	1,048.2	393	393.1	4,246	4,246.6
July 1957 Sample (S)												
Farm												
Operators	12	9.0	24	28.6	38	41.5	41	47.0	27	16.1	142	142.2
Wage earners	5	4.4	8	13.9	10	20.2	26	22.9	20	7.8	69	69.2
Nonfarm												
Proprietors	92	36.0	177	113.9	145	165.3	118	187.4	35	64.2	567	566.8
Professional	68	26.8	111	85.0	94	123.3	101	139.8	49	47.9	423	422.8
Salaried	170	171.3	519	542.8	744	787.7	949	892.8	318	305.7	2,700	2,700.3
Wage earners	133	233.8	702	740.8	1,215	1,074.9	1,262	1,218.4	373	417.1	3,685	3,685.0
Miscellaneous	30	28.8	75	91.1	99	132.3	161	149.9	88	51.3	453	453.4
All contracts	510	510.1	1,616	1,616.1	2,345	2,345.2	2,658	2,658.2	910	910.1	8,039	8,039.7

Appendix C: Four Measures of Collection Experience: Their Characteristics and Uses

DELINQUENCY RATE

Delinquency data have one important advantage for the study of the effect of changed credit terms or other economic conditions on subsequent credit experience. The first signs of collection difficulty are likely to appear in delinquency rates. Thus the relationship between delinquencies and the terms and conditions at the time loans are made would be closer in point of time than that for any other measure of collection experience except perhaps refinancing.

One of the deficiencies of delinquencies as a measure of collection experience is that the standards utilized in declaring loans delinquent vary for different banks and finance companies. Hence it is difficult to generalize on the basis of a single firm's experience, and changes in practices can distort the figures. Also, a loan on which some sort of extension is arranged (formally or informally) will escape the delinquent category.

A classification of delinquencies by duration, e.g., 30–59 days, 60–89 days, and 90 days and over, distinguishes those that occur first from those that persist and which are likely to represent more serious problems. The longer delinquencies are, naturally, more likely to result in repossession or losses.

REPOSSESSIONS

Repossession experience has proven to be an excellent measure with which to analyze the relation of collection experience to previous changes in terms. It avoids some of the problems of definition inherent in delinquency data. It represents a rather serious economic event, both for the borrower and the lender. Furthermore, although the loss rate (discussed below) may be the best measure of ultimate credit performance as a whole, its significance is sometimes blurred by fortuitous factors, such as the sale of repossessed durables in a favorable market, or by financial arrangements that involve the shifting of losses to another creditor. Repossession data have an additional advantage relative to losses in that the repossession is recorded at an earlier date.

Repossession data, like delinquency data, can be affected by changes in the creditor's policy with regard to repossession on overdue accounts. Furthermore, an additional complication concerning repossession rates arises because some contracts are purchased by sales finance companies and banks from automobile dealers under recourse agreements whereby the dealer agrees to absorb part or all of the loss encountered on contracts he originates. Recourse or repurchase agreements, naturally, alter the ultimate significance of repossession to the lender. Presumably, a given repossession rate with recourse agreements would have a different effect on lending policy than the same rate without such agreements. Unfortunately, repossession data seldom if ever include this sort of additional information.

LOSS RATES

In his study of consumer loan losses, James P. Winchester enumerated four methods which can be utilized in reporting net loss experience.[1]

First, there is net loss related to volume by year the loan was made. This method of reporting losses is seldom utilized. One of the difficulties with it is that the loss rate with respect to a given year's volume changes more or less constantly over a long period of time as old loans are repaid or charged off.

Second, net losses can be related to current volume of loans made. While this method is fairly common among banks, according to Winchester, it is rare for sales finance companies and in any case tends to understate losses where volume is growing rapidly.

Thirdly, losses can be related to volume of loans liquidated. While rare among banks, this method is fairly common among sales finance

[1] James P. Winchester, *Consumer Installment Loan Losses and Valuation Reserves*, Cambridge, Mass., 1955, pp. 17–20.

companies and is more accurate, in general, than the first two methods because it eliminates relatively new loans which have not had the same exposure to risk as the older ones.

The fourth method is to relate losses to outstandings. While this is a common method among sales finance companies, it is rare among banks. A fairly similar measure, the ratio of losses to income and reserves, is used in this study's local area data obtained from a large sales finance company.

Net losses are significantly affected by recoveries from the resale of repossessed items. Variation in the market for such items is a factor that affects the repossession rate only indirectly (by making repossession more or less profitable) and the delinquency rate not at all. This tends to reduce the correlation between net losses and credit terms or borrower characteristics at the time the loans were made.

Furthermore, loss data present problems because losses can be split in varying degree between the lending agency and the automobile dealer, who may sell the loan paper on either a recourse or a nonrecourse basis. Hence the net losses as reported by a given lender may fail to reveal the total losses on a given volume of loans, some of which the dealers themselves bear.

EXTENSIONS (REFINANCING)

A final measure of collection experience for which some data are available is extensions or refinancing. This represents an alternative to repossession (and hence loss) for the dealer on a given loan. One might expect extensions, therefore, to vary in the same direction as delinquencies, repossessions, and losses.

The major disadvantage in the use of extensions is that they do not necessarily reflect collection or repayment difficulty. Refinancing of a short maturity may even be contemplated at the time the loan is made. Many extensions are made to permit new commitments or purchases, or to consolidate other credit obligations. Because of this ambiguity, we have not included extensions in our analysis.

Nevertheless, to the extent that extensions are resorted to as alternatives to other and more drastic types of collection difficulty considered, ignoring them means ignoring one aspect of credit experience that may be related to a prior change in credit quality.

Appendix D: Repossession and Delinquency Rates on New-Car Loans Classified by Credit Terms and Borrower Characteristics, 1954–55

The data are unpublished tabulations from the National Analysts New Automobile Purchase Survey for the Federal Reserve Board (see Chapter 3, note 4).

In analyzing these data, allowance should be made for the fact (observed in Chapter 3, note 5) that offsetting fluctuations occur in the repossession and delinquency rates which can obscure the tendency for both rates to be associated with the variables used to classify the contracts. Where the contracts are cross-classified by two variables, the offsetting tendency can be tested in the following manner: (1) calculate an "expected" repossession rate for each cell in the table by multiplying the unweighted averages for the corresponding row and column and dividing by the unweighted average for the entire table, (b) subtract the expected from the actual repossession rate in each cell, (c) do the same for the delinquency rates, and (d) correlate the deviations. For Table D-15 the correlation coefficient is $-.53$; for Table D-16, $-.59$; for Table D-17, $-.21$.

TABLE D-1

Contract Down Payment Ratio, Lender Report Sample, 1954–55

Contract Down Payment Ratio (per cent)	Number of Loans			Repos-session Rate (per cent)	Delin-quency Rate (per cent)
	All	Repos-sessions	Delin-quencies		
Under 20.0	346	11	18	3.2	5.2
20.0–24.9	429	20	39	4.7	9.1
25.0–29.9	1,084	51	78	4.7	7.2
30.0–34.9	1,797	40	80	2.2	4.5
35.0–39.9	1,127	21	44	1.9	3.9
40.0–49.9	1,438	4	30	0.3	2.1
50.0 and over	1,793	2	30	0.1	1.7
Total	8,014	149	319	1.9	4.0
Information lacking	907	17	30	--	--
All contracts	8,921	166	349	1.9	3.9

TABLE D-2

Contract Down Payment Ratio, Personal Interview Sample, 1954–55

Contract Down Payment Ratio (per cent)	Number of Loans			Repos-session Rate (per cent)	Delin-quency Rate (per cent)
	All	Repos-sessions	Delin-quencies		
Under 20.0	311	10	1	3.2	0.3
20.0–24.9	275	9	8	3.3	2.9
25.0–29.9	533	7	10	1.3	1.9
30.0–34.9	991	18	19	1.8	1.9
35.0–39.9	695	8	5	1.2	0.7
40.0–49.9	920	5	9	0.5	1.0
50.0 and over	1,322	2	8	0.2	0.6
Total	5,047	59	60	1.2	1.2
Information lacking	22	5	0	--	--
All contracts	5,069	64	60	1.3	1.2

TABLE D-3

Effective Down Payment Ratio, Personal Interview Sample, 1954–55

Effective Down Payment Ratio (per cent)	Number of Loans			Repossession Rate (per cent)	Delinquency Rate (per cent)
	All	Repossessions	Delinquencies		
Under 20.0	1,382	34	24	2.5	1.7
20.0–24.9	659	6	5	0.9	0.8
25.0–29.9	581	6	11	1.0	1.9
30.0–34.9	615	5	6	0.8	1.0
35.0–39.9	413	5	5	1.2	1.2
40.0–49.9	562	4	1	0.7	0.2
50.0 and over	822	0	8	0	1.0
Total	5,034	60	60	1.2	1.2
Information lacking	35	4	0	––	––
All contracts	5,069	64	60	1.3	1.2

TABLE D-4

Original Maturity, Lender Report Sample, 1954–55

Original Maturity (months)	Number of Loans			Repossession Rate (per cent)	Delinquency Rate (per cent)
	All	Repossessions	Delinquencies		
Less than 18	856	2	9	0.2	1.1
18–23	687	5	12	0.7	1.7
24–29	3,021	42	105	1.4	3.5
30–35	3,080	87	155	2.8	5.0
36 and over	1,232	30	68	2.4	5.5
Total	8,876	166	349	1.9	3.9
Information lacking	45	0	0	––	––
All contracts	8,921	166	349	1.9	3.9

TABLE D-5

Original Maturity, Personal Interview Sample, 1954–55

Original Maturity (months)	Number of Loans			Repos- session Rate (per cent)	Delin- quency Rate (per cent)
	All	Repos- sessions	Delin- quencies		
Less than 18	556	9	4	1.6	0.7
18–23	492	5	6	1.0	1.2
24–29	1,674	16	21	1.0	1.3
30–35	1,597	30	23	1.9	1.4
36 and over	728	4	6	0.5	0.8
Total	5,047	64	60	1.3	1.2
Information lacking	22	0	0	--	--
All contracts	5,069	64	60	1.3	1.2

TABLE D-6

Effective Down-Payment Percentage and Original Maturity, Personal Interview Sample, 1954–55

Original Maturity (months)	Effective Down Payment as a Percentage of Effective Car Price					
	Under 30	30–39	40 and Over	Total	Information Lacking	All Contracts
1. Number of Contracts						
Under 30	991	592	1,119	2,702	20	2,722
30–35	1,060	343	187	1,590	7	1,597
36 and over	564	86	72	722	6	728
Total	2,615	1,021	1,378	5,014	33	5,047
Information lacking	7	7	6	20	2	22
All contracts	2,622	1,028	1,384	5,034	35	5,069

	Effective Down Payment as a Percentage of Effective Car Price				
	Under 30	30–39	40 and Over	Average	
				Unweighted	Weighted
2. Repossession Rate					
Under 30	1.9	0.8	0.2	1.0	1.1
30–35	2.2	1.5	1.1	1.6	1.9
36 and over	0.7	0	0	0.2	0.5
Average, unweighted	1.6	0.8	0.4	0.9	——
weighted	1.8	1.0	0.3	——	1.2
3. Delinquency Rate					
Under 30	1.2	0.8	0.8	0.9	1.0
30–35	1.2	1.7	0	1.0	1.2
36 and over	1.1	0	0	0.4	0.8
Average, unweighted	1.2	0.8	0.3	0.8	——
weighted	1.2	1.1	0.7	——	1.0

Note: Contracts with "information lacking" are excluded from the averages.

TABLE D-7

Borrower's Income in Year of Purchase,
Personal Interview Sample, 1954–55

Income in Year of Purchase (dollars)	Number of Loans			Repossession Rate (per cent)	Delinquency Rate (per cent)
	All	Repossessions	Delinquencies		
Under 3,000	325	5	6	1.5	1.8
3,000–3,999	502	14	8	2.8	1.6
4,000–4,999	812	10	12	1.2	1.5
5,000–9,999	2,636	26	25	1.0	0.9
10,000 and over	610	3	6	0.5	1.0
Total	4,885	58	57	1.2	1.2
Information lacking	184	6	3	--	--
All contracts	5,069	64	60	1.3	1.2

TABLE D-8

Borrower's 1955 Income, Personal Interview Sample, 1954–55

1955 Income (dollars)	Number of Loans			Repossession Rate (per cent)	Delinquency Rate (per cent)
	All	Repossessions	Delinquencies		
Under 3,000	287	7	6	2.4	2.1
3,000–3,999	463	13	6	2.8	1.3
4,000–4,999	789	8	9	1.0	1.1
5,000–9,999	2,685	28	28	1.0	1.0
10,000 and over	662	3	8	0.5	1.2
Total	4,886	59	57	1.2	1.2
Information lacking	183	5	3	--	--
All contracts	5,069	64	60	1.3	1.2

TABLE D-9

Borrower's 1955 Disposable Income,
Personal Interview Sample, 1954—55

1955 Disposable Income[a] (dollars)	Number of Loans			Repossession Rate (per cent)	Delinquency Rate (per cent)
	All	Repossessions	Delinquencies		
Under 3,000	455	11	10	2.4	2.2
3,000—3,999	690	18	6	2.6	0.9
4,000—4,999	1,058	14	14	1.3	1.3
5,000—9,999	2,320	15	25	0.6	1.1
10,000 and over	363	1	2	0.3	0.6
Total	4,886	59	57	1.2	1.2
Information lacking	183	5	3	--	--
All contracts	5,069	64	60	1.3	1.2

TABLE D-10

Net Worth of Borrower, Personal Interview Sample, 1954—55

Net Worth (dollars)	Number of Loans			Repossession Rate (per cent)	Delinquency Rate (per cent)
	All	Repossessions	Delinquencies		
Negative	186	7	3	3.8	1.6
Zero	35	4	2	11.4	5.7
1—999	351	12	3	3.4	0.9
1,000—2,999	626	1	5	0.2	0.8
3,000—4,999	440	7	6	1.6	1.4
5,000—9,999	743	6	11	0.8	1.5
10,000—24,999	1,024	5	8	0.5	0.8
25,000 and over	615	12	2	2.0	0.3
Total	4,020	54	40	1.3	1.0
Information lacking	1,049	10	20	--	--
All contracts	5,069	64	60	1.3	1.2

TABLE D-11

Liquid-Asset Holdings of Borrower,
Personal Interview Sample, 1954–55

Liquid-Asset Holdings[a] (dollars)	Number of Loans			Repossession Rate (per cent)	Delinquency Rate (per cent)
	All	Repossessions	Delinquencies		
Zero	687	34	21	4.9	3.1
1–199	747	7	17	0.9	2.3
200–499	767	6	2	0.8	0.3
500–999	650	4	2	0.6	0.3
1,000–1,999	564	3	4	0.5	0.7
2,000–4,999	518	0	4	0	0.8
5,000–9,999	155	2	0	1.3	0
10,000 and over	72	0	0	0	0
Total	4,160	56	50	1.3	1.2
Information lacking	909	8	10	--	--
All contracts	5,069	64	60	1.3	1.2

[a]The liquid asset figures represent current holdings by the borrower's spending unit at the time of the interview. They include United States Government savings bonds, checking accounts, saving accounts, and certain other savings. Currency is excluded. *Cf. Consumer Instalment Credit*, Part IV, p. 145.

TABLE D-12

Occupation of Borrower, Personal Interview Sample, 1954–55

Occupation	Number of Loans			Repossession Rate (per cent)	Delinquency Rate (per cent)
	All	Repossessions	Delinquencies		
Professional and technical	623	2	9	0.3	1.4
Clerical and sales	738	7	0	0.9	0
Skilled, semiskilled, unskilled, and students	2,267	35	40	1.5	1.8
Self-employed, nonfarm	521	8	6	1.5	1.2
Managers, officials, and proprietors	645	5	3	0.8	0.5
Farm operators	74	0	0	0	0
Housewives and retired	127	2	0	1.6	0
Unemployed	52	3	0	5.8	0
Total	5,047	62	58	1.2	1.1
Information lacking	22	2	2	--	--
All contracts	5,069	64	60	1.3	1.2

TABLE D-13

Life Cycle Status of Borrower, Personal Interview Sample, 1954–55

Life Cycle Status	Number of Loans			Repos- session Rate (per cent)	Delin- quency Rate (per cent)
	All	Repos- sessions	Delin- quencies		
Under 45 Years					
Single	512	8	6	1.6	1.2
Married, no children	563	0	2	0	0.4
Married, with children	2,231	30	36	1.3	1.6
45 Years and Over					
Single	163	2	1	1.2	0.6
Married, no children	887	11	2	1.2	0.2
Married, with children	617	11	11	1.8	1.8
Total	4,973	62	58	1.2	1.2
Information lacking	96	2	2	––	––
All contracts	5,069	64	60	1.3	1.2

TABLE D-14

Age of Borrower, Personal Interview Sample, 1954–55

Age (years)	Number of Loans			Repos- session Rate (per cent)	Delin- quency Rate (per cent)
	All	Repos- sessions	Delin- quencies		
18–29	966	17	12	1.8	1.2
30–39	1,648	14	29	0.8	1.8
40–49	1,395	19	11	1.4	0.8
50 and over	1,041	14	8	1.3	0.8
Total	5,050	64	60	1.3	1.2
Information lacking	19	0	0	––	––
All contracts	5,069	64	60	1.3	1.2

TABLE D-15

Down Payment Percentage and Age of Borrower, Personal Interview Sample, 1954–55

Age (years)	Effective Down Payment as a Percentage of Cash Selling Price				Information Lacking	All Contracts
	Under 30%	30–39%	40% & Over	Total		
1. Number Of Contracts						
Under 30	537	179	246	962	4	966
30–39	879	331	420	1,630	18	1,648
40–49	678	325	386	1,389	6	1,395
50 & over	518	190	326	1,034	7	1,041
Total	2,612	1,025	1,378	5,015	35	5,050
Information lacking	10	3	6	19	0	19
All contracts	2,622	1,028	1,384	5,034	35	5,069

	Effective Down Payment as a Percentage of Cash Selling Price			Average	
	Under 30%	30–39%	40% & Over	Unweighted	Weighted
2. Repossession Rate					
Under 30	3.2	0	0	1.1	1.8
30–39	0.8	0.9	0	0.6	0.6
40–49	1.5	2.2	0.5	1.4	1.4
50 & over	2.3	0	0.6	1.0	1.4
Average:					
unweighted	2.0	0.8	0.3	1.0	––
weighted	1.8	1.0	0.3	––	1.2
3. Delinquency Rate					
Under 30	0.6	1.1	0.8	0.8	0.7
30–39	2.3	2.1	0.5	1.6	1.8
40–49	0.9	0	1.3	0.7	0.8
50 & over	0.4	1.1	0	0.5	0.4
Average:					
unweighted	1.0	1.1	0.6	0.9	––
weighted	1.2	1.1	0.7	––	1.0

Note: Contracts with "information lacking" are excluded from the averages.

TABLE D-16

Down Payment Percentage and Income of Borrower in
Year of Purchase, Personal Interview Sample, 1954–55

Income in Year of Purchase (dollars)	Effective Down Payment as a Percentage of Cash Selling Price				Infor- mation Lacking	All Contracts
	Under 30%	30–39%	40% & Over	Total		
1. Number Of Contracts						
Under 3,000	192	55	76	323	2	325
3,000–4,999	717	250	340	1,307	7	1,314
5,000–7,499	977	417	457	1,851	11	1,862
7,500 & over	658	272	443	1,373	11	1,384
Total	2,544	994	1,316	4,854	31	4,885
Information lacking	78	34	68	180	4	184
All contracts	2,622	1,028	1,384	5,034	35	5,069

	Effective Down Payment as a Percentage of Cash Selling Price			Average	
	Under 30%	30–39%	40% & Over	Unweighted	Weighted
2. Repossession Rate					
Under 3,000	1.6	0	2.6	1.4	1.5
3,000–4,999	2.6	0.4	0	1.0	1.5
5,000–7,499	1.5	1.4	0	1.0	1.1
7,500 & over	0.8	0.4	0.5	0.6	0.6
Average:					
unweighted	1.6	0.6	0.8	1.0	--
weighted	1.7	0.8	0.3	--	1.1
3. Delinquency Rate					
Under 3,000	2.1	3.6	0	1.9	1.9
3,000–4,999	1.5	2.0	0	1.2	1.2
5,000–7,499	1.1	1.0	1.3	1.1	1.1
7,500 & over	0.6	0	0.2	0.3	0.4
Average:					
unweighted	1.3	1.6	0.4	1.1	--
weighted	1.2	1.1	0.5	--	1.0

Note: Contracts with "information lacking" are excluded from the averages.

TABLE D-17

*Down Payment Percentage and Liquid-Asset Holdings of Borrower,
Personal Interview Sample, 1954–55*

Liquid-Asset Holdings (dollars)	Effective Down Payment as a Percentage of Cash Selling Price				Infor- mation Lacking	All Contracts
	Under 30%	30–39%	40% & Over	Total		
1. Number Of Contracts						
None	441	118	118	677	10	687
1–499	904	323	284	1,511	3	1,514
500–1,999	587	244	377	1,208	6	1,214
2,000 or more	256	177	308	741	4	745
Total	2,188	862	1,087	4,137	23	4,160
Information lacking	434	166	297	897	12	909
All contracts	2,622	1,028	1,384	5,034	35	5,069

	Effective Down Payment as a Percentage of Cash Selling Price			Average	
	Under 30%	30–39%	40% & Over	Unweighted	Weighted
2. Repossession Rate					
None	5.4	3.4	1.7	3.5	4.4
1–499	1.3	0.3	0	0.5	0.9
500–1,999	0.3	2.0	0	0.8	0.6
2,000 or more	0	0	0.6	0.2	0.3
Average:					
unweighted	1.8	1.4	0.6	1.2	––
weighted	1.7	1.2	0.4	––	1.3
3. Delinquency Rate					
None	3.2	1.7	0	1.6	2.4
1–499	1.3	1.5	0.7	1.2	1.3
500–1,999	0.2	0	0.8	0.3	0.3
2,000 or more	0.8	1.1	0	0.6	0.5
Average:					
unweighted	1.4	1.1	0.4	0.9	––
weighted	1.3	1.0	0.5	––	1.0

Note: Contracts with "information lacking" are excluded from the averages.

TABLE D-18

Original Maturity and Age of Borrower,
Personal Interview Sample, 1954–55

| Age (years) | Original Maturity | | | | Infor-mation Lacking | All Contracts |
	Under 30 Mos.	30–35 Mos.	36 Mos. & Over	Total		
		1. Number Of Contracts				
Under 30	467	359	136	962	4	966
30–39	842	540	260	1,642	6	1,648
40–49	807	412	173	1,392	3	1,395
50 & over	600	277	155	1,032	9	1,041
Total	2,716	1,588	724	5,028	22	5,050
Information lacking	6	9	4	19	0	19
All contracts	2,722	1,597	728	5,047	22	5,069

| | Original Maturity | | | Average | |
	Under 30 Mos.	30–35 Mos.	36 Mos. & Over	Unweighted	Weighted
		2. Repossession Rate			
Under 30	0.6	3.3	1.5	1.8	1.8
30–39	1.0	1.1	0	0.7	0.9
40–49	1.2	2.2	0	1.1	1.4
50 & over	1.5	1.1	1.3	1.3	1.4
Average:					
unweighted	1.1	1.9	0.7	1.2	––
weighted	1.1	1.9	0.6	––	1.3
		3. Delinquency Rate			
Under 30	1.3	0.3	0	0.5	0.7
30–39	1.1	2.8	1.9	1.9	1.8
40–49	1.1	0.2	0.6	0.6	0.8
50 & over	0.3	0.7	0	0.3	0.4
Average:					
unweighted	1.0	1.0	0.6	0.9	––
weighted	1.0	1.2	0.8	––	1.0

Note: Contracts with "information lacking" are excluded from the averages.

TABLE D-19

Original Maturity and Income of Borrower in Year of Purchase,
Personal Interview Sample, 1954–55

Income in Year of Purchase (dollars)	Original Maturity				Information Lacking	All Contracts
	Under 30 Mos.	30–35 Mos.	36 Mos. & Over	Total		
		1. Number Of Contracts				
Under 3,000	166	120	39	325	0	325
3,000–4,999	614	488	210	1,312	2	1,314
5,000–7,499	969	594	291	1,854	8	1,862
7,500 & over	864	349	162	1,375	9	1,384
Total	2,613	1,551	702	4,866	19	4,885
Information lacking	109	46	26	181	3	184
All contracts	2,722	1,597	728	5,047	22	5,069

	Original Maturity			Average	
	Under 30 Mos.	30–35 Mos.	36 Mos. & Over	Unweighted	Weighted
		2. Repossession Rate			
Under 3,000	1.2	2.5	0	1.2	1.5
3,000–4,999	1.0	3.3	1.0	1.8	1.8
5,000–7,499	1.1	1.3	0.7	1.0	1.1
7,500 & over	0.9	0	0	0.3	0.6
Average:					
unweighted	1.0	1.8	0.4	1.1	––
weighted	1.0	1.7	0.6	––	1.2
		3. Delinquency Rate			
Under 3,000	1.8	1.7	2.6	2.0	1.8
3,000–4,999	1.3	1.2	1.0	1.2	1.2
5,000–7,499	1.0	1.3	1.0	1.1	1.1
7,500 & over	0.3	0.6	0	0.3	0.4
Average:					
unweighted	1.1	1.2	1.2	1.2	––
weighted	0.9	1.2	0.9	––	1.0

Note: Contracts with ''information lacking'' are excluded from the averages.

TABLE D-20

Original Maturity and Liquid-Asset Holdings of Borrower,
Personal Interview Sample, 1954—55

Liquid-Assets Holdings (dollars)	Original Maturity				Information Lacking	All Contracts
	Under 30 Mos.	30—35 Mos.	36 Mos. & Over	Total		
		1. Number Of Contracts				
None	278	300	107	685	2	687
1—499	669	567	273	1,509	5	1,514
500—1,999	679	375	158	1,212	2	1,214
2,000 & over	545	123	75	743	2	745
Total	2,171	1,365	613	4,149	11	4,160
Information lacking	551	232	115	898	11	909
All contracts	2,722	1,597	728	5,047	22	5,069

	Original Maturity			Average	
	Under 30 Mos.	30—35 Mos.	36 Mos. & Over	Unweighted	Weighted
		2. Repossession Rate			
None	6.1	5.0	1.9	4.3	5.0
1—499	0.9	0.9	0.7	0.8	0.9
500—1,999	0.3	1.3	0	0.5	0.6
2,000 & over	0.4	0	0	0.1	0.3
Average:					
unweighted	1.9	1.8	0.6	1.5	——
weighted	1.2	1.8	0.7	——	1.3
		3. Delinquency Rate			
None	1.8	2.7	2.8	2.4	2.3
1—499	1.3	1.2	1.1	1.2	1.3
500—1,999	0.6	0	0	0.2	0.3
2,000 & over	0.7	0	0	0.2	0.5
Average:					
unweighted	1.1	1.0	1.0	1.0	——
weighted	1.0	1.1	1.0	——	1.0

Note: Contracts with "information lacking" are excluded from the averages.

Appendix E: Income, Employment, and Delinquency Rates by Region, 1948–65

Personal income data are from Department of Commerce, *Survey of Current Business*, April 1966, p. 10. Nonagricultural employment data are from Bureau of Labor Statistics, *Employment and Earnings Statistics for States and Areas*, Bulletin 1307-2, p. xx, and Bulletin 1307-3, p. xxii; *Employment and Earnings and Monthly Report on the Labor Force*, August 1966, p. 31. Delinquency rates are from American Bankers Association, *Delinquency Survey*. The number of loans delinquent thirty days and over is taken as a percentage of the number of accounts outstanding.

See Table B-1 for the list of states included in each region. The regions correspond to those used in the ABA delinquency reports. Beginning in 1955, the ABA reports classify Iowa, Missouri, Kansas, and Nebraska in a separate West Central region; for comparability with earlier data we include them in the West North Central region. We classify Michigan and Wisconsin in the East North Central region, although in the ABA reports the northern parts of these states are West North Central.

The national totals for employment differ slightly from the sums of the regional data. Alaska and Hawaii are included beginning in 1960; for computation of percentage change, 1959–60, the 1960 totals, excluding Alaska and Hawaii, are $396,605,000 for personal income and 53,958,000 for employment. The national average delinquency rates are unweighted averages for nine regions, 1948–54, and for ten regions, 1955–64 (West North Central is divided into two sections); these series end in 1964 because the ABA discontinued publication of regional data.

TABLE E-1

Personal Income, by Nine Regions, 1948–65

Personal Income (million dollars)

Year or Period	Pacific	Mountain	West North Central	West South Central	East South Central	East North Central	South Atlantic	Middle Atlantic	New England	U.S. Total
1948	23,736	6,180	19,674	15,836	10,096	47,809	22,910	48,800	13,833	208,876
1949	23,947	6,218	17,999	16,655	9,607	46,017	22,990	48,702	13,657	205,793
1950	26,507	6,903	20,162	17,663	10,572	50,857	25,666	52,932	14,950	226,214
1951	30,253	7,983	21,943	19,886	11,951	57,563	29,212	57,877	16,565	253,232
1952	33,235	8,567	23,048	21,423	12,671	61,029	31,398	60,909	17,490	269,769
1953	35,331	8,758	23,463	22,134	13,279	66,325	32,777	64,860	18,528	285,456
1954	36,127	8,827	24,258	22,424	13,049	15,565	32,886	65,716	18,752	287,607
1955	39,417	9,603	24,784	23,990	14,167	70,796	35,709	69,783	20,057	308,266
1956	42,745	10,476	26,095	25,684	14,983	75,651	38,871	74,592	21,384	330,479
1957	45,437	11,352	27,874	27,442	15,652	78,642	40,821	78,750	22,487	348,460
1958	47,742	12,101	29,556	28,460	16,290	78,412	42,672	80,170	23,068	358,474
1959	52,059	12,946	30,259	29,931	17,360	83,469	45,714	84,819	24,406	380,964
1960	54,389	13,647	31,892	30,791	17,859	86,554	47,832	88,115	25,525	398,726
1961	57,659	14,435	32,941	32,419	18,867	88,077	50,332	90,889	26,565	414,411
1962	62,055	15,558	35,014	34,049	19,954	93,091	54,085	95,909	28,136	440,190
1963	66,024	16,059	36,391	35,935	21,335	97,635	57,577	99,562	29,347	462,335
1964	70,577	16,797	37,786	38,375	22,644	104,255	62,560	105,650	31,119	492,466
1965	74,796	17,815	41,077	41,078	24,407	113,075	67,616	111,996	33,159	529,890

(continued)

TABLE E-1 (concluded)

Percentage Change In Personal Income

Year or Period	Pacific	Mountain	West North Central	West South Central	East North Central	East South Central	South Atlantic	Middle Atlantic	New England	U.S. Total
1948–49	+ 0.9	+ 0.6	− 8.5	+ 5.2	− 4.8	− 3.7	+ 0.3	−0.2	− 1.3	− 1.5
1949–50	+10.7	+11.0	+12.0	+ 6.1	+10.0	+10.5	+11.6	+8.7	+ 9.5	+ 9.9
1950–51	+14.1	+15.6	+ 8.8	+12.6	+13.0	+13.2	+13.8	+9.3	+10.8	+11.9
1951–52	+ 9.9	+ 7.3	+ 5.0	+ 7.7	+ 6.0	+ 6.0	+ 7.5	+5.2	+ 5.6	+ 6.5
1952–53	+ 6.3	+ 2.2	+ 1.8	+ 3.3	+ 4.8	+ 8.7	+ 4.4	+6.5	+ 5.9	+ 5.8
1953–54	+ 2.3	+ 0.8	+ 3.4	+ 1.3	− 1.7	− 1.1	+ 0.3	+1.3	+ 1.2	+ 0.8
1954–55	+ 9.1	+ 8.8	+ 2.2	+ 7.0	+ 8.6	+ 8.0	+ 8.6	+6.2	+ 7.0	+ 7.2
1955–56	+ 8.4	+ 9.1	+ 5.3	+ 7.1	+ 5.8	+ 6.9	+ 8.9	+6.9	+ 6.6	+ 7.2
1956–57	+ 6.3	+ 8.4	+ 6.8	+ 6.8	+ 4.5	+ 4.0	+ 5.0	+5.6	+ 5.2	+ 5.4
1957–58	+ 5.1	+ 6.6	+ 6.0	+ 3.7	+ 4.1	− 0.3	+ 4.5	+1.8	+ 2.6	+ 2.9
1958–59	+ 9.0	+ 7.0	+ 2.4	+ 5.2	+ 6.6	+ 6.4	+ 7.1	+5.8	+ 5.8	+ 6.3
1959–60	+ 4.5	+ 5.4	+ 5.4	+ 2.9	+ 2.9	+ 3.7	+ 4.6	+3.9	+ 4.6	+ 4.1
1960–61	+ 6.0	+ 5.8	+ 3.3	+ 5.3	+ 5.6	+ 1.8	+ 5.2	+3.1	+ 4.1	+ 3.9
1961–62	+ 7.6	+ 7.8	+ 6.3	+ 5.0	+ 5.8	+ 5.7	+ 7.5	+5.5	+ 5.9	+ 6.2
1962–63	+ 6.4	+ 3.2	+ 3.9	+ 5.5	+ 6.9	+ 4.9	+ 6.5	+3.8	+ 4.3	+ 5.0
1963–64	+ 6.9	+ 4.6	+ 3.8	+ 6.8	+ 6.1	+ 6.8	+ 8.7	+6.1	+ 6.0	+ 6.5
1964–65	+ 6.0	+ 6.1	+ 8.7	+ 7.0	+ 7.8	+ 8.5	+ 8.1	+6.0	+ 6.6	+ 7.2

TABLE E-2

Nonagricultural Employment by Nine Regions 1948–65

Nonagricultural Employment (thousands of persons)

Year or Period	Pacific	Mountain	West North Central	West South Central	East South Central	East North Central	South Atlantic	Middle Atlantic	New England	U.S. Total
1948	4,334	1,168	3,525	3,224	2,242	10,327	5,420	10,979	3,373	44,891
1949	4,230	1,169	3,493	3,218	2,160	9,936	5,325	10,623	3,234	43,778
1950	4,384	1,223	3,608	3,333	2,247	10,368	5,564	10,876	3,345	45,222
1951	4,773	1,376	3,798	3,596	2,401	10,940	5,964	11,361	3,506	47,849
1952	5,018	1,376	3,879	3,736	2,467	11,071	6,153	11,450	3,514	48,825
1953	5,170	1,403	3,946	3,791	2,521	11,569	6,233	11,696	3,586	50,232
1954	5,140	1,386	3,880	3,751	2,458	11,055	6,122	11,342	3,492	49,022
1955	5,411	1,453	3,943	3,889	2,545	11,503	6,392	11,530	3,549	50,675
1956	5,715	1,539	4,032	4,064	2,635	11,750	6,690	11,852	3,647	52,408
1957	5,896	1,597	4,058	4,155	2,665	11,724	6,828	11,991	3,648	52,894
1958	5,852	1,622	4,012	4,125	2,634	11,071	6,784	11,600	3,534	51,368
1959	6,182	1,701	4,134	4,235	2,716	11,473	7,052	11,778	3,651	53,085
1960	6,321	1,770	4,194	4,270	2,760	11,643	7,213	11,917	3,707	54,203
1961	6,433	1,817	4,187	4,287	2,765	11,367	7,274	11,832	3,727	53,989
1962	6,729	1,877	4,272	4,418	2,861	11,662	7,550	12,056	3,799	55,515
1963	6,947	1,921	4,342	4,544	2,962	11,887	7,818	12,105	3,817	56,602
1964	7,162	1,956	4,446	4,710	3,071	12,244	8,121	12,324	3,872	58,156
1965	7,428	2,001	4,597	4,916	3,231	12,833	8,518	12,680	4,010	60,444

(continued)

TABLE E-2 (concluded)

Percentage Change In Nonagricultural Employment

Year or Period	Pacific	Mountain	West North Central	West South Central	East South Central	East North Central	South Atlantic	Middle Atlantic	New England	U.S. Total
1948–49	-2.4	0.1	-0.9	-0.2	-3.7	-3.8	-1.8	-3.2	-4.1	-2.5
1949–50	3.6	4.6	3.3	3.6	4.0	4.3	4.5	2.4	3.4	3.3
1950–51	8.9	7.6	5.3	7.9	6.9	5.5	7.2	4.5	4.8	5.8
1951–52	5.1	4.6	2.1	3.9	2.7	1.2	3.2	0.8	0.2	2.0
1952–53	3.0	2.0	1.7	1.5	2.2	4.5	1.3	2.1	2.0	2.9
1953–54	-0.6	-1.2	-1.7	-1.1	-2.5	-4.4	-1.8	-3.0	-2.6	-2.4
1954–55	5.3	4.8	1.6	3.7	3.5	4.1	4.4	1.7	1.6	3.4
1955–56	5.6	5.9	2.3	4.5	3.5	2.1	4.7	2.8	2.8	3.4
1956–57	3.2	3.8	0.6	2.2	1.1	-0.2	2.1	1.2	0.0	0.9
1957–58	-0.7	1.6	-1.1	-0.7	-1.2	-5.6	-0.6	-3.3	-3.1	-2.9
1958–59	5.6	4.9	3.0	2.7	3.1	3.6	4.0	1.5	3.3	3.3
1959–60	2.2	4.1	1.5	0.8	1.6	1.5	2.3	1.2	1.5	1.6
1960–61	1.8	2.7	-0.2	0.4	0.2	-2.4	0.8	-0.7	0.5	-0.4
1961–62	4.6	3.3	2.0	3.1	3.5	2.6	3.8	1.9	1.9	2.8
1962–63	3.2	2.3	1.6	2.9	3.5	1.9	3.5	0.4	0.5	2.0
1963–64	3.1	1.8	2.4	3.7	3.7	3.0	3.9	1.8	1.4	2.7
1964–65	3.7	2.3	3.4	4.4	5.2	4.8	4.9	2.9	3.6	3.9

TABLE E-3

Delinquency Rates on Automobile Loans Reported by Banks, Nine Regions, 1948–64

Delinquency Rate, Direct Loans (per cent)

Annual Average or Period	Pacific	Mountain	West North Central	West South Central	East South Central	East North Central	South Atlantic	Middle Atlantic	New England	U.S. Total
1948	1.362	2.130	1.791	1.263	1.459	1.112	1.529	2.066	2.070	1.642
1949	1.538	2.026	2.027	1.363	1.984	1.579	1.559	1.848	1.844	1.752
1950	1.337	1.673	1.393	.883	1.607	.999	1.311	1.758	1.835	1.422
1951	.820	1.191	1.491	.804	1.865	.891	1.095	1.588	1.359	1.234
1952	.715	.986	1.151	.870	.792	.826	.882	1.212	.939	.930
1953	.921	1.494	1.040	1.158	.706	.556	1.128	.973	.875	.983
1954	1.054	1.609	1.347	1.194	.636	.877	.845	.904	.949	1.046
1955	.678	1.168	1.121	.983	.520	.534	.602	.601	.838	.817
1956	.614	1.283	1.016	.746	.516	.575	.607	.430	.792	.760
1957	.671	1.509	.940	.704	.561	.424	.577	.399	.808	.753
1958	.693	1.634	1.120	.647	.625	.597	.667	.478	.833	.840
1959	.658	1.632	.952	.749	.555	.568	.640	.522	.596	.781
1960	1.052	1.762	1.112	.862	.756	.634	.841	.562	.729	.944
1961	1.225	1.793	1.223	1.019	.894	.781	1.001	.618	.748	1.054
1962	1.241	1.678	1.003	.777	.974	.667	.867	.543	.678	.946
1963	1.403	1.563	.870	.936	1.068	.644	.760	.569	.698	.937
1964	1.243	1.649	.933	.950	.979	.574	.806	.610	.776	.945

(continued)

TABLE E-3 (continued)

Change In Delinquency Rate, Direct Loans (per cent)

Annual Average or Period	Pacific	Mountain	West North Central	West South Central	East South Central	East North Central	South Atlantic	Middle Atlantic	New England	U.S. Total
1948–49	+.176	−.104	+.236	+.100	+.525	+.467	+.030	−.218	−.226	+.110
1949–50	−.201	−.353	−.634	−.480	−.377	−.580	−.248	−.090	−.009	−.330
1950–51	−.517	−.482	+.098	−.079	+.258	−.108	−.216	−.170	−.476	−.188
1951–52	−.105	−.205	−.340	+.066	−1.073	−.065	−.213	−.376	−.420	−.304
1952–53	+.206	+.508	−.111	+.288	−.086	−.270	+.246	−.239	−.064	+.053
1953–54	+.133	+.115	+.307	+.036	+.070	+.321	−.283	−.069	+.074	+.063
1954–55	−.376	−.441	−.226	−.211	−.116	−.343	−.243	−.303	−.111	−.229
1955–56	−.064	+.115	−.105	−.237	−.004	+.041	+.005	−.171	−.046	−.057
1956–57	+.057	+.226	−.076	−.042	+.045	−.151	−.030	−.031	+.016	−.007
1957–58	+.022	+.125	+.180	−.057	+.064	+.173	+.090	+.079	+.025	+.087
1958–59	−.035	−.002	−.168	+.102	+.070	−.029	−.027	+.044	−.237	−.059
1959–60	+.394	+.130	+.160	+.113	+.201	+.066	+.201	+.040	+.133	+.163
1960–61	+.173	+.031	+.111	+.157	+.138	+.147	+.160	+.056	+.019	+.110
1961–62	+.016	−.115	−.220	−.242	+.080	−.114	−.134	−.075	−.070	−.108
1962–63	+.162	−.115	−.133	+.159	+.094	−.023	−.107	+.026	+.020	−.009
1963–64	−.160	+.086	+.063	+.014	−.089	−.070	+.046	+.041	+.078	+.008

(continued)

TABLE E-3 (continued)

Delinquency Rate, Indirect Loans (per cent)

Annual Average or Period	Pacific	Mountain	West North Central	West South Central	East South Central	East North Central	South Atlantic	Middle Atlantic	New England	U.S. Total
1948	2.522	2.652	1.577	2.122	.991	1.596	1.926	3.071	2.005	2.051
1949	2.029	2.585	2.371	1.689	1.470	2.288	3.114	2.380	2.221	2.238
1950	2.288	2.707	2.165	1.246	1.533	2.118	1.792	2.122	1.700	1.963
1951	1.390	1.978	2.273	1.625	1.413	1.541	1.598	2.060	1.732	1.734
1952	1.399	1.891	1.484	1.928	.903	1.251	1.121	1.746	1.527	1.472
1953	1.560	2.041	2.156	2.199	1.097	1.282	1.091	1.481	1.907	1.646
1954	1.783	1.984	2.069	1.637	1.645	1.322	1.186	1.793	1.989	1.712
1955	1.287	1.724	1.652	.963	1.675	.766	.820	1.450	2.096	1.408
1956	1.379	1.738	1.533	.988	1.734	.801	.653	1.283	1.926	1.357
1957	1.421	1.925	1.424	.623	2.022	.813	.803	1.233	1.849	1.354
1958	1.540	2.088	1.627	.703	2.188	.976	1.045	1.471	2.062	1.532
1959	1.401	2.163	1.423	.704	1.343	.679	.903	1.337	1.741	1.314
1960	1.699	2.552	1.628	.836	1.198	.914	.991	1.390	1.745	1.459
1961	1.767	2.229	1.757	.879	1.195	1.052	.948	1.419	1.935	1.494
1962	1.500	2.068	1.458	.650	1.332	.874	.802	1.417	1.729	1.331
1963	1.708	2.168	1.296	.779	2.108	.936	.935	1.479	1.451	1.417
1964	1.472	2.273	1.508	.916	2.210	1.219	.909	1.524	1.438	1.497

(continued)

TABLE E-3 (concluded)

Change in Delinquency Rate, Indirect Loans (per cent)

Annual Average or Period	Pacific	Mountain	West North Central	West South Central	East South Central	East North Central	South Atlantic	Middle Atlantic	New England	U.S. Total
1948–49	−.493	−.067	+.794	−.433	+.479	+.692	+1.188	−.691	+.216	+.187
1949–50	+.259	+.122	−.206	−.443	+.063	−.170	−1.322	−.258	−.521	−.275
1950–51	−.898	−.729	+.108	+.379	−.120	−.577	− .194	−.062	+.032	−.229
1951–52	+.009	−.087	−.789	+.303	−.510	−.290	− .477	−.314	−.205	−.262
1952–53	+.161	+.150	+.672	+.271	+.194	+.031	− .030	−.265	+.380	+.174
1953–54	+.223	−.057	−.087	−.562	+.548	+.040	+ .095	+.312	+.082	+.066
1954–55	−.496	−.260	−.417	−.674	+.030	−.556	− .366	−.343	+.107	−.304
1955–56	+.092	+.014	−.119	+.025	+.059	+.035	− .167	−.167	−.170	−.051
1956–57	+.042	+.187	−.109	−.365	+.288	+.012	+ .150	−.050	−.077	−.003
1957–58	+.119	+.163	+.203	+.080	+.166	+.163	+ .242	+.238	+.213	+.178
1958–59	−.139	+.075	−.204	+.001	−.845	−.297	+ .142	−.134	−.321	−.218
1959–60	+.298	+.389	+.205	+.132	−.145	+.235	+ .088	+.053	+.004	+.145
1960–61	+.068	−.323	+.129	+.043	−.003	+.138	+ .043	+.029	+.190	+.035
1961–62	−.267	−.161	−.299	−.229	+.137	−.178	+ .146	−.002	−.206	−.163
1962–63	+.208	+.100	−.162	+.129	+.776	+.062	+ .133	+.062	−.278	+.086
1963–64	−.236	+.105	+.212	+.137	+.082	+.283	− .026	+.045	−.013	+.080

Appendix F: Quarterly Data on Automobile Contract Terms and Collection Experience for Twelve Metropolitan Areas, 1953–56

As is indicated in Chapter 3, data are for January, April, July, and October for 1953 through April 1956. They were provided by a large sales finance company to represent changes in terms and experience in twelve metropolitan areas during this period. These areas were selected on the basis of their employment experience in 1953–55 to encompass the complete spectrum of labor market situations as defined by the Bureau of Employment Security, as well as to cover the country geographically. The period to which the data apply was, of course, basically a fairly prosperous period, but it does include the mild business contraction of July 1953–August 1954. During this recession we have traced a number of the relevant economic variables by means of cross-sectional analysis. The twelve metropolitan areas and their classification with respect to adequacy of labor supply are:

	July 1953	July 1954	July 1955
Hartford	I	II	B
New York City	III	III	C
Philadelphia	III	IV-A	D
Atlanta	II	II	B
Pittsburgh	III	IV-A	D
Chicago	II	III	C
St. Louis	II	IV-A	C
Indianapolis	II	III	C
Detroit	II	IV-A	C
Dallas	II	II	B
Denver	II	II	B
Los Angeles	III	III	C

Source: *Labor Market and Employment Security*, U.S. Bureau of Employment Security, selected issues. The Bureau changed its classification in June 1955, hence the two sets of symbols. The two classifications are:

I. Labor shortage
II. Balanced labor supply
III. Moderate labor surplus
IV-A. Substantial labor surplus
IV-B. Very substantial labor surplus

A. Critical shortage
B. Few more jobs than people
C. Few more people than jobs
D. More people than jobs
E. Considerable labor excess
F. Substantial labor excess

TABLE F-1

Number of New-Automobile Contracts, Twelve Metropolitan Areas, 1953–56

Index, January 1953:100

	Area											
	A	B	C	D	E	F	G	H	I	J	K	L
1953												
Jan.	100.0	100.0	100.0	100.0	100.0	100.0	100.0	100.0	100.0	100.0	100.0	100.0
Apr.	141.3	162.2	117.3	123.1	170.0	165.8	140.2	150.9	207.1	137.1	143.8	129.2
July	165.8	172.8	118.0	120.7	161.8	172.8	154.2	174.6	220.2	155.8	146.9	138.1
Oct.	155.8	165.1	114.2	110.7	89.3	155.1	140.0	143.4	201.1	143.5	122.4	142.9
1954												
Jan.	106.8	105.4	78.8	73.8	45.2	80.6	67.1	94.4	110.2	86.7	70.4	87.8
Apr.	142.2	166.2	107.3	103.6	102.4	158.7	100.9	147.6	214.1	123.8	102.7	128.3
July	163.8	197.6	138.2	129.5	96.0	183.0	133.2	142.5	238.3	132.4	118.0	143.3
Oct.	122.7	161.4	139.7	110.7	94.9	148.3	100.6	139.6	237.2	136.4	92.4	125.0
1955												
Jan.	122.8	136.1	123.9	91.2	101.9	114.7	96.3	130.6	194.2	113.6	74.7	98.3
Apr.	183.9	246.7	192.0	137.0	160.2	179.8	167.3	184.2	277.0	172.1	135.9	164.2
July	225.7	233.4	209.4	170.5	195.1	210.0	205.8	234.3	285.3	207.2	163.9	200.5
Oct.	230.0•	294.8	236.0	185.8	226.6	198.1	201.3	256.2	306.5	234.9	163.4	198.8
1956												
Jan.	188.9	208.6	167.9	130.1	131.7	156.6	140.1	189.2	207.4	175.9	124.4	142.3
Apr.	177.5	215.8	151.4	137.0	107.7	160.6	153.3	156.5	240.3	159.7	149.9	166.5
Annual averages												
1953	140.7	150.0	112.4	113.6	130.3	148.4	133.6	142.2	182.1	134.1	128.3	127.6
1954	133.9	157.6	116.0	104.4	84.6	142.6	100.4	131.0	200.0	119.8	95.9	121.1
1955	190.6	227.8	190.3	146.1	171.0	175.6	167.7	201.3	265.8	182.0	134.5	165.4
1955 (Jan. & Apr.)	153.4	191.4	158.0	114.1	131.0	147.2	131.8	157.4	235.6	142.8	105.3	131.2
1956 (Jan. & Apr.)	183.2	212.2	159.6	133.6	119.8	158.6	146.7	172.8	223.8	167.8	137.2	154.4

TABLE F-2

New-Automobile Contracts with Down Payment of Less than 33 Per Cent, As Percentage of Total Contracts, Twelve Metropolitan Areas, 1953–56

	A	B	C	D	E	F	G	H	I	J	K	L
1953												
Jan.	15.6	19.3	30.1	13.7	29.7	9.8	8.7	27.2	7.3	4.7	7.7	10.9
Apr.	12.6	7.8	23.7	8.7	17.1	9.6	7.5	30.1	4.5	3.7	6.8	10.6
July	13.3	13.5	20.0	11.8	21.0	7.8	10.7	33.2	5.2	4.0	7.3	10.0
Oct.	17.7	9.1	17.8	8.9	14.7	6.0	12.1	37.4	1.9	3.9	8.5	11.4
1954												
Jan.	13.6	11.5	23.4	9.4	11.9	8.2	14.4	39.9	2.7	5.0	8.6	11.1
Apr.	16.7	13.8	23.1	10.1	12.4	11.6	15.4	39.4	5.9	5.2	8.1	15.9
July	25.1	22.9	28.2	20.2	17.1	14.7	24.8	37.3	13.0	11.2	11.0	19.8
Oct.	24.5	21.9	27.8	20.3	20.5	17.0	27.6	40.9	13.2	9.4	9.7	18.7
1955												
Jan.	29.2	30.2	33.7	22.7	30.2	17.0	26.1	41.3	20.5	16.0	12.4	21.8
Apr.	33.7	29.4	42.1	20.9	36.5	21.1	29.1	47.4	18.7	14.7	17.5	27.1
July	41.3	33.0	45.5	33.3	41.0	21.0	34.7	51.5	22.8	20.1	25.4	33.5
Oct.	43.3	31.0	51.2	26.2	41.0	18.4	32.3	54.9	22.8	17.6	19.7	31.8
1956												
Jan.	42.8	29.9	56.0	29.9	35.5	23.9	30.7	57.3	18.8	23.7	30.8	35.1
Apr.	36.8	33.2	57.2	33.8	38.2	23.6	31.6	57.5	20.9	19.8	21.5	37.2
Annual averages												
1953	14.8	12.4	22.9	10.8	20.6	8.3	9.8	32.0	4.7	4.1	7.6	10.7
1954	20.0	17.5	25.6	15.0	15.5	12.9	20.6	39.4	8.7	7.7	9.4	16.4
1955	36.9	30.9	43.1	25.8	37.2	19.4	30.6	48.8	21.1	17.1	18.8	28.6
1955 (Jan. & Apr.)	31.4	29.8	37.9	21.8	33.4	19.0	27.6	44.4	19.6	15.4	15.0	24.4
1956 (Jan. & Apr.)	39.8	31.6	56.6	31.8	36.8	23.8	31.2	57.4	19.8	21.8	26.2	36.2

TABLE F-3

New-Automobile Contracts with Maturities 25 Months and Over as Percentage of Total Contracts,
Twelve Metropolitan Areas, 1953–56

	A	B	C	D	E	F	G	H	I	J	K	L
							Area					
1953												
Jan.	0		0.2	0.2	0.5	1.6	0.3	63.3	20.3	19.9	6.7	1.1
Apr.	0	0.5	0.4	1.8	9.1	13.1	1.4	62.9	21.3	18.5	7.7	0.9
July	0	1.1	1.5	2.4	11.0	13.1	4.7	64.9	9.4	16.1	5.7	3.4
Oct.	0.1	1.9	0.1	1.5	9.9	7.6	7.6	69.0	6.4	15.9	10.9	4.6
1954												
Jan.	3.3	3.9	0	3.2	8.4	12.4	9.8	69.9	10.7	17.4	9.8	5.7
Apr.	9.1	11.5	27.2	13.1	12.6	25.6	20.6	67.7	20.3	21.6	12.8	17.7
July	26.5	30.8	44.0	32.9	32.6	39.8	42.3	70.8	42.7	45.4	22.8	36.0
Oct.	42.7	41.1	58.4	37.7	44.8	47.9	49.9	77.6	48.0	52.3	37.6	46.5
1955												
Jan.	45.0	42.6	59.3	41.4	47.0	42.5	49.7	69.9	54.9	50.4	40.3	45.9
Apr.	52.1	53.2	68.8	46.3	59.8	49.7	60.5	75.0	59.9	59.3	49.6	55.7
July	54.1	59.0	74.4	56.1	67.9	56.9	69.0	79.6	59.9	66.3	64.1	63.8
Oct.	71.2	62.5	74.9	55.5	68.5	59.2	72.7	82.1	65.3	69.9	67.1	65.6
1956												
Jan.	68.4	58.8	74.1	56.5	58.2	56.2	72.9	79.7	51.8	71.1	66.2	65.9
Apr.	69.7	61.7	72.7	59.2	62.8	65.3	67.9	76.4	61.3	73.7	65.4	71.3
Annual averages												
1953	0.0	0.9	0.6	1.5	7.6	8.8	3.5	65.0	14.4	17.6	7.8	2.5
1954	20.4	21.8	32.4	21.7	24.6	31.4	30.6	71.5	30.4	34.2	20.8	26.5
1955	55.6	54.3	69.4	49.8	60.8	52.1	63.0	76.6	59.9	61.5	55.3	57.8
1955 (Jan. & Apr.)	48.6	47.9	64.0	43.8	53.4	46.1	55.1	72.4	57.2	54.8	45.0	50.8
1956 (Jan. & Apr.)	69.0	60.2	73.4	57.8	60.5	60.8	70.4	78.0	56.6	72.4	65.8	68.6

TABLE F-4

Number of New-Car Repossessions During Month as Percentage of Accounts Purchased over Preceding Twelve Months, Twelve Metropolitan Areas, 1953–56

	A	B	C	D	E	F	G	H	I	J	K	L
1953												
Jan.	.087	.063	.069	.109	.030	.072	.051	.088	.117	.069	.049	.055
Apr.	.063	.059	.149	.143	.035	.050	.028	.095	.073	.037	.038	.030
July	.083	.055	.168	.066	.050	.034	.062	.087	.074	.061	.044	.072
Oct.	.130	.097	.142	.144	.122	.042	.057	.098	.160	.092	.037	.091
1954												
Jan.	.179	.114	.315	.286	.130	.085	.143	.214	.181	.153	.161	.132
Apr.	.140	.096	.251	.202	.095	.011	.134	.249	.141	.085	.143	.136
July	.216	.079	.176	.149	.204	.088	.111	.231	.139	.143	.170	.117
Oct.	.195	.100	.231	.169	.166	.033	.109	.307	.215	.177	.157	.140
1955												
Jan.	.266	.107	.242	.241	.109	.156	.187	.338	.199	.153	.156	.170
Apr.	.180	.073	.259	.113	.112	.049	.091	.237	.154	.161	.115	.100
July	.172	.056	.281	.139	.083	.103	.087	.276	.129	.139	.085	.079
Oct.	.199	.140	.410	.254	.174	.132	.101	.275	.280	.214	.129	.144
1956												
Jan.	.448	.199	.685	.414	.189	.239	.181	.599	.262	.334	.156	.239
Apr.	.270	.133	.610	.361	.370	.187	.186	.516	.249	.287	.127	.190
Annual averages												
1953	.091	.068	.132	.116	.059	.050	.050	.092	.106	.065	.042	.062
1954	.182	.097	.243	.202	.149	.054	.124	.250	.169	.140	.158	.131
1955	.204	.094	.298	.187	.120	.110	.116	.282	.190	.167	.121	.123
1955 (Jan. & Apr.)	.223	.090	.250	.177	.110	.102	.139	.288	.176	.157	.136	.135
1956 (Jan. & Apr.)	.359	.166	.648	.388	.280	.213	.184	.558	.256	.310	.142	.214

TABLE F-5

Estimated Repossession Rates, New-Automobile Contracts (Estimated by a Two-Year Weighted Moving Average to Approximate Rates for Loans as of Year of Purchase), Twelve Metropolitan Areas, 1953-55

	Area												Average of 12 Areas
	A	B	C	D	E	F	G	H	I	J	K	L	
1953													
Jan.	1.3	1.0	1.6	1.6	0.8	0.8	0.8	1.5	2.1	0.9	0.7	0.8	1.2
Apr.	1.1	0.8	1.8	1.5	0.6	0.5	0.7	1.3	1.1	0.8	0.6	0.8	1.0
July	1.3	0.9	2.1	1.7	0.9	0.5	0.8	1.4	1.3	0.9	0.8	1.1	1.1
Oct.	1.7	1.1	2.5	2.4	1.9	0.6	1.1	2.2	1.8	1.3	1.3	1.2	1.6
1954													
Jan.	2.9	1.8	4.3	3.9	3.6	1.4	2.7	4.3	3.5	2.4	2.9	2.2	3.0
Apr.	2.3	1.1	3.0	2.2	1.5	0.7	1.7	3.0	1.8	1.7	1.9	1.5	1.9
July	2.3	0.9	2.7	1.8	1.9	0.8	1.2	3.3	1.9	1.9	1.6	1.4	1.8
Oct.	3.3	1.3	3.5	2.4	1.8	1.2	1.8	4.0	2.2	2.2	1.9	1.8	2.3
1955													
Jan.	3.8	1.8	5.1	3.4	2.0	2.1	2.2	4.9	2.9	2.9	2.4	2.5	3.0
Apr.	2.6	1.1	4.2	2.4	1.6	1.3	1.2	3.9	2.1	2.3	1.3	1.5	2.1
Annual averages													
1953	1.4	1.0	2.0	1.8	1.0	0.6	0.8	1.6	1.6	1.0	0.9	1.0	1.2
1954	2.7	1.3	3.4	2.6	2.2	1.0	1.8	3.6	2.4	2.0	2.1	1.7	2.2
1955 (Jan. & Apr.)	3.2	1.4	4.6	2.9	1.8	1.7	1.7	4.4	2.5	2.6	1.8	2.0	2.5

Notes To Table F-5

Note: Inasmuch as the estimated repossession rates presented in this table have been utilized extensively in the text, it is appropriate to describe the method used for estimating repossession rates and the reasons why such estimation was necessary.

Repossession, if it is to occur, does so over a period of time after the purchase of an automobile; the down payment and maturity information presented as of the end of a year cannot properly be related to the actual repossession data for the same calendar year. Nor could any simple lagged relation significantly improve the correspondence.

The National Bureau obtained information from a large sales finance company indicating nationally the number of instalments paid before repossession occurred. About 89 per cent of all repossessions occur within the first year. By assuming arbitrarily that the rest occurred within the second year very little distortion was introduced by extrapolating the known time distribution for the first year and it was possible to obtain the following percentage distribution of the proportion of repossessions which would have occurred every three months for two years following the purchase of a car:

Number of Instalments Paid Prior to Repossession	Percentage of All Repossessions Occurring from Date of Loan Purchase
0–2 (1st Q)	34.3
3–5 (2nd Q)	26.0
6–8 (3rd Q)	17.6
9–11 (4th Q)	11.3
12–14 (5th Q)	6.8
15–17 (6th Q)	3.0
18–20 (7th Q)	.5
21 and over (8th Q)	.5
	100.0

These percentages were utilized as a moving sum in order to relate the number of repossessions to the time the loans were purchased. This method of weighting the repossession data was tested with aggregate data and found to be superior to any simple lagged method of estimating repossession rates as of the time the loan was purchased both for new-and used-automobile loans. Hence it was applied to the local area data to estimate repossession rates as of the time loans were purchased.

Because of the utilization of the moving sum method, the last three months (October, January, April) are subject to increasing error in the estimate due to the fact that the two year (8 point) moving sum is based on seven, six, and five observations respectively (adjusted to 8-point coverage). This means that a small fraction of loans is lost in the estimates, which understate the repossession rate estimate.

TABLE F-6

Late Model Used-Automobile Contracts with Down Payment of Less Than 33 Per Cent as Percentage of Total Contracts, Twelve Metropolitan Areas, 1953–56

	Area											
	A	B	C	D	E	F	G	H	I	J	K	L
1953												
Jan.	15.6	19.3	30.1	13.7	29.7	9.8	14.0	34.1	20.0	7.4	8.8	19.6
Apr.	17.2	19.1	28.9	16.8	29.9	12.6	12.3	46.4	6.5	9.2	8.9	23.4
July	15.9	25.8	23.5	18.4	38.5	13.5	12.7	39.3	2.5	9.0	8.0	22.7
Oct.	12.6	14.7	22.0	10.7	13.9	12.8	14.9	27.2	2.7	5.8	10.4	21.6
1954												
Jan.	14.5	11.8	17.6	15.0	8.4	16.2	13.1	18.2	1.2	6.0	8.9	16.3
Apr.	20.4	24.9	26.2	13.4	17.3	17.2	11.4	21.1	8.3	6.9	7.9	23.3
July	24.1	31.6	32.2	26.0	17.8	20.0	20.6	14.0	8.9	12.0	8.2	27.0
Oct.	22.3	29.1	35.7	22.7	13.3	19.5	19.3	27.6	11.1	13.4	8.0	24.8
1955												
Jan.	28.4	42.0	36.2	28.3	33.9	18.9	21.8	34.6	12.4	16.8	10.3	30.6
Apr.	35.7	42.2	35.9	33.8	44.4	27.0	24.3	36.7	19.4	17.6	11.5	32.1
July	39.3	48.0	48.6	34.5	32.9	23.9	29.1	38.8	15.9	21.6	14.7	35.8
Oct.	35.5	50.5	57.2	34.3	30.3	27.1	26.3	45.6	33.2	19.8	16.3	35.3
1956												
Jan.	41.9	49.2	59.0	41.4	33.5	29.3	24.2	46.3	28.3	25.9	16.6	42.7
Apr.	44.2	54.0	72.1	41.9	30.9	31.6	22.4	46.1	33.2	23.9	18.1	43.3
Annual averages												
1953	15.3	19.7	26.1	14.9	28.0	12.2	13.5	39.2	7.2	7.8	9.0	21.8
1954	20.3	24.4	27.9	19.3	14.2	18.2	16.1	22.7	7.4	9.6	8.2	22.8
1955	34.7	45.7	47.0	32.7	35.4	24.5	25.4	38.9	19.7	19.0	13.2	33.4
1956 (Jan. & Apr.)	43.0	51.6	65.6	41.6	32.2	30.4	23.3	46.2	30.8	24.9	17.4	43.0

TABLE F-7

Late Model Used-Automobile Contracts with Maturities of over 18 Months or 25 Months or Longer as Percentage of Total Contracts, Twelve Metropolitan Areas, 1953–56

	A	B	C	D	E	F	G	H	I	J	K	L
							Area					
Percentage With Maturities Over 18 Months												
1953												
Jan.	45.2	48.7	46.5	37.3	64.5	49.9	56.1	84.7	61.1	68.2	52.0	48.6
Apr.	41.9	50.7	45.1	38.6	62.3	53.5	48.7	79.0	68.5	59.8	46.6	48.9
July	49.2	64.2	49.4	46.7	70.1	57.9	59.5	79.0	76.0	69.3	57.5	51.4
Oct.	40.8	43.3	43.7	35.3	50.9	51.9	57.2	74.3	71.6	66.5	57.6	47.7
Percentage With Maturities 25 Months Or Longer												
1953												
Jan.	0	0	0.2	0.2	0.5	1.6	0	26.9	4.2	1.9	0.5	0
Apr.	0	0	0.4	0.4	0.3	2.9	0.1	16.3	2.5	3.9	1.1	0.1
July	0	0	0.2	0.2	0.2	1.8	0.2	12.7	0.6	2.1	0.1	0.2
Oct.	0	0	0.2	0.2	0	0.5	0.1	2.3	1.1	0.2	0	0
1954												
Jan.	0.7	0	0	0	0	1.5	0.1	4.3	1.2	1.2	0.6	0.3
Apr.	0.2	2.6	0.3	0.6	0.8	6.4	2.3	6.3	2.4	0.7	0.6	0.8
July	0.2	3.6	0.6	1.9	0.4	10.7	2.4	8.0	3.4	3.5	0.6	2.8
Oct.	0	5.1	0.7	0.3	0.5	3.3	2.7	6.4	4.0	2.0	1.4	0.8

(continued)

TABLE F-7 (Concluded)

	Area											
	A	B	C	D	E	F	G	H	I	J	K	L
1955												
Jan.	1.3	6.2	1.1	2.0	4.3	7.4	3.2	13.8	4.3	3.5	2.8	4.3
Apr.	3.3	6.7	8.2	1.8	4.2	16.8	6.3	14.5	4.4	9.1	4.2	6.5
July	3.3	11.3	9.1	4.1	2.2	11.0	9.1	12.5	12.6	6.7	4.3	4.6
Oct.	4.3	8.3	7.6	2.8	2.1	6.9	8.6	10.5	0	4.2	3.6	3.3
1956												
Jan.	12.4	22.2	13.4	8.5	7.0	12.0	8.3	23.5	7.8	11.3	9.5	8.5
Apr.	13.6	15.8	18.6	10.5	5.4	12.1	8.9	22.3	10.4	9.7	11.8	11.3

Percentage With Maturities Over 18 Months

	A	B	C	D	E	F	G	H	I	J	K	L
Annual averages 1953	44.3	51.7	46.2	39.5	61.9	53.3	55.4	79.2	69.3	66.0	53.4	49.0

Percentage With Maturities 25 Months Or Longer

	A	B	C	D	E	F	G	H	I	J	K	L
1953	0	0	0.2	0.2	0.2	1.7	0.1	14.6	2.1	2.0	0.4	0.1
1954	0.3	2.8	0.4	0.7	0.4	5.5	1.9	6.2	2.8	1.8	0.8	1.1
1955	3.0	8.1	6.0	2.7	3.2	10.5	6.8	12.8	5.3	5.9	3.7	4.7
1956 (Jan. & Apr.)	13.0	19.0	16.0	9.5	6.2	12.0	8.6	22.9	9.1	10.5	10.6	9.9

TABLE F-8

Estimated Repossession Rates, Used-Automobile Contracts, Twelve Metropolitan Areas, 1953-55

	Area												Average of 12 Areas
	A	B	C	D	E	F	G	H	I	J	K	L	
1953													
Jan.	14.7	8.1	14.4	11.3	5.3	5.8	9.3	8.3	5.7	8.0	9.4	11.6	9.4
Apr.	9.6	4.2	10.8	8.2	2.4	2.5	5.5	6.5	2.9	5.1	5.5	7.0	5.8
July	10.2	5.3	13.5	9.3	4.1	2.6	5.6	6.8	3.8	5.8	6.2	8.5	6.8
Oct.	15.0	8.7	15.9	13.4	9.1	5.4	10.3	10.0	6.4	8.9	11.5	11.8	10.5
1954													
Jan.	24.0	14.6	21.5	19.4	19.7	9.5	19.2	14.4	11.3	16.2	20.4	19.0	17.4
Apr.	13.8	6.7	12.8	10.8	10.6	7.0	10.4	8.7	4.6	8.4	12.2	11.5	9.8
July	14.0	6.6	11.8	10.4	10.5	5.4	8.2	8.6	5.5	7.1	10.6	10.5	9.1
Oct.	16.2	8.5	15.4	11.2	11.3	7.1	10.7	9.6	8.5	10.8	14.3	12.8	11.4
1955													
Jan.	15.5	7.5	14.7	10.9	5.9	8.0	9.5	9.1	9.1	10.7	12.0	12.9	10.5
Apr.	11.3	4.5	10.4	8.1	4.3	4.8	5.4	6.9	6.1	7.8	6.3	7.8	7.0
July	13.0	5.5	13.7	9.2	5.0	6.1	6.9	8.1	7.1	8.6	6.6	8.9	8.2
Oct.	15.8	7.3	16.4	11.5	8.0	8.4	8.3	10.6	10.8	11.4	9.0	10.7	10.7
Annual averages													
1953	12.4	6.6	13.6	10.6	5.2	4.1	7.7	7.9	5.0	7.0	8.2	9.7	8.2
1954	17.0	9.1	15.4	13.0	13.0	7.2	12.1	10.2	7.5	10.6	14.4	13.4	11.9
1955	13.9	6.2	13.8	9.9	5.8	6.8	7.5	8.7	8.3	9.6	8.5	10.1	9.1

Notes To Table F-8

Note: See note to Table F-5 for discussion of estimating procedure. Distribution of the proportion of repossessions which would have occurred every three months for two years following the purchase of a used car:

Number of Instalments Paid Prior to Repossession	Percentage of All Repossessions Occurring Quarterly From Date of Loan Purchase	Percentage of All Repossessions Occurring Quarterly From Date of Loan Purchase Adjusted to 1 Year Limit
0−2 (1st Q)	48.4	50.4
3−5 (2nd Q)	27.8	28.8
6−8 (3rd Q)	15.2	15.8
9−11 (4th Q)	5.0	5.0
12−14 (5th Q)		
15−17 (6th Q)	3.6	
18−20 (7th Q)		
21 and over (8th Q)		
	100.0	100.0*

*The percentages in this column were obtained by redistributing the 3.6 per cent of the second year after the purchase so as to give 100 per cent, on the assumption that all loans repossessed are repossessed within one year of the date the loan was purchased. Because of utilization of the moving sum method, the last month (October 1955) is estimated from three observations representing 95 per cent of the repossessions. It was adjusted to 100 per cent coverage, but the small fraction of repossessions thus lost causes minor understatement of the repossession rate for October 1955.

Appendix G: Some Evidence on the Effect of Credit Terms on Credit Volume

As noted in Chapter 1, the long-run upward trend in the volume of instalment credit extended in the United States has gone hand in hand with a general easing of credit terms, notably longer maturities and lower down payments. Over the short-run, also, there is evidence that an easing or tightening of terms has a corresponding effect on credit volume. Indeed, competitive practices suggest that an easing of terms is one of the important means available to lenders to achieve an increase in volume or prevent a decline. The federal government has used the credit terms instrument as a way of restricting the availability of credit. Insofar as changes in terms are associated with changes in credit quality, a connection between credit quality and quantity can be traced.

Some evidence on the relationship between credit terms and volume is provided by our local area data (Table G-1). Charts G-1 and G-2 show that areas in which the proportion of new-auto contracts with low down payments or long maturities increased the most also experienced the largest increases in the number of contracts during 1953–56. This is particularly clear when all the observations plotted are considered together, but it is also true to a degree in each of the three year-to-year periods taken separately. In 1954–55, when terms eased most rapidly, volume increased most rapidly. In 1953–54 and 1955–56, when terms eased less rapidly or tightened in a few areas, volume declined or rose only slightly.

It is interesting to note the indications in the data that without any easing of terms during this period, credit volume would have declined. This is clearly suggested by the data for 1955–56, but can also be inferred from the slope of the scatters in 1953–54 and 1954–55. That is to say, if a line through these points were extended to the left through

Year-to-Year Change in Down Payments and Volume of New-
Automobile Contracts, Twelve Metropolitan Areas, 1953–56

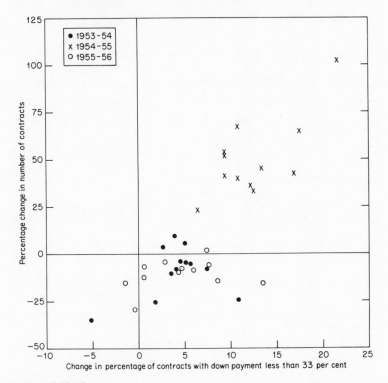

SOURCE: Table G-1.

the zero line on the horizontal scale (no change in down payments or
maturities), it would cut the vertical axis below its zero point, indicating a decline in volume. This impression from the chart is confirmed
by the regression analysis summarized in Table G-2, since the constant term in these regressions is negative in three cases out of four.

The regression analysis also attempts to take account of the possibility
that changes in maturities and down payments each have an effect on
credit volume. The coefficients of both variables are statistically significant in most of the regression equations, indicating that down payments and maturities each independently have an influence on credit
volume.

CHART G-2

Year-to-Year Change in Maturities and Volume of New-Automobile Contracts, Twelve Metropolitan Areas, 1953–56

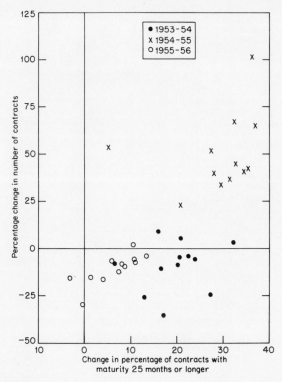

SOURCE: Table G-1.

TABLE G-1

Year-to-Year Changes in Volume, Down Payments and Maturities of New-Automobile Contracts, Twelve Metropolitan Areas, 1953–56

Area	Percentage Change in Number of Contracts			Change in Percentage of Down Payments of Less Than 33 Per Cent			Change in Percentage of Contracts With Maturities of 25 Months or More		
	1953–54	1954–55	1955–56	1953–54	1954–55	1955–56	1953–54	1954–55	1955–56
A	-4.8	42.3	-3.9	5.2	16.9	2.9	20.4	35.2	13.4
B	5.1	44.5	-6.8	5.1	13.4	0.7	20.9	32.5	5.9
C	3.2	64.1	-16.1	2.7	17.5	13.5	31.8	37.0	4.0
D	-8.1	39.9	-8.6	4.2	10.8	6.0	20.2	28.1	8.0
E	-35.1	102.1	-29.9	-5.1	21.7	-0.4	17.0	36.2	-0.3
F	-3.9	23.1	-9.7	4.6	6.5	4.4	22.6	20.7	8.7
G	-24.9	67.0	-12.5	10.8	10.8	0.6	27.1	32.4	7.4
H	-7.9	53.7	-14.2	7.4	9.4	8.6	6.5	5.1	1.4
I	9.8	32.9	-15.8	4.0	12.5	-1.4	16.0	29.5	-3.3
J	-10.7	51.9	-7.8	3.6	9.4	4.7	16.6	27.3	10.9
K	-25.3	40.3	2.0	1.8	9.4	7.4	13.0	34.5	10.5
L	-5.1	36.6	-6.7	5.7	12.2	7.6	24.0	31.3	10.8

Source: A large sales finance company. See Appendix F.

Note: Changes are computed from annual averages based on data for January, April, July and October, except that the 1956 average is for January and April only. The 1955–56 changes are therefore affected by seasonal variations, but the effect seems to be slight.

TABLE G-2

Regression Analysis of Credit Volume on Credit Terms, 1953–56

	1953–54	1954–55	1955–56 (2Q)	1953–56 (2Q)
No. of observations	12	12	12	36
Regression coefficients[a]				
a	1.13 (1.13)	3.79 (1.41)	.10 (.40)	3.23 (.72)
b	.29 (.63)	-.45 (.69)	1.18 (.34)	.95 (.34)
c	-19.33 (13.21)	15.75 (18.09)	-18.88 (2.95)	-30.25 (6.14)
T values for				
a	1.00	2.69 (S)	.25	4.50 (S)
b	.46	-.66	3.43 (S)	2.75 (S)
c	-1.46	.87	-6.39 (S)	-4.93 (S)
Multiple corr. coeff.	.36	.70 (S)	.77 (S)	.82 (S)
Simple corr. coeff.				
D and *N*	.34	.68 (S)	.25	.77 (S)
M and *N*	.19	.26	.77 (S)	.68 (S)
M and *D*	.15	.58 (S)	.26	.60 (S)

Source: Table G-1.

Note: Standard errors of regression coefficients are shown in parentheses.

[a]The regression equation is $N = aD + bM + c$ where

N: year-to-year percentage change in number of new-automobile contracts.

D: year-to-year change in percentage of contracts with down payment less than 33 per cent.

M: year-to-year change in per cent of contracts with maturity twenty-five months or longer.

S: significant at .05 level.

Appendix H: Estimation of Delinquency and Repossession Risk from Maturity and Down Payment Information on New-Auto Contracts

1. GENERAL METHOD

The objective is to derive an estimate of the subsequent rate of delinquency or repossession from a given distribution of new-automobile credit contracts, according to maturity or down payment. That is, what over-all rate of repayment difficulty could be expected when the proportion of contracts in each maturity or down-payment class is known? Furthermore, we wish to make a series of such estimates, over time, corresponding to the changing terms of contracts that actually originated and to compare such a series with delinquency and repossession rates actually observed.

For sales finance companies, we have estimated repossession risk, since the available time series with which to compare the estimates pertained to repossession and loss rates. For commercial banks, estimates of delinquency risk were made in order to compare them with the available actual delinquency rate series. The procedure was, first, to derive from the 1954–55 Federal Reserve survey of new-car purchases the delinquency and repossession rates associated with given maturity or down-payment classes of contracts. Then weighted averages of these rates were calculated, using as weights the distributions available annually or monthly of contracts according to maturity or down payment. The resulting averages show how collection experience might be expected to vary from that prevailing on contracts originating in 1954–55 in view of the variations in credit terms, other things being equal.

The following data were used for the sales finance company estimates of repossession risk:

1. Repossession rates on new-auto contracts by maturity or down-payment class, 1954–55 (Tables H-1 and H-2). These data are from the lender report sample and cover all lenders, not just sales finance companies, since separate tabulations of repossessions by type of lender were not available. Repossessions include those occurring at any time during the period between contract origination (1954 and 1955) and date of survey (June–July 1956), and the number of contracts repossessed is taken as a ratio to all contracts in the maturity or down-payment class. The lender report was used instead of the personal interview sample because it appears to give more complete coverage of credit difficulty and also to represent more accurately its relationship to length of contract. Even in the lender report sample the repossession rates for the longer contracts are probably too low, due to incomplete coverage of the entire history of the longer loans, many of which originated late in the period covered by the survey (see Chapter 3, "Interarea Analysis"). Estimates of repossession rates for 1954–55 contracts classified by ratio of contract balance to dealer cost instead of by down payment percentage also were obtained. The method is described in Section 2, below.

2. Median percentages of new-auto contracts both above and below a certain maturity, annually, 1953–61, as reported for nineteen sales finance companies by the First National Bank of Chicago. The maturity classes used in these reports changed during the period. The dividing line was at 18 months, 1953–57; 24 months, 1955–60; and 30 months, 1957–61. The divisions at 18 and 24 months were extended back to 1948 and to 1950, respectively, by using the aggregate data for two and for five large sales finance companies reported by Moore, Atkinson, and Klein.

3. Median percentages of new-auto contracts with down payment less than 33 per cent, annually, 1953–57, and with "advance in excess of dealer cost," annually, 1957–61, as reported for nineteen sales finance companies by the First National Bank of Chicago. The down-payment distribution was extended back to 1950 by using the aggregate data for five large sales finance companies reported by Moore, Atkinson, and Klein.

One series of repossession risk estimates was obtained from the maturity distributions (Table H-3) and another from the down-payment and dealer cost-ratio distributions (Table H-4). These estimates were averaged to obtain a series influenced by both aspects of credit terms (see Table 47). Finally, the risk estimates were converted to index numbers on the base of their average during 1954–55.

For commercial banks, estimates of delinquency risk were derived from the following data:

1. Delinquency rates on new-auto contracts cross-classified by maturity and dealer-cost ratio, 1954–55. The method of deriving these rates is described in Section 2, below. They pertain to all lenders, not only to commercial banks, since tabulations of delinquencies by type of lender are not available. Purchased paper and direct loans are not distinguished, for the same reason. The same limitations with respect to the rates on long-maturity contracts apply here as in the case of repossession rates, mentioned above.

2. Distributions of new-auto contracts cross-classified by maturity and by ratio of contract balance to dealer cost, as reported by a sample of commercial banks to the Federal Reserve, monthly, 1957–62. Data were used separately for purchased and direct paper. These cross-classifications are based on reports from about half the members of banks which report maturity distributions separately, and the maturity data extend one year farther back (i.e., to 1956), but the cross-classification provides more information. When the Federal Reserve survey was initiated, in August 1956, contract down-payment distributions were obtained, but after a few months these were superseded by the dealer-cost ratios. We did not use the early down-payment data. Neither did we use the distributions of used-car paper by maturity and ratio of contract balance to wholesale value, also reported monthly by the Federal Reserve. This would have been desirable since the actual delinquency rates (American Bankers Association series) with which the risk estimates are to be compared do not distinguish new- and used-auto loans, and may well be affected by shifts in their proportions. However, the data required to translate used-car terms into delinquency-risk estimates are not available from the Federal Reserve 1954–55 survey, which was confined to new cars.

3. Distributions of new-auto contracts by maturity and by dealer-cost ratio (not cross-classified), for purchased paper and direct loans by banks, as reported in the Federal Reserve new-car purchases survey for the years 1954 and 1955 (Table H-5, cols. 7 and 8).

The application of the monthly distributions to obtain weighted averages of the 1954–55 delinquency rates produced two monthly series of delinquency-risk estimates for commercial banks, one for purchased paper and the other for direct loans, 1957–64 (Table H-6). The two differ only because of differences in the maturities and dealer-cost ratios of the two categories. Roughly comparable annual estimates for 1954 and 1955 were obtained by applying the distributions in (3) above (see Table H-5). The annual estimates, 1954–55, 1957–62, were converted to index numbers by dividing by the 1954–55 average (see Table 48).

Table H-5, incidentally, permits a direct comparison of 1954 and 1955 estimates of delinquency and repossession rates by type of lender, based on the distributions of contracts according to maturity and dealer-cost ratios prevailing in those years. The maturity distributions for sales finance companies in both years were quite similar to those for banks' purchased paper, both shifting toward longer maturities in 1955. Hence the corresponding repossession and delinquency risk estimates are very nearly the same. The dealer-cost ratio distributions for sales finance companies are somewhat more liberal than those for banks' purchased paper; hence the corresponding risk estimates are higher.[1] The lowest risk estimates shown are for banks' direct loans, while those for other institutions occupy an intermediate position.

The several delinquency and repossession-risk series show to what extent, as maturities lengthen, down payments get smaller, or dealer-cost ratios increase (or as all these things happen together), collection or repayment experience tends to worsen, and vice versa. Various factors operate to make the actual rates turn out differently from the estimated risk. One of the most prominent is the business cycle. Actual delinquency or repossession rates usually worsen during a recession

---

[1] Note that the sales finance company repossession rates for 1954 and 1955 in Table H-5 differ slightly from those in Tables H-3 and H-4. The differences arise partly because the maturity and down payment or dealer-cost ratio distributions differ among the sources used, partly because the final series in Tables H-3 and H-4 are adjusted to maintain comparability with other years.

and improve during a recovery, but these changes in economic conditions will not affect the estimated risk unless the lending terms change in a corresponding way. Indeed, if lending terms tighten during recession, the estimated risk will improve while the actual ratio is worsening. Over longer periods than a business cycle, many other things that have a bearing on loan experience may change and cause deviations from the estimated risk. In short, the estimates take into account only one of the factors determining loan experience, namely lending terms, although this is, as we have seen, an important one.

Furthermore, the risk estimates apply to contracts made during a given period and to what happens to them during their ensuing life. The actual rates available for banks or sales finance companies represent delinquencies, repossessions, or losses incurred during the month or year reported, without regard to when the contract originated. Hence the actual rates incurred on loans outstanding in a given period might be expected to lag behind the estimated risks on loans originated in that period. However, the lag is probably less than a year, on the average, since repayment difficulties tend to appear early in the life of an instalment contract.

Apart from the lag, the level of the estimated rates may differ markedly from the level of reported rates because of differences in the concept of the rate that is measured (see Chapter 7, notes 1 and 3). Other sources of divergence are evident from the inadequacies and lack of comparability of the data (see especially Section 2, below). The most that can be expected, therefore, is that the estimated risk will reveal some broad tendencies corresponding to those that show up somewhat later in actual credit experience.

2. ESTIMATES FOR CONTRACTS CLASSIFIED BY RATIO OF CONTRACT BALANCE TO DEALER COST

This part of the estimation problem proved most troublesome because both the Federal Reserve and the First National Bank of Chicago have substituted the dealer-cost ratio for the down payment ratio in their current reports on the characteristics of new-auto contracts, but no comprehensive data are as yet available showing repossessions or delinquencies on contracts classified by dealer-cost ratios (see Chapter 3, note 3). What we have done is to reconstruct, out of the 1954–55 new-car purchases survey, estimates of what the repossession and delinquency rates would have been had the data been classified by dealer-cost ratios.

One of the links is provided by the fact that the 1954–55 survey did contain distributions of the number of contracts by down payment ratio (both personal interview and lender report sample) and by dealer-cost ratio (personal interview sample only). If we assume that when the contracts are arrayed separately by each of these ratios their order is substantially the same, the distributions can be matched and the dealer cost ratio that is equivalent to a given down payment ratio obtained. These will be approximately equivalent ratios for 1954–55, but not necessarily for other years when the down payment ratio may have been either more or less inflated relative to the dealer-cost ratio (see Section 3 below). We use the equivalents, however, only for the purpose of obtaining 1954–55 repossession and delinquency rates for corresponding down payment–dealer-cost ratio classes.

The three available percentage distributions are as follows:

Contract Down Payment Ratio	Personal Interview Data [a]		Lender Report Data [a]		Dealer-Cost Ratio	Personal Interview Data [b]	
	Noncum.	Cum.	Noncum.	Cum.		Noncum.	Cum.
0–9.9%	2.0	2.0	0.9	0.9	1.00 & over	23.1	23.1
10–14.9	1.6	3.6	1.2	2.1	.80–.99	36.5	59.6
15–19.9	2.6	6.2	2.3	4.4	.60–.79	21.9	81.5
20–24.9	5.4	11.6	5.3	9.7	.59 & under	18.5	100.0
25–29.9	10.5	22.1	13.5	23.2	Total	100.0	
30–34.9	19.6	41.7	22.4	45.6	Median	.85	
35–39.9	13.8	55.5	14.1	59.7			
40–44.9	9.9	65.4	9.7	69.4			
45–49.9	8.3	73.7	8.2	77.6			
50–59.9	12.5	86.2	11.1	88.7			
60–69.9	7.6	93.8	6.8	95.5			
70–79.9	4.4	98.2	3.4	98.9			
80–89.9	1.3	99.5	0.9	99.8			
90 & over	0.5	100.0	0.2	100.0			
Total	100.0		100.0				
Median	38 per cent		37 per cent				

[a] Unpublished data from National Analysts 1954–55 New-Automobile Purchase Survey for the Federal Reserve Board.

[b] *Consumer Instalment Credit*, Part IV, Table 40, p. 65; averages of the 1954 and 1955 distributions, weighted by the reported coverage ratios (23 and 34 respectively).

From these distributions the down payment classes that most closely match the dealer-cost classes in terms of the percentage of contracts included are:

Contract Down Payment Percentage	Personal Interview Data		Lender Report Data		Dealer-Cost Ratio	Personal Interview Data	
	Noncum.	Cum.	Noncum.	Cum.		Noncum.	Cum.
0–29.9	22.1	22.1	23.2	23.2	1.00 & over	23.1	23.1
30–39.9	33.4	55.5	36.5	59.7	.80–.99	36.5	59.6
40–49.9	18.2	73.7	17.9	77.6	.60–.79	21.9	81.5
50 & over	26.3	100.0	22.4	100.0	.59 & under	18.5	100.0

Thus it appears that in 1954–55 a dealer-cost ratio of 1.00 was roughly equivalent to a contract down payment of 30 per cent, .80 corresponded to 40 per cent, and .60 to about 55 per cent. The median dealer-cost ratio, .85, corresponded to a median down payment ratio of 37 or 38 per cent.

The dealer-cost ratio classes shown above, which are those used in the 1954–55 survey, are not quite the same as those used currently either by the Federal Reserve or the First National Bank of Chicago. To match the currently available classes, we adjust the preceding figures as follows: [2]

Dealer-Cost Ratio	Contract Down Payment Percentage	Personal Interview Data		Lender Report Data	
		Noncum.	Cum.	Noncum.	Cum.
1.01 & over	0–29.9	22.1	22.1	23.2	23.2
.91–1.00	30–34.9	19.6	41.7	22.4	45.6
.81–.90	35–39.9	13.8	55.5	14.1	59.7
.80 & under	40 & over	44.5	100.0	40.3	100.0
Sub-total					
1.00 & under	30 & over	77.9		76.8	
Total		100.0		100.0	

In terms of these sets of "equivalent" class intervals we obtain repossession and delinquency rates for 1954–55 from the lender report sample (Table H-7).[3] The rates provide a basis for estimating average

[2] One of the assumptions here, namely that the percentage of contracts with a dealer-cost ratio of exactly 1.00 is negligible, may be wide of the mark, but we do not know how to improve upon it.

[3] The derived relationship between dealer-cost ratios and the derived repossession rates for 1954 compare quite closely with that reported for 1958 and

delinquency and repossession risks from the 1954–55 distributions of contracts by dealer-cost ratio (Table H-5), or from the current distributions compiled by the First National Bank of Chicago for sales finance companies (Table H-4), or from the current Federal Reserve data pertaining to commercial banks (Table H-6).

Use of these rates with the current Federal Reserve data requires a further step, however, because in this case we use dealer-cost ratios cross-classified with contract maturity. Repossession and delinquency rates based on such a cross-classification do not exist, but we estimate delinquency rates in Table H-8 on the assumption that maturity and dealer-cost ratios influence the rates independently, not jointly.[4] A test of this assumption, for the only similar type of cross-tabulation that does exist, between maturity and "effective" down payment ratio (i.e., with down payment and new-car selling price adjusted for the over allowance on trade-in, if any—see below), is made in Table H-9. It shows that the method yields estimates that only roughly approximate those of a true cross-tabulation. Nevertheless, we have used the figures in Table H-8 to calculate average repossession and delinquency risks from the monthly distributions of commercial bank paper cross-classified by maturity and dealer-cost ratio, with the results shown in Table H-6.

3. A NOTE ON DEALERS' GROSS MARGINS

The dealer-cost ratio and down payment percentage permit one to calculate the dealer gross margin as a percentage of selling price. This affords a rough check on the reasonableness of the relationship between dealer cost and down payment derived in Section 2. If c is the ratio

1959 for a large sales finance company by McCracken, Mao, and Fricke (p. 138). Taking repossession rates in Table H-7 as a ratio to the rate for all contracts, the comparison is as follows:

Dealer-Cost Ratio	Repossession Rates		
	1954–55	1958	1959
1.11 and over ⎫			
1.06–1.10 ⎬	2.4	3.7	3.4
1.01–1.05 ⎭			
.91–1.00	1.2	1.4	1.5
.90 or less	0.3	0.4	0.4
All Contracts	1.0	1.0	1.0

[4] Repossession rates could be estimated similarly, but this was not done because comparable actual repossession-rate series with which to compare the risk estimates are lacking.

of loan balance to dealer cost, and d the ratio of down payment to selling price, then the dealer gross margin, m, is $1 - \dfrac{1-d}{c}$. Applying this formula to the median figures for 1954–55 (.85 for dealer cost and 37 or 38 per cent for down payment), the dealer margin is 26 or 27 per cent. Apparently the margins tend to be higher when the dealer-cost ratio is high and the down payment low, perhaps in compensation for the greater risk or because of differences in bargaining power. The figures cited in Section 2 work out as follows:

Dealer-Cost Ratio	Contract Down Payment (per cent)	Dealer Margin (per cent)
1.00	30	30
.80	40	25
.60	55	25

These calculated margins (and the down payments) are inflated to some degree by the practice of overallowing for trade-ins—i.e., instead of reducing the new-car price, the dealers increase the valuation of the used car typically traded in (which is included in the down payment). The Federal Reserve study calculated the "effective" down payment, eliminating the overallowance by substituting the estimated wholesale price of the used car for the trade-in allowance. Although no direct comparisons were made in the Federal Reserve report, the following medians for 1955 can be derived from Tables 44 and 45 in Part IV of the report:

	Dealer-Cost Ratio	"Effective" Down Payment (per cent)	"Effective" Dealer Margin (per cent)
All contracts	.88	27	17
Sales finance company, "other"	.94	24	19
Sales finance company, 4 major cos.	.92	25	18
"Other" lenders	.92	26	20
Banks' purchased paper	.88	27	17
Banks' direct loans	.77	34	14

The "effective" down payments and dealer margins are substantially lower than the contract down payments and corresponding margins, but in both cases the margin diminishes as the down payment increases and the dealer-cost ratio declines.

TABLE H-1

Repossession and Delinquency Rates for New-Automobile Contracts Classified by Original Maturity, 1954-55

Original Maturity	Number of Contracts			Repossession Rate (per cent)	Delinquency Rate (per cent)	Percentage Distribution of All Contracts
	Total	Repossessed	Delinquent			
Less than 18 mos.	856	2	9	0.2	1.1	9.6
18	588	5	10	0.9	1.7	6.6
19–23	99	0	2	0	2.0	1.1
24	2,943	40	100	1.4	3.4	33.2
25–29	78	2	5	2.6	6.4	0.9
30	2,982	80	140	2.7	4.7	33.6
31–35	98	7	15	7.1	15.3	1.1
36	1,209	29	67	2.4	5.5	13.6
More than 36 mos.	23	1	1	4.3	4.3	0.3
Total	8,876	166	349	1.9	3.9	100.0
Subtotals						
18 mos. and under	1,444	7	19	0.5	1.3	16.3
19 mos. and over	7,432	159	330	2.1	4.4	83.7
24 mos. and under	4,486	47	121	1.0	2.7	50.5
25 mos. and over	4,390	119	228	2.7	5.2	49.5
30 mos. and over	7,546	129	266	1.7	3.5	85.0
31 mos. and over	1,330	37	83	2.8	6.2	15.0
24 mos. and under	4,486	47	121	1.0	2.7	50.5
25–30 mos.	3,060	82	145	2.7	4.7	34.5
31–36 mos.	1,307	36	82	2.8	6.3	14.7
Over 36 mos.	23	1	1	4.3	4.3	0.3
Under 30 mos.	4,564	49	126	1.1	2.8	51.4
30–35 mos.	3,080	87	155	2.8	5.0	34.7
36 mos. and over	1,232	30	68	2.4	5.5	13.9

Source: Unpublished lender report data from National Analysts New-Automobile Purchase Survey for the Federal Reserve Board.

TABLE H-2

Repossession and Delinquency Rates for New-Automobile Contracts Classified
by Contract Down Payment Ratio, 1954-55

Ratio, Contract Down Payment to Contract Car Price	Number of Contracts			Repossession Rate (per cent)	Delinquency Rate (per cent)	Percentage Distribution of All Contracts
	Total	Repossessed	Delinquent			
Less than 10%	70	4	4	5.7	5.7	0.9
10–14.9	93	0	3	0	3.2	1.2
15–19.9	183	7	11	3.8	6.0	2.3
20–24.9	429	20	39	4.7	9.3	5.4
25–29.9	1,084	51	78	4.7	7.2	13.5
30–34.9	1,797	40	80	2.2	4.5	22.4
35–39.9	1,127	21	44	1.9	3.9	14.1
40–44.9	779	4	14	0.5	1.8	9.7
45–49.9	659	0	16	0	2.4	8.2
50–59.9	890	0	20	0	2.2	11.1
60–69.9	541	2	8	0.4	1.5	6.8
70–79.9	272	0	0	0	0	3.4
80–89.9	76	0	1	0	1.3	0.9
90–99.9	14	0	1	0	7.1	0.2
Total	8,014	149	319	1.9	4.0	100.0
Subtotals						
Under 30	1,859	82	135	4.4	7.3	23.2
30 & over	6,155	67	184	1.1	3.0	76.8
Under 35	3,656	122	215	3.3	5.9	45.6
35 & over	4,358	27	104	0.6	2.4	54.4

Source: Unpublished lender report data from National Analysts New-Automobile Purchase Survey for the Federal Reserve Board.

TABLE H-3

Maturity Distribution of New-Automobile Contracts and Estimated Repossession Risk, Sales Finance Companies, 1948–65

Percentage Distribution

	A		B		C		D		E	
	18 Mos. & Under	19 Mos. & Over	18 Mos. & Under	19 Mos. & Over	24 Mos. & Under	25 Mos. & Over	24 Mos. & Under	25 Mos. & Over	30 Mos. & Under	31 Mos. & Over
1948	78	22								
1949	53	47								
1950	48	52								
1951	97	3			95	5				
1952	51	49			100	0				
1953	28	72	16.7	83.3	90	10				
1954	22	78	13.8	86.2	81	19				
1955			9.1	90.9	61	39	32.1	67.9		
1956			6.7	93.3	36	64	21.9	78.1		
1957			6.2	93.8	30[a]	70[a]	20.3	79.7	56.1	43.9
1958							17.2	82.8	36.1	63.9
1959							13.4	86.6	23.2	76.8
1960							13.7[a]	86.3[a]	19.2	80.8
1961									22.0	78.0
1962									18.6	81.4
1963									15.3	84.7
1964									14.6	85.4
1965									13.7	86.3
Reposs. rate (%), 1954–55	0.5	2.1	0.5	2.1	1.0	2.7	1.0	2.7	1.7	2.8

(continued)

TABLE H-3 (concluded)

	Weighted Average Repossession Risk (per cent), Based on Columns					Final Estimated Repossession Risk (per cent)[b]
	A	B	C	D	E	
1948	0.9					1.0
1949	1.3					1.4
1950	1.3		1.1			1.4
1951	0.5		1.0			0.6
1952	1.3		1.2			1.4
1953	1.7	1.8	1.3			1.8
1954	1.7	1.9	1.7			1.9
1955		2.0	2.1	2.2		2.0
1956		2.0	2.2[a]	2.3		2.1
1957		2.0		2.4	2.2	2.2
1958				2.4	2.4	2.4
1959				2.5	2.5	2.5
1960				2.5[a]	2.6	2.6
1961						2.6
1962						2.6
1963						2.6
1964						2.6
1965						2.6

Source: Columns A, C—Moore, Atkinson, and Klein, "Changes in the Quality of Consumer Instalment Credit", Table 22; Columns B, D, E—First National Bank of Chicago, "Instalment Sales Finance Company Ratios," successive issues.

aFirst six months.

bBased on column E for 1957-65; D (reduced by 0.2 points) for 1955-56; B for 1953-55; A (raised by 0.1 points) for 1948-52. Column C was not used.

TABLE H-4

Distribution of New-Automobile Contracts by Down Payment and Dealer-Cost Ratio, and Estimated Repossession Risk, Sales Finance Companies, 1950-65

| | Contract Down Payment Ratio | | | | Ratio Of Contract Balance To Dealer Cost | | Weighted Average Repossession Risk (per cent) Based on Columns | | | Final Estimated Repossession Risk (per cent)[b] |
| | A | | B | | C | | | | | |
	Under 33%	33% & Over	Under 33%	33% & Over	1.01 & Over	1.00 & Under	A	B	C	
Percentage Distribution										
1950	8	92					1.4			1.0
1951	3	97					1.2			0.8
1952	10	90					1.4			1.0
1953	14	86	29.9	70.1			1.6	2.1		1.2
1954	21	79	40.3	59.7			1.8	2.4		1.5
1955	33	67	52.0	48.0			2.2	2.8		1.9
1956	35[a]	65[a]	57.2	42.8			2.3[a]	3.0		2.1
1957			60.4	39.6	32.1	67.9		3.1	2.2	2.2
1958					28.6	71.4			2.0	2.0
1959					33.0	67.0			2.2	2.2
1960					32.1	67.9			2.2	2.2
1961					33.0	67.0			2.2	2.2
1962					35.0	65.0			2.3	2.3
1963					38.4	61.6			2.4	2.4
1964					38.8	61.2			2.4	2.4
1965					40.0	60.0			2.4	2.4
Reposs. rate (%), 1954–55	4.4	1.1	4.4	1.1	4.4	1.1				

(Continued)

Notes to Table H-4

Source: Column A—Moore, Atkinson, Klein, *"Changes in Quality"*,
Table 29. Columns B, C—First National Bank of Chicago, "Instalment
Sales Finance Company Ratios," successive issues.

The repossession rates, 1954-55, are from Table H-2, column 5. For
the contract down payment distributions the class "30.0 and over" in
Table H-2 was considered most nearly comparable to the class "33
per cent and over" here, because it includes a large volume of contracts at the 33 per cent level. For the method of deriving repossession
rates for contracts classified by ratio of contract balance to dealer
cost, see Section 2 of this appendix.

aFirst six months.

bBased on column C for 1957-65; Column B (reduced by 0.9 points)
for 1953-56; Column A (reduced by 0.4 points) for 1950-52.

Table H-5

Estimates of Repossession and Delinquency Risk, by Type of Lender, 1954 and 1955

1. Estimates for 1954

	1954-55		Sales Finance Cos.			Banks			
	Reposs. Rate (per cent) (1)	Delin. Rate (per cent) (2)	Four Major (3)	Other (4)	All (5)	Purch. Paper (6)	Direct Loans (7)	Other Inst. (8)	All Lenders (9)
			Percentage Distribution Of Contracts						
Contract Maturity (mos.)									
Under 30	1.1	2.8	53	46	51	52	79	61	59
30–35	} 2.7a	5.0	37	42	38	36	14	27	31
36 and over		5.5	11	11	11	12	6	11	10
Total			101	99	100	100	99	99	100
			Percentage Of Sample Reporting						
			14	4	18	8	7	3	37
			Percentage Distribution Of Contracts						
Dealer Cost Ratio									
Under .60	0.1	1.7	19	b	19c	20	26	b	22
.60–.79	0.3	2.1	18	b	18c	26	28	b	23
.80–.99	2.1	4.2	42	b	42c	38	35	b	38
1.00 and over	4.4	7.3	21	b	21c	15	11	b	17
Total			100	b	100	99	100	b	100
			Percentage Of Sample Reporting						
			7	2	9	4	4	2	23
Weighted Average Repossession Risk (per cent), based on									
Contract Maturity			1.9	2.0	1.9	1.9	1.4	1.7	1.8
Dealer Cost Ratio			1.9	b	1.9c	1.6	1.3	b	1.6
Maturity and Cost Ratiod			1.9	2.0	1.9c	1.8	1.4	1.7	1.7
Weighted Average Delinquency Risk (per cent), based on									
Contract Maturity			3.9	4.0	3.9	3.9	3.3	3.7	3.8
Dealer Cost Ratio			4.0	b	4.0c	3.6	3.3	b	3.7
Maturity and Cost Ratiod			4.0	4.0	4.0	3.8	3.3	3.7	3.8

(Continued)

Table H-5 (concluded)

2. Estimates for 1955

	1954-55		Sales Finance Cos.			Banks			
	Reposs. Rate (per cent) (1)	Delin. Rate (per cent) (2)	Four Ma-jor (3)	Oth-er (4)	All (5)	Purch. Paper (6)	Di. rect Loans (7)	Oth-er Inst. (8)	All Lend-ers (9)

Percentage Distribution Of Contracts

Contract Maturity (mos.)									
Under 30	1.1	2.8	28	33	29	33	63	46	38
30–35		5.0	46	42	45	42	26	33	40
36 and over	} 2.7	5.5	26	25	26	25	9	20	22
Total			100	100	100	100	98	99	100

Percentage Of Sample Reporting

			21	6	27	13	11	5	57

Percentage Distribution Of Contracts

Dealer Cost Ratio									
Under .60	0.1	1.7	12	13	12	16	23	12	16
.60–.79	0.3	2.1	19	15	18	18	32	18	21
.80–.99	2.1	4.2	36	34	36	40	32	36	35
1.00 and over	4.4	7.3	33	38	34	25	12	34	27
Total			100	100	100	99	99	100	99

Percentage Of Sample Reporting

			12	3	15	7	7	3	34

Weighted Average Repossession Risk (per cent), based on									
Contract Maturity			2.3	2.2	2.2	2.2	1.7	2.0	2.1
Dealer Cost Ratio			2.3	2.4	2.3	2.0	1.3	2.3	2.0
Maturity and Cost Ratio[d]			2.3	2.3	2.2	2.1	1.5	2.2	2.0

Weighted Average Delinquency Risk (per cent), based on									
Contract Maturity			4.5	4.4	4.5	4.4	3.6	4.1	4.3
Dealer Cost Ratio			4.5	4.7	4.6	4.2	3.3	4.6	4.2
Maturity and Cost Ratio[d]			4.5	4.6	4.6	4.3	3.4	4.4	4.2

Notes to Table H-5

Source: Columns 1 & 2––Tables H-1 and H-7. Columns 3–9––
Consumer Instalment Credit, Part IV, Tables 43 and 45 (maturity data
are from the lender report sample, dealer cost ratio data are from the
personal interview sample).

aThe rates for the two maturity classes separately are 2.8 and
2.4 respectively. They are consolidated here because the decline in
rate for the longest maturity is probably spurious, see Chapter 3.

bData not shown in source because of too few cases.

cFour major companies only.

dSimple average of two preceding lines.

Table H-6

Estimated Delinquency Risk, New-Automobile Contracts, Commercial Banks, 1957-66
(percentage of loans delinquent at some time during their life)

Purchased Paper

Year	Jan.	Feb.	March	April	May	June	July	Aug.	Sept.	Oct.	Nov.	Dec.	Annual Aver.
1957	n.a.	5.23	5.07	5.23	5.33	5.09	5.20	n.a.	n.a.	4.91	5.04	5.02	5.05a
1958	5.51	5.63	5.69	5.56	5.63	5.37	5.37	5.50	5.42	5.48	5.59	5.52	5.37a
1959	5.79	5.74	5.82	5.69	5.69	5.70	5.69	5.85	5.74	5.60	5.77	5.83	5.68
1960	5.74	5.87	5.64	5.80	5.79	5.82	5.83	5.88	5.83	5.78	5.72	5.78	5.78
1961	5.81	5.91	5.87	5.84	5.99	5.79	5.92	5.99	5.97	5.84	5.75	5.62	5.81
1962	6.16	6.17	6.10	5.99	6.10	5.98	6.05	6.00	5.97	5.95	5.90	6.00	5.94
1963	6.38	6.30	6.28	6.22	6.26	6.14	6.24	6.27	6.30	6.16	6.07	6.22	6.16
1964	6.21	6.36	6.33	6.28	6.26	6.38	6.50	6.47	6.36	6.33	6.40	6.28	6.35
1965	6.46	6.51	6.40	6.44	6.48	6.46	6.42	6.45	6.52	6.45	6.37	6.38	6.37
1966						6.56							

Direct Loans

Year	Jan.	Feb.	March	April	May	June	July	Aug.	Sept.	Oct.	Nov.	Dec.	Annual Aver.
1957	n.a.	3.07	3.18	3.05	3.33	3.13	3.22	n.a.	n.a.	3.01	3.11	3.00	3.13a
1958	3.51	3.58	3.53	3.39	3.59	3.41	3.59	3.65	3.50	3.47	3.30	3.70	3.39a
1959	3.64	3.90	3.81	3.78	3.82	3.48	3.71	3.97	3.74	3.73	3.77	3.75	3.65
1960	4.08	4.19	3.88	4.19	4.26	4.03	3.96	3.94	4.15	4.12	4.16	3.97	3.94
1961	4.39	4.48	4.46	4.47	4.51	4.31	4.35	4.25	4.52	4.23	4.25	4.39	4.24
1962	4.53	4.48	4.47	4.68	4.71	4.69	4.68	4.74	4.71	4.49	4.43	4.50	4.55
1963	4.73	4.86	4.55	4.62	4.72	4.60	4.60	4.85	4.69	4.52	4.49	4.69	4.61
1964	4.74	4.62	5.14	5.19	4.89	4.82	4.92	5.00	4.90	4.93	4.80	4.68	4.79
1965	5.00	4.64	4.60	4.72	4.63	4.97	4.96	5.02	5.05	4.91	4.92	4.89	4.94
1966						4.59							

Notes to Table H-6

Source: Estimated by computing weighted averages of 1954-55 delinquency rates cross-classified by maturity and dealer-cost ratio (Table H-8), using as weights the Federal Reserve monthly percentage distribution of new-auto contracts reported by commercial banks. The second of the two distributions reported for a given month is used, without regard to the variation in the sample of banks covered from month to month. No seasonal adjustment required.

ᵃPart of year.

Table H-7

Repossession and Delinquency Rates for Dealer-Cost-Ratio Classes, 1954-55

Contract Down Payment Ratio (per cent)	Equivalent Dealer Cost Ratios[a] (1)	Number of Contracts			Repossession Rate (per cent) $[(3) \div (2)]$ (5)	Delinquency Rate (per cent) $[(4) \div (2)]$ (6)
		Total (2)	Repossessed (3)	Delinquent (4)		
0–29.9	1.00 & over	1,859	82	135	4.4	7.3
30–39.9	.80–.99	2,924	61	124	2.1	4.2
40–49.9	.60–.79	1,438	4	30	0.3	2.1
50 & over	.59 & under	1,793	2	30	0.1	1.7
0–29.9	1.01 & over	1,859	82	135	4.4	7.3
30–34.9	.91–1.00	1,797	40	80	2.2	4.5
35–39.9	.81–.90	1,127	21	44	1.9	3.9
40 & over	.80 & under	3,231	6	60	0.2	1.9
0–29.9	1.01 & over	1,859	82	135	4.4	7.3
30 & over	1.00 & under	6,155	67	184	1.1	3.0
Total		8,014	149	319	1.9	4.0

Source: Compiled from Table H-2.

[a]The top set of class intervals is used in the Federal Reserve 1954-55 new-car purchases study, the second set in the First National Bank of Chicago's survey of sales finance company ratios, and the third in the Federal Reserve survey of bank loans.

Table H-8

Estimated Delinquency Rates for New-Automobile Contracts Classified by Maturity and Dealer-Cost Ratio, 1954-55

Dealer-Cost Ratio	Maturity				
	24 Mos. & Under	25 – 30 Mos.	31 – 36 Mos.	Over 36 Mos.	Total[a]
	Delinquency Rate (per cent)				
1.01 and over	4.9	8.6	11.5	7.8	7.3
.91 – 1.00	3.0	5.3	7.1	4.8	4.5
.81 – .90	2.6	4.6	6.1	4.2	3.9
.80 and under	1.3	2.2	3.0	2.0	1.9
Total[b]	2.7	4.7	6.3	4.3	4.0

[a]From Table H-7, column 6.
[b]From Table H-1, column 5.

The estimates in each maturity-dealer-cost-ratio cell are obtained by assuming the same pattern within each column and row as that shown by the marginal column and row, e.g., the entry in the upper left corner is $\frac{2.7}{4.0} \times 7.3 = 4.9$.

This method assumes that the association of delinquency rates with dealer cost ratio is independent of maturity and that the association with maturity is independent of dealer-cost ratio.

TABLE H-9

Test of Method of Estimating Delinquency Rates Within Maturity-Down Payment Classes on Assumption of Independence

Effective Down Payment Ratio (%)	Maturity			
	Under 30 Mos.	30 – 35 Mos.	36 Mos. & Over	Total
10–29	1.2(1.2)	1.2(1.4)	1.1(1.0)	1.2
30–39	0.8(1.1)	1.7(1.3)	0(0.9)	1.1
40 & over	0.8(0.7)	0(0.8)	0(0.6)	0.7
Total	1.0	1.2	0.8	1.0

Source: Special tabulations of personal interview data from National Analysts. New-Automobile Purchase Survey, 1954-55, for Federal Reserve Board.

[a]Parenthetic entries are computed by the method used in Table F 8, i.e., on the assumption of independence.

Index